On or About December 1910

Studies in Cultural History

ON OR ABOUT DECEMBER 1910

*Early Bloomsbury
and Its Intimate World*

PETER STANSKY

HARVARD UNIVERSITY PRESS
CAMBRIDGE, MASSACHUSETTS
LONDON, ENGLAND

First Harvard University Press paperback edition, 1997

Library of Congress Cataloging-in-Publication Data
Stansky, Peter.
  On or about December 1910 : early Bloomsbury and its intimate
world / Peter Stansky.
    p. cm.—(Studies in cultural history)
  Includes bibliographical references and index.
  ISBN 0-674-63605-8 (cloth)
  ISBN 0-674-63606-6 (pbk.)
  1. Bloomsbury (London, England)—Intellectual life—20th century.
2. Woolf, Virginia, 1882–1941—Friends and associates. 3. Authors,
English—England—London—Biography. 4. Intellectuals—England
—London—Biography. 5. Bloomsbury (London, England)—Biography.
6. Artists—England—London—Biography. 7. Bloomsbury group.
I. Title II. Series.
DA685.B65S73 1996
820.9′00912—dc20   96-17588
[B]   CIP

To my readers, particularly Billy and Marina

Contents

Illustrations

On or About December 1910

Introduction

Unexpectedly and perhaps belatedly, England in 1910 entered the story of a modernism that since the turn of the century had had a number of its major events occur on the Continent. One might assume that England ought to have claimed an important role in the story earlier, if only because it was so dominant in so many other ways—though its leading position in the West was being challenged by Germany. That fateful rivalry climaxed in the two world wars, both of which England "won" and both of which marked the decline of England's power.

But there was a very special quality to what was happening in England in the years before the First World War. As elsewhere in Europe, there was a triumph of opulence, indeed vulgarity, alongside the continuation of intense poverty, the more paradoxical in England because of its acknowledged position of being the head of the most powerful Empire in the world. Perhaps the symbolic culminating event of those prewar years was the funeral in 1910 of the rich and vulgar king Edward VII, attended by a panoply of monarchs. In retrospect, looking back after the devastation of the First World War, that Edwardian event was taken to represent the funeral of the Europe, or certainly the England, of the nineteenth century, and what the historian G. M. Young called its flash Edwardian epilogue.

———

In November and December of 1910 the critic and painter Roger Fry assembled in London the exhibition "Manet and the Post-Impressionists" (a term that he invented, and that has become canonical). The exhibition proved explosive. No doubt remembering its impact, Virginia Woolf later wrote in one of her best-known phrases, "on or about December 1910 human character changed." For Woolf character was all important: "our marriages, our friendships depend on it." She was concerned with the more conscious manifestation—character rather than innate nature—but also character in a newer "modern" sense, not the mere externals on which in her view the realist Edwardian novelists, Galsworthy, Wells, and Bennett, had depended, but something deeper and different.

Mr Bennett and Mrs Brown, the essay in which Woolf made her remark, was written in 1924. It arose out of a dispute she was having with Arnold Bennett, who had accused her, in a mention of her novel *Jacob's Room,* of being unable to depict character. Woolf, discussing how a novelist might choose to write of Mrs Brown, a lady seen in a railroad carriage, aligned herself against Bennett the realist with such "modern" writers as E. M. Forster, T. S. Eliot, Lytton Strachey, James Joyce, and D. H. Lawrence, the generation that came to the fore in the decade after 1910. (In the context of the actual events of 1910, there is a certain irony in her attacking Bennett, for he had been an outspoken defender of the Post-Impressionists.) In the paragraph that follows the remark, Woolf admits that such events don't happen quite as suddenly as she had suggested:

> I am not saying that one went out, as one might into a garden, and there saw that a rose had flowered, or that a hen had laid an egg. The change was not sudden and definite like that. But a change there was, nevertheless; and, since one must be arbitrary, let us date it about the year 1910. The first signs of it are recorded in the books of Samuel Butler, in *The Way of All Flesh* in particular; the plays of Bernard Shaw

continue to record it. In life one can see the change, if I may use a homely illustration, in the character of one's cook.

(It is a wonderful image of British society as it was—writing in 1924, Virginia Woolf, a figure on the left in many ways, would nevertheless assume that most of her readers, down to the bottom of the middle class, would employ a cook, and she may well have been right in the 1920s.)

> The Victorian cook lived like a leviathan in the lower depths, formidable, silent, obscure, inscrutable; the Georgian cook is a creature of sunshine and fresh air; in and out of the drawing-room, now to borrow *The Daily Herald,* now to ask advice about a hat. Do you ask for more solemn instances of the power of the human race to change? . . . All human relations have shifted—those between masters and servants, husbands and wives, parents and children. And when human relations change there is at the same time a change in religion, conduct, politics, and literature. Let us agree to place one of these changes about the year 1910.[1]

Woolf was having something of a joke in her mention of a specific month, as she acknowledges even in the final sentence of the long passage I've quoted, where she writes "about the year 1910." But her choice of the year and the month will serve as a principle of organization or point of departure for this book.

My discussion will touch on contemporary political events and social disturbances, but its culmination will be the Post-Impressionist show itself at the end of the year. It is not only hindsight that makes that exhibition seem so important. Almost from its first day, it was recognized as significant, even though so many disliked it and thought it a counterpart to the anarchism that they saw about them in political society. It was the challenge of a new world, a new reality.

English writers, especially at the time we are considering, tend to be more deeply embedded within the middle classes of their society than might be true on the Continent. Certainly the Bloomsbury writers, in revolt though they were in many ways, could not have been more middle to upper-middle class. Indeed, they themselves were far more within the "establishment" than most of the Edwardian writers about whom Woolf complained. Galsworthy was of middle-class background, but Bennett and even Wells—radical though he was—were outsider figures intensely anxious to enter the world that counted. The members of Bloomsbury were in that world already, and hence might treat it with more disdain.

The changes and threatened transformations of the English state—a relation between politics and the making of modernity—have been brilliantly suggested by George Dangerfield in *The Strange Death of Liberal England*. Published first in the United States in 1935, it is a book that remains an extraordinary narrative tour de force. Whether one agrees with him or not, Dangerfield has done much to shape the debate about the prewar period in England, a fine demonstration that insight and imagination are still among the most important of historical skills. He begins his study with one of the major events of 1910, the appearance in the sky of Halley's comet, which Asquith observed on shipboard returning to England from France on May 7, 1910 just after he learned of the death of Edward VII.

During 1910 some of the most important institutions of the English state were being severely challenged. When politics and artistic and personal events are put together, perhaps one can even presume to say that human character changed "on or about December 1910."

It was a time, as Dangerfield emphasizes, when Liberal England was being battered by labor unrest, Irish unrest, and increasingly violent agitation on behalf of votes for women. Between 1910 and 1914 there were some fears of revolution from the left and the right—the right becoming in fact more revolutionary. How valid such fears were can never be known, for the outbreak of the war removed that particular danger. Certainly the state was becoming more anarchic, more uncontrolled, more "modern." So too was the world of art.

Political and artistic divergences reached a semi-crescendo in December 1910, as Woolf, presumably only half seriously, suggests. The younger members of the Bloomsbury group, among them Lytton Strachey and Maynard Keynes, moving toward thirty, had not yet done a great deal and might almost be called embryos, in the language of the Cambridge secret society, the Apostles, to which Strachey and Keynes belonged. Strachey in 1910 was involved in making a career as a young literary figure in London, having failed to secure a fellowship at Trinity College, Cambridge. Keynes was teaching at Cambridge. Both were pursuing their complicated love lives centering on Strachey's cousin, the painter Duncan Grant. They were also spending much time conversing with Vanessa Bell, now married to their Cambridge friend Clive Bell, and her sister, Virginia Stephen, who would marry Leonard Woolf in 1912. (Woolf, who had also been at Cambridge and an Apostle, had been in Ceylon as a civil servant since 1904, and was now holding the post of an Assistant Government Agent there. He kept in touch through letters, mostly from Strachey.) Virginia was in the country in the early part of 1910, recovering from a nervous breakdown, one not as serious as her similar attacks in 1904 and 1913. Except when ordered by her doctors to do nothing but rest, she was writing a few reviews as well as working fitfully on her first novel, *The Voyage Out*. So far as the public world was concerned the younger members—the heart of Bloomsbury—were quite invisible.

Roger Fry, however, was forty-four and well-known in 1910. He had studied science at King's College, Cambridge, and was an Apostle. Contrary to his family's wishes, he had planned to make a career of painting, at which he was not particularly adept, and as a connoisseur and an art critic, at both of which he was to be much more successful. At first, under the influence of Bernard Berenson, he distinguished himself in the Italian field, and his first book was a study of Bellini. In 1903 he was a founder of the *Burlington Magazine*, and in 1906 he became curator of European paintings for the Metropolitan Museum in New York, then dominated by J. P. Morgan. But Fry could spend much time in Europe on museum business, and in January of 1910 he re-met Clive and Vanessa Bell in the railway station at Cambridge—a chance meeting of three acquaintances that by the year's end would have reverberations for the history of Bloomsbury and for the history of modernism.

Fry had been on increasingly bad terms with Morgan and was presently fired from the Metropolitan—a relief. He was free now to explore French contemporary art. In the fall of that year he, Clive Bell, Desmond MacCarthy, and Lady Ottoline Morrell went to Paris to select paintings for an exhibition at the Grafton Gallery, which happened to have a gap in its schedule. By creating the name Post-Impressionism, Fry arbitrarily and perhaps misleadingly appeared to create a movement.

The Apostles had been concerned with what they considered the world of appearance and the world of reality, one of the themes of E. M. Forster's *Howards End,* published that year. For Fry himself, at that moment, appearance was possibly the world of appreciation and connoisseurship, while the "new painting" seemed to herald a different reality, where form was more important than the picture it purported to represent, where self-expression and one's immediate reaction were important to the artist, and where the views of one's uneducated cook or maid might have as much significance as those of a highly educated and cultivated viewer. Fry wrote rather vividly about this in his essay "Retrospect," published in *Vision and Design* in 1920:

> I tried in vain to explain what appeared to me so clear, that the modern movement was essentially a return to the ideas of formal design which had been almost lost sight of in the fervid pursuit of naturalistic representation. I found that the cultured public which had welcomed my expositions of the works of the Italian Renaissance now regarded me as either incredibly flippant or, for the more charitable explanation was usually adopted, slightly insane. In fact, I found among the cultured who had hitherto been my most eager listeners the most inveterate and exasperated enemies of the new movement. The accusation of anarchism was constantly made. From an aesthetic point of view this was, of course, the exact opposite of the truth, and I was for long puzzled to find the explanation of so paradoxical an opinion and so violent an enmity. I now see that my crime had been to strike at vested emotional interests. These people felt instinctively that their

special culture was one of their social assets. That to be able to speak glibly of Tang and Ming, of Amico di Sandro and Baldovinetti, gave them a social standing and a distinctive cachet. . . . It was felt that one could only appreciate Amico di Sandro when one had acquired a certain considerable mass of erudition and given a great deal of time and attention, but to admire a Matisse required only a certain sensibility. One could feel fairly sure that one's maid could not rival one in the former case, but might by a mere haphazard gift of Providence surpass one in the second. So that the accusation of revolutionary anarchism was due to a social rather than an aesthetic prejudice. In any case the cultured public was determined to look upon Cézanne as an incompetent bungler, and upon the whole movement as madly revolutionary.[2]

Fry may have exaggerated, and, as with almost everything, there were notable precursors. But there is no doubt that this was the "special moment" for the introduction of modernism to England.

As English society itself was gradually becoming more democratic and "modern," so too, perhaps, were its artistic expressions. A contemporary critic, Christina Walsh, writing in the Labour paper, the *Daily Herald,* remarked: "The Post-Impressionists are in the company of the Great Rebels of the World. In politics the only movements worth considering are Woman Suffrage and Socialism. They are both Post-Impressionist in their desire to scrap old decaying forms and find for themselves a new working ideal."

Fry and his friends assembled a large exhibition, with paintings, drawings, bronzes, and pottery pieces, including twenty Cézannes, twenty-two Van Goghs, and thirty-six Gauguins, as well as some Matisses and Picassos. There were thousands of visitors to the Grafton Gallery. The common assumption has been that the exhibition was received with universal derision; in fact, there were some favorable notices. But such influential defenders of earlier new art as Robert Ross and D. S. MacColl turned vehemently against this latest manifestation. The success of the show and its reception will be among the questions explored in the pages that follow.

I

Virginia Woolf I

Many dates could be assigned for the beginning of Bloomsbury, beginning with the birth of Virginia Woolf in 1882, or even earlier if one wished to consider her parents. No doubt 1904, the year of Sir Leslie Stephen's death, was an important formative date. That year his four children, Vanessa, Thoby, Virginia, and Adrian, set up housekeeping on their own in the Bloomsbury section in London at 46 Gordon Square. Starting in 1905, Thoby's friends from Cambridge would come to their Thursday evenings. Another crucial date was 1899, the year Lytton Strachey, Leonard Woolf, Clive Bell, Thoby Stephen, and Saxon Sidney-Turner entered Trinity College, Cambridge.

Serious as these young people might be, and frivolous as well, intelligent as they undoubtedly were, their discussions may not have been, at least at first, especially remarkable, although the level was more serious than at the dinner parties to which George Duckworth dragged Vanessa and Virginia or at the dances during the London season attended by those who were similar to the Stephen children in terms of age and class. Much to the disapproval of their half-brothers, George and Gerald Duckworth, the young Stephen orphans, all over twenty-one, were unchaperoned. (The Duckworth brothers have, quite properly, received a bad press, and they did great harm to Virginia through their sexual molestations of her. In her memoirs Virginia depicts them, particularly George, as extremely conventional and stupid. But they both had rather interesting careers. George worked as an unpaid private secretary for Charles Booth, assisting him on his great multi-volume *Life and Labour of the People in London*, and devoted much of his life to serving as Secretary of the Royal Commission on Historical Monuments. His younger brother Gerald founded the publishing firm of Duckworth, which would publish Virginia's first two novels.)[1]

Undoubtedly it was unusual for a group of young men and women of their class to meet in such a way. Virginia Stephen, and most of her friends, had great pleasure in gossip, and she was a genius at it, making it up when the natural material was not rich enough. One thinks of the young people as chatting away, but indeed they were content to sit in silence if there wasn't anything good enough to say.

Bloomsbury was shaped to a considerable degree by G. E. Moore's *Principia Ethica*, published in 1903, in particular his emphasis on the importance of beautiful objects and of personal relations. But it would be wrong to assume that this set of beliefs meant that conversation was warm and loving, although there was a basic assumption that they were good friends. The most-quoted Bloomsbury remark was a question: "What exactly do you mean?" One would not be allowed to get away with sloppy thinking, and received opinions were highly suspect. "Personal relations" did not mean unreflective support. Rather, one had an obligation to be honest and tell others one's opinion, for their own good, of course.

What was unusual about their conversation, unusual even now, but certainly so in England before the First World War, was their willingness to chat openly about their own and others' sexual lives. This did not come about immediately but after they had known each other for some while, after Vanessa Stephen and Clive Bell had married in 1907. Perhaps Vanessa was influenced by Clive's worldliness. After their marriage Bloomsbury had two locations, the Bells remaining at 46

Gordon Square; Virginia and Adrian moving to 29 Fitzroy Square and in 1911 to 38 Brunswick Square. The latter address became something of a "commune," with Maynard Keynes and the painter Duncan Grant living on the ground floor and Leonard Woolf, who had returned from Ceylon after seven years there, on the top floor. The men were willing to share with Virginia and Vanessa a sexual frankness, more common among sophisticated undergraduates, that they had developed at Cambridge. Their closeness was intensified by Woolf, Strachey, and Keynes being members of the Apostles, and by Keynes and Strachey's openness about their homosexual pursuits.

In a memoir Virginia captured the moment of this change, in 1908, in a well-known anecdote, perhaps an exaggeration but undoubtedly suggesting the spirit of the group.

> It was a spring evening. Vanessa and I were sitting in the drawing room. The drawing room had greatly changed its character since 1904. The Sargent-Furse age was over. The age of Augustus John was dawning. . . . The door opened and the long and sinister figure of Mr Lytton Strachey stood on the threshold. He pointed his finger at a stain on Vanessa's white dress.
>
> "Semen?" he said.
>
> Can one really say it? I thought and we burst out laughing. With that one word all barriers of reticence and reserve went down. A flood of the sacred fluid seemed to overwhelm us. Sex permeated our conversation. The word bugger was never far from our lips. We discussed copulation with the same excitement and openness that we had discussed the nature of good.[2]

At about this time, Keynes remarked of economics that "nothing except copulation was so enthralling," and he would pursue both in his conversation, the latter perhaps more with closer friends. Clive Bell remembers another episode "of epoch making character" at the same time involving Lytton Strachey, even more vivid, and also in mixed company. "Lytton had described someone or other as 'lowering'. 'How lowering' enquired Adrian. 'To the prick' replied Lytton."[3]

———

There can be no doubt that the Stephen sisters were at the center of Bloomsbury, and virtually its only women. Without them it might have been little more than a group of men friends who continued to meet, having known one another at university. The sisters had committed themselves to careers. They were young, Vanessa having turned thirty and Virginia twenty-seven in 1909, and they were still best known as daughters of the eminent late-Victorian man of letters Sir Leslie Stephen. Vanessa was at work on her painting and Virginia on her writing, publishing her first piece in 1904, a book review of W. D. Howell's *The Son of Royal Langbrith,* in the *Guardian,* an Anglican High Church publication of small circulation. They and their friends might not have been much different from other young people of good birth and small private incomes trying to make their way in the cultural world of London.

In 1904 the four Stephen orphans had given up the family house in fashionable Kensington to move to respectable but distinctly unfashionable Bloomsbury. There was no clear "head of household." Vanessa was twenty-five and for seven years had had the terrifying job of being in charge of the Hyde Park Gate house after the marriage then death of her half-sister Stella. Thoby, then all of twenty-four, studying for the bar, was hardly a figure of substance and maturity, despite his nickname of "The Goth," reflecting his powerful face and build. The four Stephens had a firm position in the "intellectual aristocracy." They were descended through their father from the "high Victorian intellects" of the Clapham sect of the early nineteenth century. Their grandfather was Sir James Stephen, "Mr. Mother-Country," the prominent under-secretary for the colonies, and their uncle, Sir James Fitzjames Stephen, the judge and conservative utilitarian. Sir Leslie had married as his first wife Minny Thackeray, daughter of the novelist. She died in 1875, and he married secondly Julia Jackson Duckworth, a daughter of one of the Pattle sisters, well-known for their beauty and to the more cultivated part of London society through their association with the Little Holland House set. Julia's aunt was the great pioneer photographer Julia Margaret Cameron.

Members of the great professional classes of Victorian England, the Stephen children had some financial security that allowed them to pursue what careers they pleased, bolstered by those "golden islands" that were part of the middle-class landscape of the Schlegel sisters of Forster's *Howards End.* Thoby was destined for the bar; Adrian as well. The sisters might or might not earn money, and certainly it would have been within the tradition of their own family—which included the authors Lady Ritchie, Thackeray's daughter and their step-aunt, and Caroline Stephen, their father's sister—to do so. Writing in particular was one of the few professional careers open to middle-class women. Virginia was increasingly prolific as a reviewer. In 1907 she started her first novel, *Melymbrosia,* which was to be completed and published, as *The Voyage Out,* in 1915. Because of the state of her mental health during 1910 she did comparatively little work on the novel that year. Indeed the little work she did do on it at the beginning of the year may have helped bring about her breakdown in March.

The middle classes were far from immune to heart-wrenching trage-dies, and the Stephen family seemed almost unusually marked by illness, mental and physical. Leslie Stephen's first wife had died young, and their daughter was mentally retarded. His second wife, Julia Duck-worth, died in 1895 at the age of forty-nine, a devastating blow for the adolescent Virginia and an intensification of the congenital gloom of Sir Leslie. Virginia's first cousin, the brilliant writer J. K. Stephen, died young and mad in 1892. Her half-sister Stella died in 1897, only three months after her marriage.

Most tragic of all, Virginia's beloved older brother, Thoby, died of typhoid in 1906, at the age of twenty-six. His friendship at Cambridge with Clive Bell, Maynard Keynes, Lytton Strachey, and Saxon Sydney-Turner had led him to bring them to the Thursday evening "at homes" that the Stephen sisters started shortly after moving to Gordon Square. Perhaps in reaction and grief, Thoby's death on November 20 brought the Stephen sisters emotionally closer to his friends. Vanessa, who had refused Clive Bell before, most recently only twelve days before Thoby died, agreed to marry him two days after Thoby's death. The men who were interested in Virginia romantically at that time—and who proposed to her—were Walter Lamb and Hilton Young, also Thoby's contemporaries at Cambridge.

Lytton Strachey, although a homosexual, proposed to Virginia a year and a half later and was accepted. Almost instantly they both realized that it was a mistake, yet it was a possibility that did not completely disappear over the next year or so. The beginning of Leonard Woolf's romantic interest in Virginia can be found in his correspondence with Lytton, without the physical presence of Virginia herself. Strachey had written to Woolf that he had proposed to Virginia, but that they had both thought better of it. Such ideas were on these young men's minds, for on February 1, 1909, Woolf wrote to Strachey that he wished to marry Virginia, even though he had only met her a few times. It is hard to know how serious he was. "Do you think Virginia would have me? Wire to me if she accepts. . . . I wonder if after all Virginia marries [Saxon Sydney-]Turner."[4] While Vanessa had not abandoned the possibility that Lytton would marry Virginia, Lytton himself continued his matchmaking ways in a letter to Leonard in August 1909: "You must marry Virginia. She's sitting waiting for you, is there any objection? She's the only woman in the world with sufficient brains; it's a miracle that she should exist; but if you're not careful you'll lose the opportunity. . . . She's young, wild, inquisitive, discontented, and longing to be in love. If I were you I should telegraph."[5] Although Woolf was very taken with the idea, he declined to telegraph; instead he planned to propose to her when he returned in December 1910. But he did not come back to England until June 1911, and did not propose until early the following year. Virginia finally accepted; they were married in August 1912.

When Leonard returned in 1911 his most vivid impression was how much his friends' style had changed. One might hazard a guess that there had almost been a change in human character from the world he had left for Ceylon seven years earlier to the world he found on his return.

The social significance of using Christian instead of surnames and of kissing instead of shaking hands is curious. Their effect is greater, I think, than those who have never lived in a more formal society imagine. They produce a sense—often unconscious—of intimacy and freedom, and so break down barriers to thought and feeling. It was this feeling of greater intimacy and feeling, of the sweeping away of formalities and barriers, which I found so new and so exhilarating in 1911. To have discussed some subjects or to have called a (sexual) spade a spade in the presence of Miss Strachey or Miss Stephen would seven years before have been unimaginable; here for the first time I found a much more intimate (and wider [than Cambridge]) circle in which complete freedom of thought and speech was now extended to Vanessa and Virginia, Pippa [Strachey] and Marjorie [Strachey].[6]

There was, however, even a certain formality about the decision to use first names. In a letter in July 1909 to James Strachey, Vanessa wrote, with the salutation "Dear James": "Do you mind if we use Christian names? It seems rather absurd not to. Will you & Mr. Mallory come to tea on Sunday?"[7] Indeed, it was probably Lytton who introduced this tiny but significant change, calling Clive and Vanessa by their Christian names for the first time when he came to congratulate them on their engagement.[8] In his memoir of Strachey, Bell remarks of this change in the salutation of letters. "All begin 'Dear Bell' or 'My dear Bell'; the first beginning 'Dear Clive' is of November 25th, 1906. This is a date in the history of Bloomsbury. It was at the time of my engagement to Vanessa Stephen that we took to Christian names, and it was entirely Lytton's doing. No question here of drifting into a habit, the proposal was made formally when he came to congratulate us. The practice became general. . . . Henceforth between friends manners were to depend on feelings rather than conventions."[9]

To a considerable degree Leonard, in marrying Virginia, was taking on her custodianship, which previously Vanessa had largely exercised. Virginia was mentally fragile, heir to the instability of the Stephens and damaged to an unknown degree by the sexual molestations of her half-brothers. She would have a serious nervous breakdown the year after her marriage, and whether rightly or wrongly Leonard sought out medical opinion on the advisability of their having children. She had had her first breakdown at the time of her mother's death in 1895. In 1904 she had had another breakdown and in May of that year had attempted suicide. In 1910 she had had a less devastating breakdown. Some of the year was spent recovering; the standard medical recommendation of the time was for quiet, rest, and food. Yet much of this year was also an intensely active time for her, in public matters such as the *Dreadnought* affair and her involvement in the cause of women's suffrage. Privately there was her continuing flirtation with Clive—these were the years when she was closest to him—while Vanessa was preoccupied with the two-year-old Julian and her pregnancy with Quentin.

The Stephen sisters were not political activists; for them the most important world was that of art. Virginia was, however, a feminist. She began the new year in 1910 by volunteering to work for the women's suffrage cause. On New Year's Day, she wrote to her Greek tutor, Janet Case: "Would it be any use if I spent an afternoon or two weekly in addressing envelopes for the Adult Suffragists? I dont know anything about the question. Perhaps you could send me a pamphlet, or give me the address of the office. I could neither do sums or argue, or speak, but I could do the humbler work if that is any good. You impressed me so much the other night with the wrongness of the present state of affairs that I feel that action is necessary."[10]

Perhaps the most active suffragist in their circle was Lytton's sister, Marjorie. (Lytton's sister-in-law Ray Strachey would become a prominent figure in the movement and its historian.) The previous October Vanessa had written about a visit with Marjorie rather dismissively in a letter to Lytton which was mostly devoted, but not too explicitly, to a friend's wedding night: "Marjorie dined with us last night & seems to be rapidly going off her head about suffrage. I made her very angry too by saying that women were more hysterical than men."[11]

Because of illness that year, Virginia wrote far less than any year since 1904. She did only four reviews for the *Times Literary Supplement,* in contrast to sixteen the previous year. Her reviewing would continue to dwindle until after the publication of *The Voyage Out*. She was anxious to devote more time to her novel. To the extent that reviewing was financially significant, she was under less pressure: in 1909 she inherited £2500 on the death of her aunt Caroline Stephen.

2

The Dreadnought *Hoax*

In February 1910 the most significant event in Virginia Woolf's exterior life was the notorious *Dreadnought* hoax. (In the eyes of some, for Bloomsbury the year began and ended with jokes: the *Dreadnought* hoax in February and the Post-Impressionist Exhibition in November.) On February 7, a group of friends, including Virginia, boarded the H.M.S. *Dreadnought,* at that time the most powerful battleship in the world, posing as the Emperor of Abyssinia and his suite.[1] Or so the story has been told quite a few times. It was canonized in Adrian Stephen's brief account published by the Hogarth Press in 1936, the year of the death of Horace Cole, who had, with Adrian, been the main force behind the lark. From that time, and perhaps before, the episode was always described as a visit by the emperor himself. On the surface of it, this was improbable as the emperor was a fairly well-known international figure. There are interesting theoretical ramifications in the whole enterprise. Presumably there was some conscious choice that the group should impersonate Ethiopians, although their costumes, highly elaborate, were not accurate. They would be disguised with dark skin color and beards. At the same time, they would be expected to be less dark skinned and have more "European" features than Africans from farther south on the Continent. Here was a group of disrespectful young people choosing to impersonate a group of the "other," but in a rather elegant way and at an exalted rank.

Being Ethiopians was also an intriguing choice for other reasons. Ethiopia had been within the British sphere of influence earlier in the nineteenth century. But later in the century the Italians tried to make the area their sphere of influence. In 1889 Menelek had become emperor with Italian support. In 1891 he broke with the Italians and in 1896 defeated them, a great blow to Western prestige and domination, at the battle of Adowa. It was a rare triumph against the Western powers. One doubts that this victory was in the mind of the hoaxers in 1910, but their choosing to be Ethiopians certainly suggests some degree of subversive thought about the concept of Empire, particularly as Britain had tacitly supported, through various agreements, the Italian attempts to subdue Ethiopia. In the wake of the Ethiopian victory, Italy, France, and Britain all made treaties with Ethiopia recognizing, in varying degrees, the independence of the country. It was a great achievement for the Ethiopian emperor. By 1910 Menelek, weakened by illness, was much less in control and the Germans were fishing in the troubled waters of his empire. He died in 1911.

But in fact the group did not claim to include the emperor, despite Adrian's later statements to the contrary, but rather passed itself off as Prince Makalen and his suite who had come to England to visit Eton (Cole's old school—needless to say the visit did not take place) as a possible educational establishment for children of the royal house. In some senses the episode was rather silly and trivial, but it led to questions in Parliament, and it is of some significance in illuminating Bloomsbury's attitude toward the state, the empire, and the navy. In any case, it is quite a splendid story that bears retelling. It has been told before not only in Adrian Stephen's account in 1936 but in an article by Joseph Hone in the *Listener* in 1940, and in Quentin Bell's biography of Virginia Woolf. The first two are not quite in agreement with one another. I will also examine the official side of the story, as found in the records of the Admiralty in the Public Record Office.

Virginia Woolf's own view toward the navy may be suggested in a passage in *The Voyage Out*, which she was working on at the time. The ship in the novel, *Euphrosyne*, is taking Rachel Vinrace, the heroine of the book, on the voyage that will end in her death. It passes the British Mediterranean Fleet and dips its flag. The Dalloways, a much less attractive couple in this novel than they are in *Mrs Dalloway*, are worldly in not a particularly pleasant way. Richard Dalloway, rather crudely, both awakens and plays with Rachel's sexuality with his unsolicited kiss. The Dalloways are thrilled by the navy, Clarissa saying to her husband: "Aren't you glad to be English?" The passage goes on:

> The warships drew past, casting a curious effect of discipline and sadness upon the waters, and it was not until they were invisible that people spoke to each other naturally. At lunch the talk was all of valour and death, and the magnificent qualities of British admirals. . . . Life on board a man-of-war was splendid, so they agreed, and sailors, whenever one might meet them were quite especially nice and simple. This being so, no one liked it when Helen remarked that it seemed to her as wrong to keep sailors as to keep a Zoo, and that as for dying on a battle-field, surely it was time we ceased to praise courage.[2]

The British navy was hardly a laughing matter—although an equivalent to the *Dreadnought* episode might have been taken far more seriously in Germany. Anglo-German naval rivalry was one of the great themes and political facts of the period and undoubtedly one of the causes of the First World War. The *Dreadnought* was not only a particular ship but also the first of the new class of powerful battleship, the very symbol of the British navy's assertion of its continuing superiority over the German navy and its determination to maintain its position as the most powerful navy in the world. The public had demanded eight more of the same class of ship to be built, as in the slogan "We want eight. And we won't wait."

The General Election that had taken place in January had partially been waged over the issue of the Dreadnoughts. In 1909 Lloyd George, the chancellor of the exchequer, in order to raise enough money to pay for the old age pensions he had inaugurated and to finance the building of the ships, had introduced, among other methods, land taxes which the House of Lords considered confiscatory. The House of Lords, contrary to precedent, but claiming that they were acting in protection of the constitution, defeated the Budget. The Liberal government, headed by Herbert Asquith, called a general election. Lloyd George was the most colorful speaker in the campaign, asserting that a fully equipped Duke cost far more than a fully equipped Dreadnought. Contrary to the predictions, the Liberals won, although their majority was down from their great victory of 1906. The Budget was passed, and the power of the House of Lords would be a dominant issue in politics for the rest of the year.

Certainly the navy and the *Dreadnought* were fairly potent symbols of the state, an adventuresome target for young Bloomsbury to take on. Horace de Vere Cole, the originator of the hoax, was himself not a member of Bloomsbury, but as a contemporary and good friend of Adrian's at Cambridge he was a frequent visitor to Virginia and Adrian's house in Fitzroy Square. Cole was a member of a wealthy family with literary connections, being a great-nephew of the Anglo-Irish poet Aubrey de Vere. Born in 1881, he went to Eton, served in the Boer War, where he became quite deaf, and entered Trinity College, Cambridge, in 1902. He did not bother to take his degree, and one has the impression that he devoted most of his undergraduate days to planning pranks, although he was also interested in art and poetry. The same year as the *Dreadnought* hoax, his sister Annie Cole became engaged to Neville Chamberlain, about to launch his political career. Needless to say, the couple were quite disapproving of Horace's antics and of the *Dreadnought* episode in particular. When Annie asked her fiancé's opinion of the hoax he reported to his sister: "I was obliged to say what I did think, but fortunately it appeared that was her opinion too and she was not at all inclined to be proud of her brother's exploit. It appears that he is 28. I think he must be a little mad."[3] This was the same Miss Cole who was painfully teased by Virginia and Clive through excessive compliments at a Bloomsbury gathering in July 1909.[4]

Adrian had participated in Cole's previous hoax, in March 1905, persuading the mayor of Cambridge to receive, at the town's Guildhall, the Sultan of Zanzibar's uncle, played by Cole, accompanied by a party in costume and color, a suite of three natives and one Englishman. Adrian, writing about both episodes later, seemed to have enjoyed promoting the rank of the leading participants: in the first, the uncle to the Sultan himself, and in the second a leading prince to the Emperor of Abyssinia. There is a certain irony in this, as at the very beginning of his account he claims that he has no literary ability ("at least one of them involved in the hoax [Virginia] is so much better qualified in almost every way") but that it is "all but impossible for me to tell a lie," presumably also a contrast to Virginia, who was known for her elaborations of stories. Few were offended by the Cambridge lark, and the University declined, despite the urging of the deeply irritated town officials, to ask the young men to leave. As Adrian later wrote: "The person hoaxed was only a Cambridge tradesman (he kept a chemist's shop), whereas naval officers, as one critic said, were 'different'—they were 'men of honour.'"[5]

Adrian and Cole had created other practical jokes: pretending to be navvies digging up Piccadilly, giving a party in Birmingham where all the people invited had "bottom" as the last part of their names.[6] Cole was much more in the circle of the painter Augustus John than in Bloomsbury's, most notably years later, in 1928, when Cole married Mavis Wright, much younger than himself, as a second wife, and John had a son by her, Tristan Hilarius John de Vere Cole.[7] Was this the ultimate practical joke?

The tweaking of authority had been Adrian and Cole's idea from the start. Adrian's earlier plan when they were still at Cambridge was that Cole and himself should go to Alsace, then occupied by Germany, don German officers' uniforms, and somehow lead a group of German soldiers across the border into France and see what might happen. Adrian appeared to be quite convinced that they could carry it off, but they settled on the milder Zanzibar caper. Five years later they decided on a more ambitious hoax: a royal Abyssinian party to visit the royal navy.

The day of the hoax they discovered, or perhaps already knew—either way it added to the excitement—that the Stephens' cousin William Fisher was the chief staff officer on the *Dreadnought*.[8] (His brother H. A. L. Fisher was already an eminent historian and would be, during the First World War, Lloyd George's education minister, and eventually Warden of New College, Oxford, and holder of the Order of Merit. Perhaps his greatest contribution was introducing state scholarships to universities. William himself would become an admiral and a knight.) That the families were not very close decreased the chances of recognition, helped by costumes and make-up. Not to be recognized was essential if they were to achieve their aims. As Quentin Bell remarked, "The object of their excursion was to hoodwink the British Navy, to penetrate its security and to enjoy a conducted tour of the flagship of the Home Fleet, the most formidable, the most modern and the most secret man o' war then afloat, H.M.S. *Dreadnought*."[9]

The number of the participants began to dwindle, and two days before the prank, Virginia and Duncan Grant were asked to join as part of the royal suite. Anthony Buxton, another contemporary from Cambridge and Eton, a tall athlete, was to be the most important prince, inaccurately referred to as the emperor in the later accounts and also in his obituary in the *Times;* Adrian was to be the German interpreter; and Cole, Cholmondeley of the Foreign Office. Duncan, Guy Ridley, and Virginia were the other princes in the suite.

On the ship Buxton was introduced as "Ras el Mendax," rather an amalgam of an Ethiopian title and the real name of Emperor Menelek, who was also known as Prince Makalen. It is unknown who invented the title. Perhaps Cole was deliberately running a risk that any of the naval officers with some classical training might recognize the Latin word for mendacious, particularly familiar to generations of English schoolboys from the tag line *splendide mendax,* in a Horatian ode in praise of the one Danaid, Hypermnestra, who alone of the fifty sisters, did not murder her husband and cousin on their wedding night. It is not clear what feminist implications this story might have, but certainly the group thought of the enterprise as "splendidly mendacious."[10]

The *Dreadnought* hoaxers. *Left to right:* Virginia Stephen, Duncan Grant, Adrian Stephen, Anthony Buxton, Guy Ridley, Horace Cole.

Virginia did not get along easily with Adrian—Vanessa too found him hard to talk to unless they were reminiscing about family—so perhaps this was an effort to be nice to him, or perhaps she was taken with the excitement of the venture. Although a teaser herself, Virginia hated his teasing, so perhaps he goaded her into participating. Eventually he would become a psychiatrist after the war, led into it by his wife, Karin Costelloe. At this time he was qualifying for the bar, but spent much of his time mooning around 46 Gordon Square and pursuing, not too intensely, an affair with Duncan. The month before there had been talk of his embarking on a three-year course to become a legal historian, perhaps in the steps of Leslie Stephen's biographer, the great historian F. W. Maitland. As Vanessa wrote to Lytton: "Adrian has changed his profession once more. He is going to be a legal historian which may mean that he will have to spend one year at Oxford, one at Cambridge

& one in Paris as a preliminary to real work. This at least is Sir Frederic Pollock's advice to whom Virginia made him write in the heat of the moment. He is very enthusiastic about it now. I rather fear a second collapse. His [piano?] recital at the A.D.A. [?] ended in a complete breakdown."[11] Apparently nothing came of this plan.

Vanessa was horrified at the idea of the hoax as dangerous for Virginia's health. As she remarked five days after the episode, also commenting on the event and making clear her attitude toward Cole, in a letter to a close friend, the painter Margery Snowden:

> Our chief excitement this week you may have read about in the halfpenny press. I wonder if you would be very much amused or would think it rather silly as I am inclined to.... All was arranged when several hitches occurred & some of the people gave it up. They were beginning to think they couldnt go. Cole was getting frightened & Adrian was the only person who was really keen about it. They found there would only be 3 or 4 of them, & they thought that wouldnt be enough—when they asked the Goat [a family nickname for Virginia] to go too. She agreed—rather, I admit, to our horror—for Cole is really an intolerable bore. He is very rich & very vulgar—throws his money about.... Then they got Duncan Grant to go too. It all went off perfectly.

Vanessa was unhappy that Cole might become a more intimate part of her circle.

> The reason we object to it is that Cole will now pervade Fitzroy Sq—he is already doing so—& will probably make himself quite at home there now that he can consider himself on friendly terms with the Goat as well as with Adrian—the Goat having hitherto rather avoided him. It also seemed to us in another way a pity to drag her into it—for if they had been discovered as everyone thought they would be, the sailors would certainly have revenged themselves by some violent practical joke on them & it would have then been very awkward when it was found that one of them was a woman.[12]

The morning of February 7 (not February 10 as it is given in most accounts), employees of Willy Clarkson's, a professional costumer, came to 29 Fitzroy Square at seven in the morning in order to transform four of the participants into Abyssinian nobility. The four mistakenly did this before having breakfast, only to discover that they would harm their disguises by eating, and hence were starved the rest of the day.[13] The party then went to Paddington, where the stationmaster, surprised that he had received no advance notice but apparently not taking alarm, formed a reception committee and provided special carriages. Once the party had set off and could not be stopped, a telegram was sent to the commander-in-chief of the Home Fleet in the name of Charles Hardinge, at that time permanent undersecretary of state at the Foreign Office. Cole had located a post office in the West End where he thought no questions would be asked as it was exclusively staffed by women!

The telegram is preserved in the Admiralty papers as having been handed in at the St. James Street post office at 3.2 P.M. and received at 3.3 P.M. It read as follows: "C in C Home Fleet Portland Prince Makalen of Abbysinia [sic]; and suite arrive 4.20 today Weymouth he wishes to see dreadnought. Kindly arrange meet them on arrival regret short notice forgot wire before interpreter accompanies them Harding [sic] Foreign Office."[14] According to Adrian, a friend with the rather splendid name of Tudor Castle actually sent the telegram. Adrian thought quite wrongly that his own name was never discovered by the authorities. Sending the telegram was actually the only crime committed in the enterprise, it being a fraud to forge someone's name, in this case that of the distinguished Sir Charles Hardinge, who later in the same year would be created a baron and made Viceroy of India. Executing a hoax, even one that cost the taxpayers money, was not a crime as long as money was not extracted by means of it. The commander-in-chief of the Home Fleet to whom the telegram was sent was Sir William Henry May. Born in 1849, he had been in the navy since 1863, had been Third Sea Lord when the Dreadnought program was initiated, and would become an admiral of the fleet in 1913.

On the train the two chief conspirators, Cole and Adrian, had a grand meal, much to the distress of the Abyssinians, who had to make do with buns bought at the station at Reading and consumed behind drawn blinds. They were met at the station at Weymouth by the admiral's flag-lieutenant in cocked hat and sword. All went smoothly, red carpet at the station, one horse-drawn cab and one automobile, launch to the ship, sailors drawn up, flags flying, welcoming band on the ship (it hadn't been able to find the Abyssinian national anthem so it had played Zanzibar's instead, which of course was ironically appropriate), inspection of the ship. Adrian started with a few words in Swahili that Cole had taught him on the way down, then switched to remembered bits of Virgil and Homer. "When I was a boy I had spent years on what is called a classical education, and now I found a use for it."[15]

According to Hone, Cole and Adrian had themselves a good tea on the ship, claiming that the starving princes had already eaten. In Stephen's version, none of them ate, making the claim that because of the Ethiopians' religion, their food had to be prepared in special ways—Stephen saying that they were all apprehensive about their make-up, for even in his case it included a false beard. At this point, William Fisher appeared, demanding to know who Adrian was. Cole was quite concerned that Fisher had recognized his cousin, but when Cole replied that he was a German interpreter, Fisher expressed fury that a German was on the ship. The party, which inspected the ship for forty minutes, went off after the playing of "God Save the King" and an attempt, politely declined, at the station by Cole to invest the flag lieutenant with the Imperial Order of Ethiopia. Buxton lost half his moustache from a sneeze, but by this time he was in the train and was able to present only half his face to the cheering onlookers. Cole was particularly pleased to hear later that while they were on the ship a launch carrying royalty—a son of Prince Louis of Battenberg—crossed the bow of the *Dreadnought* and was reprimanded for doing so while the Abyssinian royal party was on board.

The hoax might have remained secret, as they had decided not to tell the newspapers. But as with the Zanzibar caper, Cole could not resist publicizing his exploit. He even went so far as to inform the Foreign Office. (Vanessa believed, or so she said in her letter to Marjorie

Snowden, that Clarkson's, the costumer, had let the cat out of the bag.)
The next day Hardinge telephoned the Admiralty with the information,
as noted in an Admiralty memorandum written on February 14: "A man
of the name of Cole called there [the Foreign Office] this morning &
stated that he had secured recently the reception on the Dreadnought
of a party of some three or four persons in the guise of Abyssinian
visitors to this country & he gave the F.O. to understand that the visit
was a deliberate hoax. The circumstances seemed to be very curious &
the inclination of the F.O. was to regard the man as mad, but at the
same time Hardinge thought it right that the Admiralty should be
informed."

This was contrary to what the majority of the group had wished and
expected. As Quentin Bell writes of Virginia's return to her house: "'Oh
Miss Genia, Miss Genia!' exclaimed Sophy as her employer, exhausted,
dishevelled, blackened and bewhiskered, let herself into No 29 Fitzroy
Square late that evening. The press should be told nothing. That at all
events was the view of the majority. They had been charmingly entertained, treated in fact with such kindness that they felt rather guilty,
and, at any rate, the joke had gone far enough."[16] A letter is preserved
from Virginia's cousin Dorothea Stephen, written some weeks later,
criticizing Virginia's participation in the hoax, and intimating that she
was led into such foolishness because of her lack of religious beliefs![17]
Clive Bell and Lytton Strachey also disapproved of the hoax, presumably sharing Vanessa's anger and concern that Cole was putting Virginia's psyche at risk, but both Virginia and Duncan were irritated at
Clive's disapproval.[18] Virginia wrote to Violet Dickinson on February
14 that the hoax was "now a dull story. Two interviewers have been
today, and one wishes for my portrait in evening dress! Also what age,
and creed am I."[19] The Press, presumably, had discovered the names of
the hoaxers but refrained from publishing them.

On February 9, Admiral May wrote to Graham Greene. There is no
indication in the Admiralty papers how he had already discovered it was
a hoax, unless the Admiralty had alerted him to the call the Foreign
Office had received. Graham Greene would be the most active official

figure in the handling of the situation. He had had a long career in the Admiralty civil service, starting in 1881. He was at this point the Admiralty's assistant secretary, and would become permanent secretary of the admiralty, and be knighted, in 1911. The episode does not appear to have hurt anyone's career. (Needless to say, this being England, Graham Greene was the novelist's uncle.[20] The civil servant apparently used Graham as part of his last name, without a hyphen, or at least he is so addressed in the official documents.) May wrote:

> There were four Abyssinians, accompanied by a F.O. official and an interpreter. The F.O. official was very deaf & talked for some time with Commanders Fisher and Willoughby & with whom he claimed several mutual acquaintances. From the telegram I naturally concluded Sir Charles Hardinge had forgotten to send the telegram & had then short-circuited the Admiralty. The telegram was not received until 3.45 pm [?] & the train by which they were travelling arrived at 4.20 pm so I had no time to wire to the Admiralty. The party were not 3/4 of an hour on board as they left at 5.30 & went by 6 pm train to London. The F.O. official said he had been in the Embassy at Rome. . . . Willoughby now says he thinks the interpreter had a false beard. The Abyssinians were in native dress & appeared to be genuine.

The story became public knowledge on Saturday, February 12, in stories in the *Express* and the *Globe.* The subheadline in the latter read "An Amazing Story" and continued, "For sheer impudence the exploit beats the imposture of Voigt at Koepenick, and no expense was spared to ensure its success." In this story as well as the one in the *Daily Telegraph* on February 14, a comparison was made with the well-known hoax of the Captain of Koepenick. That had caused a sensation in October 1906 when the poverty-stricken Voigt had marched into the Town Hall of Koepenick, a suburb of Berlin, and had impersonated a German officer. It was illegal in Germany to don any uniform to which one was not entitled, and in any case he also acquired money by the ruse. He was sentenced to jail for four years, served two, and later joined the Barnum circus. The episode, particularly in the stage version, by Carl

Zuckmayer in 1931, has been taken to stand for a German propensity automatically to defer to authority.

The cases were quite different in many ways, but both were dedicated, at least in part, to making fun of the military institutions of the state and as such presented a considerable challenge to the powers of government as to how best to deal with such "subversive" activities. In the English case, the participants were upper middle class, and indeed Cole spent a great deal of money to bring off the hoax. No doubt their class position protected them to an extent, but the state, in this case, was in some difficulty as the only illegal act was the forging of a telegram. (Voigt had been prosecuted for donning a uniform in order to extract money; the Dreadnought hoaxers had done neither.)

The story in the *Globe* had some errors such as that "one of the gentlemen . . . belongs to a noble family" and that two of the group were from the costumers, accompanying the Abyssinians "resplendent as dusky princes" as attaché and interpreter. The costumer commented to the reporter from the *Globe:* "The commander of the party was absolutely reckless in his expenditure. . . . Dissatisfied with imitation jewelry, he went out and purchased quite £500 worth of precious stones. . . . They were provided with short, crisp, curly black beards and the most complete sets of nigger lips." The telegram had been printed in the *Express* and "it must regretfully be said, adds the 'Express,' bore the name of a high official, whose lightest wishes were likely to be received with respect."

The *Globe* story went on: "With characteristic hospitality, the officers of the battleship strove their utmost to shower honours and attentions on their guests. The attaché from the Foreign Office was charming, and his explanations were complete. . . . [He] informed one of the officers that the 'princes' were on a visit to this country in order to make arrangements for sending their sons and nephews to school at Eton." At this point one of the notorious moments in the visit was recounted. Perhaps Cole created it for the newspapers or perhaps it happened but was not included in either Adrian's or Hone's accounts. According to the *Globe,* the princes "murmured in chorus," as a form of appreciation, "bunga,

bunga." The *Express* had the "bunga, bunga" story in somewhat more detail. "At every fresh sight they muttered in chorus, 'Bunga, bunga,' which, being interpreted, means 'Isn't it lovely?' That is to say, three of the 'princes' did but the fourth 'prince' being afraid to reveal her naturally treble voice, assumed a cold, and murmured 'chuck-a-choi, chuck-a-choi,' by which she intended to convey her great appreciation of the surroundings." "Bunga, bunga" became associated with the visit, and apparently for some time afterward boys shouted "bunga, bunga" at men from the ship when they strolled around Portland and Weymouth.[21]

Duncan Grant wrote of the escapade to Keynes on February 9 that they were greeted by a "lovely young lieutenant" and that there was a "full regiment of Marines drawn up on the deck playing Yankee Doodle, streaming flags in every direction & the Admiral and full staff drawn up on deck to receive us. Can you believe it? They were perfectly charming." On February 12 Keynes replied: "Until I saw you on the poster of today's Daily Express I didn't altogether credit your story. But there it is set out in print—so I suppose I must believe you. What a lunatic affair! Are you going to be jailed for it?"[22]

Further stories appeared in the newspapers on Monday, February 14, adding some glorious details to the hoax. The *Daily Mirror* had a long account, based on the version supplied (by Cole?) on Saturday. Here the full false names of the group are given: Herbert Cholmondeley of the Foreign Office; George Kauffman, the German interpreter. Cholmondeley and Kauffman are identified as the main actors in the Zanzibar hoax, Cholmondeley as the Sultan (no longer his uncle) and Kauffman as the Grand Vizier. The four Abyssinians are named in the article as Prince Makalen, chief Prince of Abyssinia, Prince Sanganya, identified, correctly, as the sister of the interpreter, Prince Mandox, and Prince Mikael Golen. The story describes their clothing:

All the princes wore vari-coloured silk sashes as turbans, set off with diamond aigrettes, white gibbah tunics, over which were cast rich flowing robes and round their necks were suspended gold chains and jewelled necklaces. Their faces were coloured a deep brown with a specially-prepared powder, and half hidden under dark false beards and moustaches, while, except in the case of the lady, their hair was dyed black and crisply curled. The young lady's make-up—she is described as very good looking, with classical features—was precisely the same as that of the other princes, save that her long hair was bound up tightly on the top of her head, and she wore a black curly wig. They also all wore patent leather boots which, Oriental fashion, tapered to a point, the ends projecting fully six inches beyond the toes. White gloves covered the princes' hands, and over the gloved fingers, they wore gold wedding rings—heavy, plain circlets, which looked very impressive. Prince Makalen, as chief of the royal party, had an additional ornament. This was the real Imperial order of Ethiopia—a star-shaped jewel, in the centre of which was a sapphire-like piece of glass. . . . The total value of the jewelry worn by the princes was at least £500.

Here the language reported was neither Swahili nor Greek nor Latin but rather gibberish, of which a sample is given: "Yembo inscara milu berango scutala bonga astema hevashi shemal." An eighteen-gun salute was declined, on the basis that the ship did not have an Abyssinian flag. (Adrian gave the reason as a reluctance to cause the sailors the trouble of cleaning the guns.) Cole told the naval officers that Makalen was Menelek's first cousin, and he explained the suddenness of their visit by the fact that they had hastily left Paris because of floods there.

In the same issue on a different page, the *Mirror* ran a photograph identified as the Abyssinian princes, putting "A" under the picture of the interpreter and "B" under that of the Foreign Office official. Those identifications were correct, but unfortunately the picture was of the Zanzibar hoax of some years before, so that both Adrian and Cole were in costume. Two days later the paper ran a large reproduction of the correct photograph, which the group had had taken before it set out, under the title "How the officers of H.M.S. Dreadnought were hoaxed: photograph of the 'Abyssinian princes' who have made all England laugh." All the participants are identified by the names they took for the hoax, Virginia as "the young woman of the party who disguised herself as 'Prince Sanganya.'"

The same day the *Daily Telegraph* ran the story, beginning: "Not since the Captain of Koepenick made the world laugh by his surprising exploit has so successful a practical joke been perpetrated as was enacted last week on board the battleship Dreadnought, the flagship of the Commander-in-Chief of the Home Fleet." This story points out that a Chinese Naval Mission, recently in the country, had been treated with great courtesy and allowed to inspect men-of-war. Such visits were usual, and the *Telegraph* reassured its readers that "Foreign visitors . . . are not shown anything which is in any degree confidential, but are merely shown round the ship with courtesy." The paper identifies Fisher as the brother of one of the participants, rather than first cousin of two. It also has Virginia's name wrong: "with delicious irony, the lady in the party. who was dressed in male attire, chose to be called 'Prince Mendax.'" The *Pall Mall Gazette,* in a brief editorial comment the same day, concluded by commending the hoaxers to the extent "that neither their aims nor their methods are at variance with good nature and decent fellowship."

The *Daily Mirror* on February 15 published an interview with Virginia, without giving her name. This article took a calm attitude toward the hoax, claiming that the officers of the *Dreadnought* were amused by it: "With that keen sense of humour which is one of the characteristics of the British naval service, they freely admit that the hoaxers scored heavily, and, far from bearing them any ill-will, they give them full credit for their successful and audacious trick." The article also states that the previous Sunday Captain Richmond of the *Dreadnought* met Cole and Stephen (only their pseudonyms are given in the story) and that they smiled at one another and shook hands, Richmond claiming that the officers of the ship "laughed heartily in appreciation when they learned they had been hoaxed." Cole apparently had received an invitation to take a cruise in a British warship, but that he had declined. Various ladies had written him asking to participate in the next hoax.

The interview with Virginia that follows makes her sound a rather empty-headed society lady. "'I had only two days' notice of the adventure,' she said, 'and I entered into it because I thought I would like the fun. . . . As a matter of fact, the only really trying time I had was when I had to shake hands with my first cousin, who is an officer on the Dreadnought, and who saluted me as I went on deck. I thought I should burst out laughing, but, happily, I managed to preserve my Oriental stolidity of countenance." In a second story in the *Mirror,* the paper reported that possible new names for the ship were being bandied about in Plymouth: the Abyssinia, the Aethopia, the Dark Horse, the Black Bess. Members of the Atlantic Fleet, at Dover, in rivalry to May's Channel Fleet "were vastly amused at the Dreadnought hoax, and there were many jokes about Abyssinia princes during coaling operations yesterday. Especially pleased are the men at the idea of the Dreadnought crew being turned out to salute black princes."[23]

The same day a local paper, the *Western Daily Mercury,* in a column entitled the "Bunga Bungle," reported on its interview with two chauffeurs. An order had come for one large car, but as the firm didn't have one available, two smaller cars were sent to meet the train. But only one was needed for the trip to the ship, as Lieutenant Willoughby had appeared with a horse cab. The drivers reported on the grave demeanor of the royal party, as well as the anxiety to be returned to the station in time to catch the six o'clock train back to London, for which the two cars would be needed. The article pointed out that in addition to offering the Grand Cross of Abyssinia to the admiral and the lieutenant, "they tendered the two chauffeurs and the Jehu [a fast driver] each a handsome douceur, and there was no red tape regulation to compel the latter to renounce the genuine gift." The high literary style of the local correspondent is consistent to the end:

> The revelation of the hoax has been the cause of an unrestrained flow of badinage among the sailors. The unfortunate lieutenant is now greeted with the familiar "Bunga bunga" on every hand, while among the ship's company the great joke is the Bunga bungle, and "Bunga bunga" is the prevalent password. "Bunga bunga" also appears to be gaining popularity in civic circles, and when a sailor of the Dreadnought passes along he hears, sotto voce, mocking "Bunga bunga" from some tickled landlubber.[24]

Perhaps an appropriate concluding press report was the full page the *Dorchester Mail* devoted to the story on February 18. It began:

> It is perfectly reasonable to assume that the all-absorbing topic in the official circles of the British Admiralty at present is the daring and skilfully perpetrated hoax. . . . Five young men, and one young woman, all of them extremely well connected and all of them well-to-do, carried out this joke on the Admiralty, the British Navy, and H.M.S. Dreadnought in particular. . . . It is safe to say that for sheer impudence and brazen effrontery, the amazing episode has never had an equal.

As in the story in the *Mercury,* the *Mail* emphasized the royal party's haste to make the six o'clock train. "They hardly waited for the motors to halt before they leapt out and hurried on to the platform." About "the girl" in the party, the *Mail* revealed that she had come to the plan late because of a male defection, and that she had "stepped into the breach and the breeches."[25]

Two days earlier, on February 16, the same day it ran the correct photograph on its front page, the *Daily Mirror* had carried another story claiming that, either through being cut out or blacked out by ink, the record of the visit had been removed from the logbook of the *Dreadnought.* Perhaps this was in reaction to the rather light tone the paper had taken the previous day. There had been a further development. In the original story it had been noted that the flag-lieutenant who had greeted the party and seen it off at the train had been offered by Prince Makalen the Imperial order of Ethiopia that he was wearing, but that the officer had declined it, as he could not accept it without permission. Now, according to this new story, the officer had discovered the real identity of Cholmondeley (Cole) and had written him requesting the Order, and Cole was sending it to him. At the bottom of the column there was a short further item entitled "Music-Hall Version" about a song being sung at the Pavilion Music-Hall at Weymouth:

> Mr. Medley Barrett, the comedian, was received with roars of laughter when he sang, on entering, to the tune of "The Girl I Left Behind

Me," the following doggerel verse:—When I went on board a Dreadnought ship, / Though I looked just like a costermonger, / They said I was an Abyssinian prince, / Because I shouted "Bunga-bunga." Though the rhyme is somewhat strained, the joke was thoroughly appreciated. The Dreadnought is at sea at present, and the common rumour has it that Admiral May intends to keep her out of port as much as possible until the joke has died down a little.

The stories do add even more drama. The hoax was clearly a sensation of the moment and put the Admiralty in a difficult situation. What was it to do? Authority is always awkwardly placed when it has been made mock of, as any action it might take is likely to make it look even more foolish. Should one rise above the situation or attempt to punish the perpetrators?

The issue now was how the civil service would react to the incident. Reginald McKenna was the First Lord of the Admiralty in the Cabinet. He was not yet involved, although he would be, and he was kept apprised. The First Sea Lord was Sir Arthur Wilson, a holder of the Victoria Cross in 1884 and an Admiral of the Fleet since 1907; in 1912 he would receive the Order of Merit. On February 12 Graham Greene sent him a note:

> I have telephoned to the Treasury Solicitor & he says that unless some injury or the obtaining of money or secret information can be alleged against the party there would be no case for an action, but there may be an offence against the Post Office Acts in the sending of a telegram in an assumed name with an intention to deceive. He will look up the question. In the meanwhile I presume no further action need be taken. The Solicitor is inclined to agree with Sir Ch. Hardinge that it would do more harm than good to attempt to deal with this hoax in legal proceedings, & that the best plan would be to do nothing. As I said, I think Sir E. Grey [Edward Grey, the Foreign Secretary] intended to speak to the First Lord on the subject.

But the honor of the navy was at stake and the incident would not end so quickly. On February 13 Admiral May wrote to Graham Greene:

I had expected to hear from you about this Abyssinian hoax. . . . Can anything be done to punish the ring leaders; in the first place can the law touch people who send false telegrams in the name of high officials? Will the Foreign Office or the Admiralty move in the matter & prosecute. Will the Admiralty take the opinion of the Law officers of the Crown & let me know if it is against the law. Do the Admiralty wish me to report the matter officially. If so, please return the telegram. My Flag-Commander [Fisher] feels sure that he can name two of the men & the woman & can give the addresses. Please let me have a telegram tomorrow & reply to questions that you know about as I want to know before I go to sea for two days early on Tuesday morning.

Graham Greene telegraphed to May that action was being considered, as he noted to the First Sea Lord: "As you wished to discuss the action to be taken with the First L[ord] I have simply sent a telegram to Sir W May to the effect that by your directions I have seen the Solicitor & Public Prosecutor . . . & that the desirability of taking legal action was being considered. This will satisfy Sir Wm that the question is being considered now officially."

The next day May wrote a formal letter to the Admiralty: "I beg to call their Lordships' attention to the visit of six persons, four of them in disguise [actually five counting Adrian] to the 'DREADNOUGHT' on the 7th instant. . . . I would point out the possible danger to the public service of fictitious telegrams . . . being sent of Officers in command of H.M. Navy."

Graham Greene wrote on February 14 a formal report on the episode. That afternoon he visited Mellor, the Treasury solicitor, and Sir Charles Mathews, the public prosecutor. Mathews said that ordinarily the solicitor to the post office would handle the offense but that he might be able to take it up if it were considered in the general realm of public administration. In any case the issue would have to come before the magistrate in the police court where the telegram had been sent, in Great Marlborough Street, and the magistrate would decide whether to issue a summary fine of forty shillings or to send the case to a high court, that is, "whether the Magistrate considered that it was a mere joke or whether it might be classed as a serious offence."

There was the further issue that even if the sender of the telegram was not part of the party, the others might be guilty if "one of the party aided and abetted in sending the telegram." As recorded in this memorandum, the Admiralty had concluded that the telegram had been written out by Cole and sent by

> a servant or an agent to take to the Post Office after the departure of the party by train. . . . It appears, therefore, a matter for consideration by the First Lord and the Secretary of State for Foreign Affairs, as to whether the Public Prosecutor should be instructed to take any action, or to investigate the circumstances with a view to advising whether they were such that a prosecution might be undertaken with a possibility of success. It will be seen from the attached letter that Sir William May desires that the matter should be seriously considered from the point of view of whether a prosecution were or were not, possible.

To this document, the First Sea Lord wrote a short addition:

> The serious part of this affair is the forging of a telegram from one high Government Official to another, and this, if not taken serious notice of, is likely to lead to repetitions which might have much more serious consequences and also to throw doubt on genuine telegrams, which might occasion serious inconvenience. Propose to write to the Foreign Office and Sir William May to ask them to furnish all the evidence in their possession against any person suspected of forging the telegram in order that it may be laid before the Public Prosecutor to see whether it is sufficient to obtain a conviction and if so that he should be asked to prosecute. Even though the Magistrate would probably deal with the case summarily and therefore by a fine only, it would be made clear that the offence was liable to imprisonment which would probably be inflicted on a repetition of the offence.

The same day the memorandum was initialed by McKenna, presumably approving the course of action. There is one final set of initials, on

February 16, probably Graham Greene's, circling back to him for action.

On that day, Graham Greene wrote a formal letter to Admiral May reviewing the situation. He reported that he had shown May's original letter of February 9 to the First Sea Lord. "There was nothing in the papers then about the incident & we hoped the villains would be content with what they had done & avoid publicity. So I was asked to communicate with the F.O. & the Solicitor as to the legal position & as to whether action should be taken, if so decided, by the F.O. or Admiralty."

Apparently the hoax had become known, as May's first letter indicated as early as February 9, through Cole's inability or unwillingness to keep his mouth shut. On February 17 Hardinge wrote to Graham Greene, in connection with a possible prosecution, that "Mr Horace Cole is apparently the ringleader of the hoax, and it was from him that the persons who originally informed a member of this Department learnt, in private conversation, of what had been done on February 7th." The letter goes on, giving a nice indication of the functioning of private knowledge and/or the class system: "I am, however, sure that you will agree that it cannot be expected that these gentlemen should consent to make statements to be used as evidence for the purpose of convicting Mr. Cole of acts which he detailed to them in the course of private conversation." He then hoped that similar evidence could be found that would not be protected by the gentlemanly code: "evidence of a more direct and primary character."

Graham Greene continued in his letter to Admiral May:

On the Saturday, however, the Press began to publish details of the hoax & the matter of course assumed a more serious aspect, though the offence remained the same.

On my return [from the country] on Monday Sir A. Wilson asked me to see both the Solicitor & the Public Prosecutor, & the result of my interview was, as I telegraphed to you, that the only legal action which could be taken was on the ground of the infringement of Section 11 of the Post Office Protection Act (1884).

The Section lays down that the sending of a forged telegram, whether with intention to defraud or not was punishable on summary conviction by a fine not exceeding £10 or on conviction on indictment by imprisonment up to 12 months with or without hard labour.

The operation of the Act would, however, be largely in the hands of the Magistrate & he might dismiss the case with say a 40/-fine only. It is therefore a matter for consideration whether, if evidence can be obtained as to the actual sender & forger of the telegram, the result of the trial would be satisfactory from the point of view of "authority." Certainly it would be unfortunate if officers had to appear to give evidence before a Magistrate in the prosecution of a serious charge & then the case was dismissed with a light fine & possibly some humourous remarks from the Magistrate.

The newspapers only would gain in excellent "copy" for their writers & scribblers!

In the Admiralty's papers there is a draft of the formal request to May for a full account because of the fear of "the serious results which may follow if no attempt is made to prevent the telegraph from being abused in such a manner as to mislead officers in the conduct of their duties." May replied to Graham Greene informally on February 17:

> I agree with you that it is no use prosecuting unless there is a very good chance of the offenders being punished on conviction or indictment with imprisonment. . . . I take it the Public Prosecutor would exercise a strong influence on the decision of the Magistrate.
>
> The difficulty appears to me to get hold of the sender of the telegram, as it was probably sent by some servant after the party had left London by train.
>
> If there is any chance of the Magistrate dismissing the case with a fine of 40/ then we had much better not prosecute.

Also on the 17th, May submitted his official account to the Admiralty, which adds some details, such as that "knowing Sir Charles Hardinge personally and there being no time to confirm the telegram by asking the Admiralty, I decided to give the so called prince the usual honours and show him the ship." The flag lieutenant was the Hon.

P. R. H. D. Willoughby, a son of the Earl of Ancaster (he would be killed in the First World War), who was sent to the Weymouth Railway Station "to meet the party, which consisted of four dark skinned persons in Oriental costumes, and two Europeans." According to this report, Cole

> evaded the question when asked for his own name by pretending that he was deaf [he was in fact deaf as a result of fighting in the Boer War] and could not understand what was being said. Later on when on board 'DREADNOUGHT' he gave his name as Cholmondeley. . . . I left the party after receiving them and went on shore. . . . Mr. Cholmondeley, now known to be Mr. Horace Cole, conversed with Flag Commander Fisher for some time and talked about mutual acquaintances. He informed him that Prince Makalen was a cousin of the Emperor Menelik, and asked that a gun salute might be given him. This was not done. It was also stated that the party had come to England to see the Public Schools, with a view of having their sons educated in this country, and that they were going down to visit Eton the following day, and subsequently Germany. The party left the ship at 5.30 pm, escorted by my Flag Lieutenant, who reports that on landing at Weymouth the man purporting to be Prince Makalen offered him a decoration, which, however, he declined to accept. Flag Commander Fisher can identify three of the party, viz., the Foreign Office Official, the Interpreter and the woman. He also informs that two of the party are Mr Adrian Stephen and Miss Stephen of 16[sic] Fitzroy Square, London.

One would guess, but cannot be sure, that Fisher also told May that the Stephens were his cousins. It must have made the whole incident even more embarrassing. Two days later the matter was turned over to the Director of Public Prosecutions.

On February 24 McKenna had to answer questions in Parliament whether any breach of the law had been committed. He replied that that was being investigated. McKenna's line was to dismiss the matter as "the work of foolish persons." Further questions were asked on March 2, and the First Lord promised to pursue the question of whether special white gloves had been purchased for the occasion, presumably at the expense of the state.[26]

Almost the final document in this tempest in a teapot, but one that involved many prominent figures and has the further intriguing aspect that a player in it became one of the most important writers of this century, was produced on March 9. Presumably the parliamentary questions gave a further impetus to the desire to conclude the matter. Charles Mathews prepared a confidential report for Graham Greene, in which he states that thanks to a police inquiry it had been discovered that the sender of the telegram was Tudor R. Castle of 33 Addison Road, Kensington. The further information is more or less the same as recorded before, except that it gives the exact time of the departure of the train from Paddington—12:40—and adds the detail that the party traveled from Paddington on the Great Western Railway but returned on another line. Castle communicated with the G.W.R. Company in order to secure a refund for the return part of the ticket, a quite ludicrous economy, considering how much Cole had spent on the enterprise. Mathews had obtained both a copy of the original telegram from the post office and the letter from Castle to the railway company and established that they were in the same handwriting—contrary to the earlier theory that the telegram was in Cole's hand. "Mr. Gurrin, the Handwriting Expert, has, so far as he can judge from a cursory examination of the photographs, no reason to doubt that the two documents are in the same handwriting." Mathews also believed that Castle played the interpreter. Greene notes on the margin that "This is not certain." As we know, it was Adrian Stephen. Mathews concludes:

> In these circumstances, I am of opinion that the evidence available is sufficient to justify the issue of a Summons against Mr. Castle, under section 11 of the Post Office Protection Act, 1884, for forging the telegram in question, and that a prosecution of Mr. Castle for that offence would result in a conviction. The question, however, as to whether or not such a prosecution should be instituted is one of policy, and is for Their Lordships [of the Admiralty] and not for me, to decide.

On the cover page of the memorandum there are various notations and initials indicating that Graham Greene, Wilson, and McKenna had all read Mathews's report. Wilson requested on March 12 that a letter be sent to May asking him if he wished Castle to be prosecuted. McKenna read the memorandum the same day, but made no comment. An unknown civil servant noted that "Mr Adrian Stephen one of the party told me that he was himself the interpreter & the photograph bears this out." On March 19 a letter was sent to May. On March 23 May replied, closing the episode officially. He was "pleased to inform Their Lordships that after consideration of Sir Charles Mathews' opinion expressed officially and semi-officially, and in view of the time that has now elapsed since the occurrence, I am of opinion that it would be better on the whole not to proceed with the prosecution of the person who sent the forged telegram." What is not stated explicitly in these documents is that the risk would be that acting now, when the nine-day wonder had calmed down, would revive the whole story. It was likely that the British navy would be made to look foolish once more with not very much punishment being handed out to the splendidly named Tudor Castle, who had had the least to do with the whole enterprise.

Reactions to the hoax were, however, taking place on a more private level, at the highest in the involvement of the Cabinet minister, Reginald McKenna, and at the lowest on the part of the young naval officers who felt that the honor of the navy had been besmirched. In 1940 Virginia Woolf gave a talk to the Women's Institute at Rodmell, the village where she and Leonard lived at Monk's House. By then, for the second time in the century, the worldwide militarism that was in part represented by the *Dreadnought* had engulfed the country in war. Only a fragment of the talk has survived, but in it she said that Adrian and Duncan Grant had gone to see McKenna, the First Lord of the Admiralty, about the matter. She had written at the time about the visit in a letter in early March to Violet Dickinson: "Adrian and Mr Grant saw McKenna. He merely laughed at them, and supposed they had to save themselves. When they said that they wished to apologise in order to get the officers out of the scrape, he was amazed. He said that it was ridiculous to suppose that anyone on board could be blamed for an instant. In fact, he seemed to think the suggestions impertinent, and said that an apology was not to be thought of."[27]

In her talk about the hoax years later she remarked:

> The truth was I think that Mr McKenna was secretly a good deal amused, and liked the hoax, but didn't want it repeated. At any rate he treated them as if they were school boys, and told them not to do it again. But we heard afterwards that one result of our visit had been that the regulations were tightened up; and that rules were made about telegrams that make it almost impossible now to repeat the joke. I am glad to think that I too have been of help to my country.[28]

One wonders what would have happened if, by chance, the perpetrators, as in the German case, had not been of the same class as those who were the victims of the hoax. The hoaxers were, after all, such who could speak to a Cabinet minister on equal terms, the son of Sir Leslie Stephen and a member of a cadet branch of the family of a prominent Scottish laird. McKenna might already have known of their brilliant friend Keynes, with whom he was to work closely when Chancellor of the Exchequer during the First World War. He would not have known that Grant had just told Keynes he was falling in love with Adrian.

The young naval officers decided to take steps on their own. But it was all rather decorous, and fitted into appropriate action for the upper classes. Hence, the next move in the comedy was that Willie Fisher came to see Adrian and bawled him out. "Did we realise that all the little boys ran after Admiral May in the street calling out Bunga Bunga? Did we realise we owed our lives to the British Navy? Did we realise that we were impertinent, idiotic? Did we realise that we ought to be whipped through the streets, did we realise that if we had been discovered we should have stripped naked and thrown in the sea?"[29]

Apparently, however, the conventions of the navy forbade Fisher to punish Adrian because he was a relation,[30] but Adrian foolishly provided the other names. It is not known what punishment, if any, was meted out to Buxton and Ridley. (Buxton became a major in the First World War, and later a distinguished naturalist and author. Yet in his obituary in the *Times* it was his role, incorrectly stated as the emperor rather than the emperor's cousin, a mere prince, that was given greatest prominence.)[31] Otherwise English common sense prevailed. Fisher visited Cole, and they agreed that an exchange of punishments would do, with six taps of a cane on his rear from Fisher to Cole, and then return taps—why?—from Cole to Fisher! Fisher and fellow officers also visited the Grants at breakfast time, kidnapping Duncan, to the consternation of his mother. Duncan's father, a retired army major, was more understanding, remarking to his wife, "I expect it's his friends from the Dreadnought." Duncan was taken to Hampstead Heath, but he wouldn't fight. He received two ceremonial taps. The officers offered to drive him home, particularly as he was in his slippers, but he declined and returned by tube.[32]

In his pamphlet, Adrian has a reverse order, that he and Duncan went to see McKenna after rather than before the visits that saved the honor of the navy. They wished to apologize; according to Adrian's account, McKenna was only interested in pleas for mercy, and when they were not forthcoming, dismissed the young men.

One further newspaper clipping from March 14 is preserved in the official file, from the *Daily Express*, which had carried one of the first stories. It reports that the hoaxers had been "caned by indignant officers." The story continues: "It was found impossible to bring home to these foolish offenders against the dignity of the British Navy any actual breach of the law. The Navy, however, has taken the matter into its own hands, and the 'Express' is now able to announce that punishment—informal, but none the less vigorous—has been meted out to the ringleaders in this stupid practical joke." The story does not sound quite correct, as it has five princes rather than three—one was excused because of illness and "the 'lady prince' was absolved." According to this account, one of the offenders was summoned to London from the country and ordered to go to Admiral May's residence. After being kept waiting twenty minutes, he

received a curt message from the Commander-in-Chief that his presence was not desired. The two other "princes" who were the instigators of the hoax were dealt with less leniently. Young naval officers have a more violent way of administering justice than admirals. They invited one of the "princes" to meet them in a certain house in London, and administered six strokes with a cane. The second of the two "princes" met with a similar punishment on the following Sunday afternoon. Like his fellow "prince," he also submitted to the castigation with lamb-like docility. The officers of the Dreadnought now feel that the honour of the Navy is satisfied.

It was all very public school, and presumably provided Virginia with further evidence of the silliness of the military mind.

As Quentin Bell suggests, this episode, without arrests and without too much high indignation, taken so much less seriously than the parallel episode in Germany that formed the basis of the play *The Captain from Köpenick,* nevertheless may have been a factor that helped persuade Virginia of masculine foolishness. It was also, of course, funny and in the English tradition of undergraduate hoaxes. But, if it is not putting too much weight upon it, it also suggests questions about the nature of the state—that its values, which had taken their modern form during the nineteenth-century development of nationalism, should not be regarded too seriously.

The *Dreadnought* and its sister ships, and their rivals being built in Germany and elsewhere, were important factors in the coming of war. They represented public, military values. The question of how many warships would be built was still a matter of debate. The Liberals, despite being the party of "Peace, Retrenchment and Reform," felt they had no choice but to give into the demands of the time; for better or worse, they prepared Britain for war. The hoax's implication of the foolishness of the military had no effect in sidetracking the juggernaut that was to come. It is also intriguing that four of the six were disguised as Africans and that one of the six was cross-dressing. Although the sex change of *Orlando*, published eighteen years later, was a kind of love letter involving Vita Sackville-West, it is possible that the robes worn on the *Dreadnought* that day had something to do with the central hinge of that dazzling fantasy. The change—"he was a woman"—took place while Orlando was Ambassador to Turkey.[33] The flowing robes that the princes wore were rather androgynous but the beards were certainly masculine. For Cole and probably for the others as well, carrying off a grand hoax was the dominant motive. Yet the episode does suggest that in their irreverent fashion, Virginia, Duncan Grant, Adrian, and his friends were also striking a blow in February 1910, minor as it might be, for private values and against war.

3

Virginia Woolf II

The *Dreadnought* episode did not interfere with Virginia's commitment to helping the suffrage cause in a small way, addressing envelopes, but it wasn't her world—even though later in the year she would attend some suffrage meetings. Years afterward, she would capture the atmosphere of the suffrage movement in her second novel, *Night and Day*, published in 1919. As she wrote to her great friend Violet Dickinson in late February 1910: "I spend hours writing names like Cowgill on envelopes. . . . The office, with its ardent but educated young women, and brotherly clerks, is just like a Wells novel. . . . I wish you would enlighten me upon human nature. The deeper one gets, the muddier it is."[1]

Perhaps because of the excitement of the *Dreadnought* hoax and the pressure of working on her novel, as she did until March, Virginia was moving closer and closer to a crisis. She may have thought that she was near finishing the novel. Certainly later in her life it was just that point—finishing a book and relinquishing it—that brought her to the verge of a breakdown. Dealing with the delirium and death of Rachel Vinrace, the central character of *The Voyage Out*, also may have unnerved her.[2]

In 1908, she had started work on the novel then called *Melymbrosia* and had consulted with Clive about it. There is the nice touch that the name of the ship in the novel, owned by her father, that takes Rachel on her fatal voyage, is the *Euphrosyne,* one of the three Graces, standing for merriment. It was also the title of the collection of verse that Clive had contributed to in 1905 as had, anonymously, Strachey, Woolf, Walter Lamb, Sydney-Turner, and A. F. Bell, no relation. Discussion of the novel-in-progress provided the context for the great intensity of Clive and Virginia's relationship in these years, as Clive was very pleased to be taken seriously as his sister-in-law's artistic adviser and provided the model for the lover in the book, Terence Hewet. The other major male figure, St. John Hirst, was modeled on Lytton. The two were depicted as great friends in the novel. But at this moment, or sometime later in the year, they had had a quarrel. Clive was being possessive about Vanessa and Virginia, and had gone so far as to forbid Lytton to visit Gordon Square. On January 1, 1911, Virginia wrote to Lady Ottoline Morrell: "I suppose you have heard of the terrible ructions which have split our world in two since you went away? The plan is now to give a fancy dress ball, where Clive shall be a Guardsman, and Lytton a ballet girl, and they will embrace before they discover, and make it up. But quarrels are really rather exciting."[3]

Virginia's weak health was a bridge to attention from Vanessa, and also from Clive. Though living apart in Bloomsbury, she and the Bells frequently spent time in the country together, as well as seeing one another constantly in London. This was the period of Clive and Virginia's closest relationship, an ardent flirtation which had started in 1908. As he wrote to her in May of that year: "I wished for nothing in the world but to kiss you. . . . What does matter is that we should not leave unsaid or undone those things which, by some divine emotion, we know we ought to say and do."[4]

They were intellectually and emotionally in tune in these years to a greater degree than they would be at any other time. Clive felt proud of himself for being, in his view, the first to recognize Virginia's genius.[5] Perhaps deliberately, Virginia was driving a wedge between herself and

Vanessa, punishing her sister for changing their relationship by marrying Clive. By 1910, however, the sensual tone of Clive's relationship with both sisters was less intense, perhaps because Clive had resumed seeing Mrs. Raven-Hill, his mistress before his marriage. Vanessa's pregnancy with Quentin may have been a factor as well. But Clive was clearly not happy with the idea of Virginia being involved with another man, and this may have been another reason for the fight with Lytton. Despite his homosexuality, there was still a possibility that Lytton might marry Virginia, even though their engagement in 1909 had only lasted overnight. Clive wrote to her in September 1910:

> To speculate on what exactly it is you want to say to the man you will love is not a congenial occupation: that way ill-temper and irritation lies, if not madness. You'll see what a jolly, hearty, well-[?], affectionate, slap-you-on-the-back-with-a-tear-in-one-eye, manly, pseudo-insouciant, "damme"-don't-care-a-rap-have-a-cigar-old-chap attitude I shall take up about your marriage in the future. But I hope you're going to write something about women first, before your sharp edges get blunted in the bed.[6]

Unsure of herself, not yet attached to Leonard, Virginia was grateful for Clive's advice on her novel. Indeed, the emotional triangle in *The Voyage Out* echoed her situation: Rachel's fiancé Terence Hewet derived from Clive; Helen Ambrose, her aunt, resembled Vanessa; Rachel, herself.

Vanessa, still in love with Clive, missed him terribly when he was away. But she was preoccupied with the infant Julian, and by 1910 she was pregnant with, she was convinced, a daughter who was to be named Clarissa. She was a young mother, and she was also fussing about Virginia, who was racked by severe headaches. There were renewed consultations with George Savage, a distinguished specialist on mental problems, who had been Virginia's doctor when she had her suicidal breakdown in 1904, after her father's death.[7] He had also been Leslie Stephen's doctor and treated Virginia without fee, at least in her earlier crisis, which placed her under a moral obligation to continue with him.[8]

Savage in 1910 continued the treatment he had prescribed at the time of her more serious breakdown in 1904. It was standard treatment for a neurasthenic rather than for a lunatic: rest, sleep, and nourishment. The official diagnosis was loss of nerve force, not of reason.[9] (Eventually, Virginia would express her resentment against him; he presumably served as one of the models for the pompous establishment physician Sir William Bradshaw in *Mrs. Dalloway*.) Following his counsel, she spent three weeks with the Bells and Adrian in a boarding house by the sea at Studland, in Dorset.

They had gone to Studland for the first time the previous Autumn, and in a letter of invitation to Lytton Strachey, before the quarrel, Vanessa provided a description: "It is a place near Poole Harbour, & sounds attractive country—but I must warn you that we shall be in lodgings, probably uncomfortable ones. I only know that the rooms are rather small. If it is fine it won't so much matter as there is a large beach very near. Virginia is going to be in the other lodgings there."[10]

In a letter of April 2, 1910, to Saxon Sydney-Turner, Clive provides an amiable picture of their life at Studland: "The weather is glorious, and the beds only rather lumpy. . . . The principal disagreements are hard beds, shoulders of mutton, pork, Semolina pudding, ill-trained cats, uproarious dogs and occasional excess in asserting of individualities. The great events of the day are the morning and afternoon posts; so you have a chance of creating [with a letter] a great deal of wholesome excitement and serving an eager and appreciative public."

Virginia was being closely watched, and Adrian, a few days later, wrote to Sydney-Turner about her health: "she is to all appearance as well as I have ever seen her; she spends most of her time in the open air, plays patience, eats her meals, on the whole, with avidity, & takes her medicine without too many protestations."[11]

Lytton Strachey commented, with some exaggeration and in a sense from a hostile camp, in a letter to Duncan Grant: "Did you hear that Virginia had a nervous breakdown, and went off with the rest of the Bloomsbury set to Studland? They're all still there—quarreling, I gather, from morning to night in their lodging house; but apparently it's

Virginia and Clive at Studland. Taken by Vanessa Bell.

doing Virginia a great deal of good."[12] Strachey in fact was staying close by, farther down the coast at the Cove Hotel in West Lulworth with Rupert Brooke. He was having quite a good time, although Bell did not envy him. As he wrote to Sydney-Turner: "Lytton, I understand, is caring for his body and asserting his individuality not far from us, at Lulworth, with Rupert Brooke, who enjoys himself, I hope, better than I should in his place." In the same letter he gave a good report of Virginia: "The patient, I think I may say, is restored to her wonted health. We are all fairly happy, and moderately amiable."[13]

Yet the stay does not sound like a complete success, although Clive put the best face on it in a letter to Lady Ottoline Morrell: "Our invalid grows daily less placid and more caustic, which may be regarded as a very good sign, and a return to normal conditions. Normal conditions, I may say, are not very well suited to close quarters in a lodging house, but they are encouraging." He continued in the letter to comment on Lytton:

> Poor Lytton Strachey; he has fallen ill again and must leave London and all its intrigues; he leaves it, however, with that comely young poet, Rupert Brooke;—a poor substitute for your Tuesday evenings—to which he is careful to tell me he has been invited—but still a substitute. Dust and Ashes! He has some thought of joining us, it appears, and I hope if I dissuaded it will not be imputed to me for uncharitableness. A knot of decrepit Byrons and Chateaubriands asserting their individualities [clearly a favorite phrase] round a patent-stove affords an atmosphere depressing for a convalescent, or, indeed, for one that is whole.[14]

In part flattery, but in part true, the rest of the letter suggests that Clive would rather be at Lady Ottoline's spacious salon (even if he had its usual day wrong) at Bedford Square than at the seaside boarding house.

That spring the Bells went to stay with the Waterlows in Rye, in the house of Waterlow's father-in-law, the famous jurist Sir Frederick Pollock. Sydney Waterlow, born in 1878, was slightly older than the Bells. He had entered the diplomatic service in 1900 after being a brilliant classical scholar at Trinity, but in 1905 had left the service determined to return to the classics. He had married Alice Pollock in 1902. The marriage was unhappy, undoubtedly not helped by Bloomsbury's opinion that she was quite stupid. At this period Sydney was becoming closer and closer to Bloomsbury, particularly to Virginia, to whom he would propose unsuccessfully in 1911 although he was not divorced until 1913.[15]

Waterlow was also a good friend of Henry James, who was living in Lamb House in Rye. After dinner, as Clive reported to Virginia, he and Waterlow discussed, with much praise, Virginia's unsigned review of Emerson's Journals that had appeared in the *Times Literary Supplement* on March 3. (In that review, one has a sense of Virginia identifying with the young Emerson, as she too was already struggling with the emergence of a style of her own: "In the pages of his diary one can see how his style slowly emerged from its wrapping, and became more definite and so strong that we can still read it even when the thought is too remote to hold us.")[16] Clive and Waterlow also discussed both Lytton and Virginia, Clive reporting that on the latter "I was peculiarly lucid & acute, and one illustration by means of which I explained what I meant by 'the artist's vision of a situation' was so remarkable as to be almost worth remembering." He concludes his letter saying that Vanessa wished to remind her to make an appointment with Dr. Savage, and adds an injunction of his own: "Do try to sleep well & be better before I come back."[17]

In June Virginia took another holiday with the Bells at Blean, near Canterbury. She was there for almost a month, recording her stay in amusing letters to Saxon Sydney-Turner and others. But at the end of the time she was still depressed (Blean doesn't sound all that diverting) and still having her severe headaches. Savage decided that more drastic action should be taken: a nursing home. For part of this time, Vanessa left Virginia and Clive at Blean together and went back to London to await her child's birth, which would not, however, happen until mid-August.

While in London Vanessa wrote frequently to Clive and Virginia, still at Blean, about the doings of 46 Gordon Square. Reading her

Virginia and Julian at Blean. Taken by Vanessa Bell.

letters, one appreciates how important servants were to middle-class life of the time, with the constant comings and goings of various individuals for lunch, tea, and dinner, let alone the need for help in looking after the two-year-old Julian. The young men, Adrian, Saxon, and Duncan, spent much of their time there, Saxon in particular. Vanessa appeared to be a little skeptical of the intensity of the passion between Adrian and Duncan.[18]

There can be no question, however, of the love and rapport between the two sisters, even if now clouded by the close relationship that had developed between Clive and Virginia. Upon her return to London Vanessa wrote a letter full of news of Adrian's doings, of the exhibition at the Friday Club, and of seeing everyone at the opera. Yet there is a sense of envy of Virginia, with her "green suspicious eyes," and Clive for being together: "She, I see, will fling it [the letter] down—& then finger it again & re-read scraps in the hope of finding something between the lines (as if there were any interstices in my simple pages). . . . Adrian has reduced Duncan to tears by abusing the Stracheys—dont repeat this—& Marjorie is supposed to have changed her views & now finds men attractive."[19]

Two days later Vanessa wrote an overly protesting letter to Clive—in the animal language of lovers (with Vanessa being a Dolphin, a frequent conceit)—about buying, ostensibly as a birthday present for Clive, a sketch by Duncan, *Lemon Gatherers*. She felt they were likely to receive about a thousand pounds as gifts at the time of "Clarissa's" birth, so the picture could be afforded.[20] Very conscious of missing Clive, she wrote to him some days later: "Your poor little bed-fellow is so lonely of a morning."[21] And in a letter a few days later: "You do make me astonishingly & continuously happy."[22] In letters in August and September, when she was in London just having given birth and Clive was out of the way with Julian at Seend, she frequently mentioned with pleasure the thought of Clive rushing up the stairs to her bedroom. She was still very much in love with him even though she knew and seemed to accept that he was once again seeing his former mistress, Mrs. Raven-Hill, whom she referred to in letters to him as "your whore."

These years, before Virginia's marriage to Leonard, were when the relationship between the Bells and Virginia was at its most complex. Clive, who found it hard to cope with fatherhood, enjoyed the emotional excitement of his relationship with Virginia and probably would have gone to bed with her if she had been willing. As he wrote to her in a rather heavy-handed fashion about their forthcoming time in Blean: "I know I shan't be disappointed with Blean and you know why, but you'll only think I'm trying to win you back to a good temper with compliments."[23] Considering her mental state, it might have been inconsiderate to press upon her the strength of his feelings. The same day she wrote to him—the mails were so good then that one letter may well have been in response to the other:

> It is very doubtful whether a woman of my defective taste should write a letter of affection. . . . All I wanted to say was—how very much attached to you I am, and how much pleasure you give me. I see that I never did understand so much as I thought: perhaps I didnt have the chance. The future will be made much more pleasant by being more appreciative of you. I cant go on to say in what directions I am more appreciative, being stupid with paying bills, but I think that if you saw what I meant you would be pleased. I expect that what I mean will wear through in time.[24]

Clive was just beginning his own literary career in these years. Up until 1909 he had been little more than a young man about town, with an interest in literature, and with literary friends. He himself thus far had published hardly anything at all. In 1905 he had contributed to the collection of anonymous poems entitled *Euphrosyne*. That same year he had published a verse translation from the Latin and in 1906 a negative review of G. M. Trevelyan's study of George Meredith, both in the *Cambridge Review*. But in 1909 and 1910 he contributed thirty pieces to the *Athenaeum*, and in fact he edited it for three weeks in the summer of 1910. In his writings then there was no particular indication of his interest in art. All the pieces were literary with the exception of a rather dismissive obituary of the *Punch* cartoonist Linley Sambourne; he was probably chiefly familiar with Sambourne's work through the coincidence that two other *Punch* artists, G. D. Armour and Leonard Raven-Hill (the husband of Clive's mistress), were Wiltshire neighbors of his parents. His reviews also included a favorable one, but with some criticisms, of *Howards End*, in December 1910.[25] The meeting with Fry and the subsequent Post-Impressionist Exhibition were to change the direction of his writings dramatically; the publication of *Art* in 1914 and its exposition of the doctrine of significant form would mark him thereafter primarily as an art critic. It was an interest he had had for a long time—he had been uncommon in having a reproduction of a Degas in his undergraduate rooms, and he had sought out artists on his visits to Paris in earlier years. But the events of 1910 gave him his professional identification.

Virginia, although only two and a half years younger than Vanessa, regarded her in an almost daughterly way, yet combined with an amorous intensity. She had resented Vanessa's marriage to Clive, and her flirtation with him was, in part, a kind of revenge. The sisters' relationship certainly survived this; the closeness between them was probably the most intense emotional relationship of their lives, even more so for Virginia than for Vanessa. But the flirtation also changed their relationship; Vanessa may have never completely forgiven Virginia for it, and it may have helped prepare the way for a change in the nature of Clive and Vanessa's intimacy, although their becoming friends rather than lovers did not happen until the next year.

On Dr. Savage's recommendation that she needed more careful supervision, Virginia went as a patient to Jean Thomas's nursing home, Burley, in Twickenham outside of London, where she would stay from the end of June until the middle of August. The decision came up fairly quickly, because as late as June 25 Vanessa was asking if they would all spend the rest of "a cheerful summer at Studland? You with your brains teeming with new ideas & producing all kinds of works—& I at last quit of Clarissa."[26] But perhaps Vanessa was whistling in the dark; only two days earlier she had written about Savage's feeling that more drastic action—the nursing home—was necessary. Or was it that Studland would be for September, after the stay at the nursing home?

Once the decision was taken to go to Twickenham, Virginia wanted to get on with it and leave Blean a few days earlier than intended. As she wrote to Vanessa about the nursing home: "I've no doubt it will be damnable, and the thought of the nurses and the food and the boredom is disgusting; but I also imagine the delights of being sane again. He [Savage] says he wont insist on complete isolation, so I suppose I shant be as badly off as I was before." She was also in some sort of consultation with her half-brother George but was finding him rather obtuse. "I think I shall say [to George] that I expect to be confined next month, and let him muddle it out for himself. He will suspect Saxon, and take immediate steps to have him promoted [in the civil service]. He will also run down to Brighton, and negotiate a settlement with Saxon père."[27]

Vanessa was extremely supportive, writing Virginia frequently, not expecting answers as Virginia was advised to write as little as possible. Vanessa took very seriously Savage's diagnosis of the situation.[28] She was also anxious that Virginia not think that she had urged the rest cure upon Savage.[29] Virginia found the need to rest extremely boring, but she was committed to that course of action. A month later she wrote to Vanessa: "I feel my brains, like a pear, to see if its ripe; it will be exquisite by September."[30]

Letters from Vanessa to Virginia, written in July, provide a vivid sense of Vanessa's concern, the difficulties Virginia presented as a patient, as well as a sense of Bloomsbury life. They are addressed to "Billy," a shortened version of another nickname, Billygoat. The letters have that characteristic of good humor and regard with which one frequently writes, perhaps not effectively, to the sick. Savage didn't want Virginia to have visitors at first nor indeed too many letters, suggesting to Vanessa that she only write once or twice a week.[31]

The letter of July 17 begins: "I heard what I expected from Clive—that you are seducing the household of the hitherto respectable Miss Thomas & that your own lusts are increasing at the same time. Perhaps you find massage conducive to lust. I can imagine it might be.

Really, what with your cultivation of Sapphism with a Swede at Twick-enham & Lytton's of Sodomism with Swedes in Sweden, which apparently is the breeding house of vice, you will be a fine couple worthy of each other."[32] Vanessa was in the last stages of pregnancy, and presumably it was harder for her to visit. She was fearful that Clarissa might be born on the train to Twickenham. Clive came to visit instead; but it would almost appear that Vanessa had a certain pleasure in throwing them together. According to Clive, Miss Thomas, the proprietor of the nursing home, was extremely fond of Virginia. Vanessa was also consulting with both Savage and Miss Thomas. This ran the risk, not uncommon in such situations, that the patient would feel that her relations and the professionals were conspiring against her.

Vanessa, in a letter of July 20, told Virginia what she had been up to in London, claiming that life was rather dull, but it may well have given her a sense of all she was missing: tea with Ottoline just before she left for a trip—

> She was moribund & Philip looked miserable. . . . Adrian & Duncan came in & did not make matters better. Everything dragged & Ottoline was too limp to do anything. . . . A. & D. came back to supper here & afterwards we tried to re-create the hysterical merriment that overcame us at Blean one evening when we talked of funeral scenes, but without success. We also raked out some of the many thousand letters that Granny wrote to Mother but they proved dull too. . . . Everyone agrees that the summer has been a mournful one, whether on account of your disease or the King's death, does not seem to be certain. Of course Clarissa also has not added gaiety to the scene.[33]

Vanessa was also seeing Marjorie Strachey, Lytton's sister, who came for a gossip, telling Vanessa that "she has at last fallen in love with a man" who Vanessa thought might be Duncan. At the same time, Marjorie talked of her infatuation with Mary Berenson during a trip to Florence. She seemed quite concerned about getting married. "She certainly is not attractive physically & I can't well imagine anyone marrying her. She made a lot of enquiries about the prevention of babies, a subject of which she seemed to be quite ignorant & which apparently interests her as much as it does Ottoline."[34] Marjorie reappeared for dinner a week later, discussing women's suffrage, to which she was devoting quite a bit of time.

A visit from Clive at Twickenham does not seem to have been a success, as it brought about Virginia's most common symptom: intense headaches. The breakdown may have had something to do with the flirtation between herself and Clive; its incestuous overtones may have revived some bad memories of her relations with her Duckworth half-brothers. In a rather loving letter to Virginia for her birthday the following January 25, Clive wrote, "I am amazed at some things, the way I have been managed since Twickenham days amongst others. Shall we ever talk of that I wonder? Well, it's not only in feminine powers of management that you have grown. I admire you more than ever. I think you're more beautiful, more charming, and more like a genius than when you were twenty-eight."[35]

On July 29 Vanessa wrote a long concerned letter about Virginia's health, refuting the charge of conspiracy. Much to Vanessa's distress, Virginia had seen her innocuous letter to Miss Thomas in which she wrote that she hoped Virginia would stay at the nursing home as long as necessary to be better. Virginia interpreted that as a desire to keep her there far too long. Perhaps the gossipy letter of July 20, which Vanessa had undoubtedly written in an attempt to amuse, had given the impression that Vanessa did not care about her health. Savage had said that she would be well in three or four weeks. As Vanessa wrote, "I think Miss T., though I quite agree with you as to her being emotional etc. is also very sensible & intelligent & does understand your health & constitution generally very well. I expect that Savage does too, but evidently he has either been wrong twice—first when he said you would be cured in 3 weeks & secondly when he said you would be perfectly well in 4—or else, as I think probably in the second case, he cant bring himself to order you to do what he knows you would hate." She went on: "I think it is clear that you arent well yet. If you were you wouldn't have a bad head all day as the result of 2 hours with Clive the day before."

Vanessa thought that if Virginia returned to London too soon she would exhaust herself, particularly as she would be rushing to see "Clarissa." "We shall both get very cross & very much agitated." Reporting Miss Thomas's analysis of the situation, that Virginia should accept the need for careful living for a few days, Vanessa added: "you can't be trusted to act with sense unless you are constantly told of the need for you to do so." Now that they were no longer living together, Vanessa could not look after her constantly. "Even if it does land you in a lunatic asylum or make you a permanent invalid, I see that you must be left to your own devices. I have only written all this, which I know will make you very cross, because you seem to think that I am trying to arrange matters for you secretly." Vanessa worried that Virginia would leave the nursing home too soon and have another breakdown that would be even worse. At the same time, she had to be supportive of Virginia's wish to leave. Vanessa presented a bleak picture of life in London in the summer, she involved with "Clarissa," Clive at work (he was now much occupied with the editing of the *Athenaeum*), Adrian away.[36]

Miss Thomas, who had become fond of Virginia, would not be free herself, because of other patients, until the middle of August, to travel with Virginia. Vanessa could be a little impatient with Virginia, or perhaps she saw it as rather a way of teasing her to get better. She certainly did not trust her to look after herself. "You might just as well be giving up the time to having babies as to having these attacks, as far as your brains are concerned."[37]

It is unclear whether Virginia remained at Twickenham until the middle of August, when she and Miss Thomas went on their two-week trip to Cornwall, or left sometime earlier to spend some time in London. (There is a gap in Vanessa's frequent letters to her between August 8 and August 26.) Talking and writing were Virginia's greatest pleasures, and even when she was no longer at the nursing home she was to have a quiet routine prescribed by Dr Savage: resting after lunch for an hour, no coffee after lunch, and getting to bed by eleven.

Perhaps it also made Vanessa's life a little simpler that Virginia was in Cornwall with Miss Thomas when "Clarissa," who turned out to be a boy, was born on August 19.[38] By August 1 Vanessa thought it might be a boy: "It seems so absurd to go on waiting here for Clarissa whose existence I am beginning to doubt. I think she must be a boy, or she'd be more considerate in her time of arrival."[39] There was the problem of his name, as boys' names had not been thought of. Vanessa wished to call him Claudian, but hated the nickname Claud. The Bells appeared to be in a Latinate mood; as Gratian was another possibility, and that was the baby's name for a while. Vanessa remarked with apparent pleasure on what she imagined would be Adrian's and Virginia's reaction to the name. "How they will dislike 'Gratian.' I'm sure they hope for Leslie or James."[40] Gerald Duckworth, she reported, was quite exercised about it: "Just think of the poor chap at school. I said yes—but perhaps he wont go to school—on which I thought he would have apoplexy. . . . Tomorrow when Saxon comes I am going to get him to go carefully through the dictionary with me so as to be sure that we arent missing something better than Gratian—which however I like more as I think of it."[41] Two days later she had switched to Claudian.[42] There seemed to be a general concern about the name. That same day Keynes wrote to Grant: "I have not heard about Vanessa's male child. What are they going to call him? Are they going to try again for a female?"[43]

Some days later Stephen seemed a possibility. "Stephen Heward [a Bell family name] Bell doesnt sound bad—but I dont quite take to Stephen as a Christian name. It sounds to me rather pompous & not beautiful. But it is respectable & distinguished . . . The choice seems to me to be between Stephen—I can be reconciled to. Quentin, I like. Cyprian I like. Claudian I really like best I think but perhaps the danger of Claud is too great. Saxon likes Jovian but he'd be called Jo inevitably."[44]

The issue was still unsettled in December, although Claudian then seemed more favored, when the Bells and the boys were spending Christmas with Clive's family in Wiltshire. (Vanessa spent her time reading *Clayhanger;* her sister-in-law *Howards End.*)[45] Clive wrote to Virginia: "Claudian still suffers for lack of a name. I believe it would be much better to stick to the one he's got, though I don't much care for it, and let him take another for himself if he wants one when he is older.

Otherwise, I vote for Fabian or Christopher, neither of which Vanessa can abide. I doubt whether there will be any change. Julian [now almost three] says Quentin would be best."[46] Finally, following Julian's advice, they decided on Quentin, with Claudian as the second name.

Until the middle of October Virginia would continue to be out of London, searching for health: first in Cornwall, with Jean Thomas. She reported to Sydney-Turner a scene that she would use in *The Voyage Out:* "Last night we crept under the windows of the grand hotel, and saw Miss Mickle and Mr Thomas Dunhill playing Brahms to a great drawing room full of dowagers and athletes."[47] Virginia became quite close to Jean Thomas and appreciative of her devotion. She would visit her in the months to come, noted in her letters the antics of those in the nursing home, and did not take badly Miss Thomas's exhortations to become an active Christian in order to avoid insanity.[48]

In late August Clive, rather disconcertingly, one would think, for Virginia, wrote to her:

I am not easy; never, since you came back from Twickenham, have you been quite yourself. You haven't yet recovered your wonted vitality, your devilry, your "je ne sais quoi", have you? You're not entirely the Virginia that I used to know, though you've become more so since the early summer. What I want you to do is to let me know, from time to time, what you think about yourself. I should attach far more importance to that than to the most elaborate medical or physiological details. Will you simply tell us whether you feel yourself to be going forward or going back or stationary; and tell us quite honestly?[49]

There is evidence that she was still closer to Clive than she would be later in her life, and on September 4 she wrote him a long letter, presumably in reply to his in late August, in which she reviewed the three most important elements in anyone's life: health, love, and work.

I remember that you asked me some searching questions about my health. I feel that this fortnight [in Cornwall] has done a great deal of good, and brought back that kind of spring which has been lost all this time. . . . As to my being recovered, I think there is no doubt. You will find me scarlet and brown and I believe, fatter.

With regard to happiness—what an interesting topic that is! . . . My conclusion upon marriage might interest you. So happy I am it seems a pity not be happier; and yet when I imagine the man to whom I shall say certain things, it isn't my dear Lytton, or Hilton [Young, who had also proposed to her in 1909] either. . . .

I have been thinking of Thoby all the time here; I suppose it is the birds. . . . I hope to work on Women every morning at Studland. I have only one book here—a small Pope. I fumble the words, awkwardly, with a kind of awe, like a rustic. That world becomes astonishingly far away. How odd—that one writes oneself![50]

Quite a few letters appear to be missing, as the next one to Clive, on September 8, remarks: "I'm very sorry that I didn't write before, but I thought you saw all my letters to Nessa; and I was purposely very lazy. But I did write, as a matter of fact; and didn't send it, when Nessa's letter came, as I thought it looked like asking for Lytton's letter. However, waiting didn't do any good apparently; and I suppose I have made you angry."[51] Her state of mind was still fragile. Vanessa had written to Clive about her the previous day: "She saw it was necessary to be very careful for a long time & that she would now do anything to avoid these headaches. She told me she had written to you & had asked you to help her to avoid emotional scenes! I think she really has no idea that they may in any part be due to her as much as to you."[52]

There was a further family holiday at Studland starting September 10, in which Clive joined part of the time. But mostly this vacation belonged to the sisters (and Vanessa's sons), what one might regard as the truest heart of Bloomsbury. Vanessa was in the difficult position of looking after her sister as well as her children; Virginia was not, presumably would never be, completely recovered. It was particularly difficult as part of the problem was Virginia's relation to Clive, complicated by Clive's quarrel with Lytton. Vanessa and Virginia often talked about Lytton, Virginia stating that marriage with him was quite impossible—but it is striking that such a marriage was still not totally out of her mind.[53] Virginia's doctor, Savage, was disturbed about the relationship with Clive and felt that the solution was for Virginia to marry, preferably an older man.[54]

Clive had gone to London, and by now he was on his way to Paris to meet with Fry and Desmond MacCarthy to select pictures for the exhibition. There was a contrast between the more exotic experience of Clive in Paris and that of Virginia and Vanessa with Julian and the still named Claudian (and servants) at the beach at Studland: Julian playing in the sand and trying to involve his mother—"he was almost in tears yesterday because he couldnt make us understand the song about Grace Darling"; in contrast to Clive in Paris—"I wonder whether you'll come across a new genius in Paris & even perhaps invest in one of his works."[55]

On September 26, while Virginia was in Studland, her review of *Mrs Gaskell* by Mrs Ellis H. Chadwick appeared in the *Times Literary Supplement*. It was her last publication in a year in which she wrote only four reviews, and it was lightly scathing. The book, subtitled "Haunts, Homes, and Stories," dealt with the surrounds of a writer. (Such a review can be taken as a rebuke to the "Bloomsbury industry" and does, it must be admitted, make one feel a little uneasy about this very enterprise. On the other hand, Virginia feels that there are some writers who deserve such attention. Let us consider her in that number.) She writes that Mrs. Gaskell

> would have opened [the book under review] with a shiver and dropped it with a laugh. It is delightful to see how cleverly she vanishes. . . . The surprising thing is that there should be a public who wishes to know where Mrs Gaskell lived. Curiosity about the houses, the coats, and the pens of Shelley, Peacock, Charlotte Bronte, and George Meredith seems lawful. One imagines that these people did everything in a way of their own; and in such cases a trifle will start the imagination when the whole body of their published writings fails to thrill.

Most of the review ignores the book, and rather comments on Mrs. Gaskell. Woolf makes an intriguing differentiation, with some anticipation of *Mr Bennett and Mrs Brown*, between the Victorian novelist and the modern one, although in contrast to the later essay, Galsworthy is here held up as a figure of praise.

> Compare the strike in *North and South,* for example, with the *Strife* of Mr Galsworthy. She seems a sympathetic amateur beside a professional in earnest. . . . Able by nature to spin sentence after sentence melodiously, they [mid-Victorian novelists] seem to have left out nothing that they knew how to say. Our ambition, on the other hand, is to put in nothing that need not be there. What we want to be there is the brain and the view of life; the autumnal woods, the history of the whale fishery, and the decline of stage coaching we omit entirely.

There would appear, in the review, to be some sense of the turmoil of the poor in that very year. "Because they are strange and terrible to us, we always see the poor in stress of some kind, so that the violence of their feeling may break through conventions, and, bringing them rudely into touch with us, do away with the need of subtle understanding. But Mrs Gaskell knows how the poor enjoy themselves; how they visit and gossip and fry bacon and lend each other bits of finery and show off their sores."[56]

Clive used his genuine concern for Virginia's health as a semi-ironic reason for maintaining their rather flirtatious correspondence. On October 10 she was back in London.[57] The next month, she wrote him a complicated letter about his handling of the situation when they were interrupted while having tea together—a letter that suggests how important it was to them both that they should talk *tête-à-tête.*[58] He wrote to her on Christmas day from his parents' house in Wiltshire: "You have been neglectful; really you ought not to be: a day without a letter means nightmares of your trembling on the threshold of a mad-house." His style was that they were writing colleagues and he wished to maintain his position as her consultant. He told her what he had written, including a review of the short book C. J. Holmes had rapidly brought out surveying the Post-Impressionist Exhibition and several other reviews, and went on, "Why wont you ever send me anything you write? I'm intensely curious to know how your mind's been moving these last three months? Where are you now? Is it possible you're really never caught by the current? Are you altogether a duck's back to influence? I suppose so, but let me see."[59]

Nevertheless, she had recovered sufficiently to recommit herself to the novel, about to change its name from the obscure *Melymbrosia* to *The Voyage Out*. She worked on it to some extent in the last three months of the year. Then from January to April 1911 she wrote eight chapters of a new draft. She did not finish it until March 1913, and largely because of her serious breakdown that year it was not published until 1915.[60] In many ways it is a traditional first novel, recounting the education of its central character, who can be taken to stand for the author herself. It seems as if it were going to end in a traditional way: the happy marriage, now that they are both ready, of the young couple. What is subversive in *The Voyage Out*, and reflects Woolf's own concerns, is the intensity of the relationship between Rachel and her aunt, who is partially derived from Vanessa; it is even more important that, rather than marrying, at the end of the novel Rachel dies of a tropical disease.

Looking back on the novel in 1916, Virginia made to Lytton Strachey a comment—while being rather critical about her work and saying that she had not reread it since publication—that might also be made about a Post-Impressionist painting. "What I wanted to do was to give the feeling of a vast tumult of life, as various and disorderly as possible, which should be cut short for a moment by the death, and go on again—and the whole was to have a sort of pattern, and be somehow controlled."[61]

She was now taking up her old life in London, including going about on visits, in mid-October to Mrs Pearsall Smith at Iffley outside Oxford—Bertrand Russell's and Bernard Berenson's mother-in-law, whose granddaughters, also there at the time, were to marry Lytton's brother Oliver and Virginia's brother Adrian. She also visited her old friend Madge Vaughan, whose husband had become Headmaster of Wellington. Writing to Violet Dickinson in mid-November she indicated her activities, with some acerbity. "My time has been wasted a good deal upon Suffrage. We went to two meetings, at which about a dozen people spoke, like the tollings of a bell. . . . It was at the Albert

Hall. The only amusement was that a baby cried incessantly, and this was taken by some as a bitter sarcasm against a woman having a vote." She was also increasingly dismissive of her half-brother George, who called on her: "He looked like a valet; and I do not think that my bitter remarks about him were wrong."

But she had resumed writing, working on a review of a book on the first Duke and Duchess of Newcastle. It would be published in the *Times Literary Supplement* in February; in it she discussed the difficulties of the Duchess as a literary woman. "The Duchess, with her folio volumes, her odd manner of dress and behaviour, was a laughing stock in London."[62] In 1911 she would publish only two reviews, and in 1912 only one, but not, I believe, as in 1910 because she was ill but because she was working on *The Voyage Out*. For most important, she wrote in the letter that "next week I begin my work of imagination."[63] And two weeks later she wrote again about the book: "I am seething with fragments of love, morals, ethics, comedy tragedy, and so on; and every morning pour them out into a manuscript book. Never shall I write a review again."[64]

At the end of the year Virginia Woolf committed herself to a fairly dramatic change in the pattern of her life. No doubt one reason was the view that London, with its excitements, was bad for her health and that it might be a good idea to have a permanent base in the country. She visited for the first time since 1897, with the thought of finding a house to rent or buy, the part of Sussex that would become identified with the group, staying with Adrian at the Pelham Arms in Lewes. Clive favored such an acquisition if he could visit: "Will you have a little spare-room in your cottage and invite me to sleep in it often? If so I'm all in favour of the purchase."[65] She was having quite a wonderful time in Lewes, as she reported to Vanessa on Christmas Day.

> The eccentricity of our appearance is magnificent. Adrians hair flows like a crazy poets; then we bought him a Harvest hat for a shilling, a strawberry roan colour, suited for an August afternoon.
> I wear a bright purple cloak, over my red dress, with a smart black toque. . . .

Yesterday by the way (Adrian will tell the story) I got past the ticket inspector with a dog ticket. Hans had mine. . . .

We have just discovered that one can telephone from here; Duncan can be talked to for two pence. Adrian comes up beaming, from Love, I suppose. I withdrew discreetly.[66]

On the 27th she wrote again, with a long account of the rather dreary lunch she had with Sydney-Turner and his mother at her home, a sort of clinic, in Brighton. And then two days later she wrote to Clive about a review, of which he must have sent her a draft, he had written of Trelawny's letters that would appear in the *Athenaeum* on January 7. She was glad he wrote, even though "that old Bitch [Vanessa] left off suckling her whelps and wrote." She claimed to have found it difficult to read the review: "With Adrian and Duncan swarming on the floor, making it like the bottom of an alligators tank, one gets no chance of reading. But I read your review with great pleasure. . . . You are much sturdier on your legs than you were; you stride over the ground, and plant words firmly, in a way I admire." She reported on her pleasure at receiving invitations from Ottoline and Molly MacCarthy; she reported that Jean Thomas was coming for a night, and that Adrian had just left. "As for my writing—you will have to wait for Mel[ymbrosia]. to see what has become of it. . . . I should say that my great change was in the way of courage, or conceit; and that I had given up adventuring after other people's forms, as I used."[67]

In January she rented, for £19.10s a year, the first of her three Sussex houses, where she would be for only a year before moving to Asheham. It was a rather plain semi-detached house on the main street in the village of Firle. She renamed it Little Talland House, after Talland House, so significant and beloved as the location of family vacations in St. Ives in Cornwall. She had reembarked upon the major commitment of her career, the writing of her first novel; she had acquired, with Adrian perhaps there from time to time, a country home of her own; and her health appeared to have been restored. These were good reasons that when Virginia Woolf looked back upon December 1910, she came to the conclusion that it was then that human character had changed.

4

Artists and Others

Beyond her own immediate private circumstances, the public event that inspired Virginia Woolf more than a decade later to remark about the change in human character was the Post-Impressionist Exhibition which opened in November 1910. Of course in an official sense the death of the king in May meant a change from the Edwardian to the Georgian age, which would fit nicely with the literary scheme she enunciated in *Mr Bennett and Mrs Brown.* The influence of Roger Fry on his young friends, with whom he became acquainted in Bloomsbury in 1910, was also decisive in the making of the group.

For Fry too his meeting, or rather re-meeting, with young Bloomsbury was crucial: it provided him with a group of like-minded people, notably Clive Bell and the painters Vanessa Bell and Duncan Grant, who agreed with him about art and participated with him in the evolution of his ideas. He needed their support as he became less the traditional English art critic and more the exponent of modernism in art in England. Vanessa had met Fry casually in the years before, but if she and Clive had not encountered him at the station in Cambridge in January 1910, and then continued their conversation with him in a compartment on the Cambridge-London train, Bloomsbury as we came to know it might never have existed.[1] The addition of Fry and later in that year of E. M. Forster carried weight, though the style was already set: a gathering of near-contemporaries with quite a few shared assumptions and experiences. It was significant also that the group was not exclusively male nor was its tone determined by the lady of the house as would have been true at a more conventional "at home" or evening party. Perhaps most important, these were young people not willing automatically to accept the conventions and received opinions of the day.

With Virginia Woolf, Lytton Strachey, and E. M. Forster, Bloomsbury's impact upon literature was to be more commanding than upon the visual arts. Although the reputation of Vanessa Bell and Duncan Grant as painters has fluctuated over the years, they were certainly influenced in their work, as were many other British painters, by Roger Fry.

What was it in Fry's own life in 1910 that led him to create the Post-Impressionist Exhibition? That "artquake" had among its beginnings the fortuitous coming together of personalities, not only as we have seen, Fry and the Bells, but also Lady Ottoline Morrell, with whom Fry would have a very brief affair, and who during this year came closer to Bloomsbury, continuing her always rather off-center relationship with the group. There would be the involvement of other players: the painter Henry Lamb, Lytton Strachey, Desmond MacCarthy. Strachey was already a very intimate figure in the group, despite his quarrel with Clive, Henry Lamb less so (although his brother Walter thought himself romantically interested in Virginia).

The year 1910 was a turning point for Fry. It was then that his career changed direction and he moved from being a more or less traditional critic concerned with the art of the Renaissance and its sequels to an advocate of the latest developments in contemporary art. Although he was trained as a scientist while an undergraduate at King's College, Cambridge, from 1885 to 1888, where he was also an Apostle, his fondest wish was to be a painter, somewhat to the distress of his distinguished Quaker family. His father, Sir Edward, was a judge, and his sister, Margery, made a significant mark as a prison reformer—in the Quaker tradition. The Frys were part of the cousinhood of Frys, Rowntrees, and Cadburys, all Quakers and renowned for their connection with the making of chocolate, which made them rich.

Fry had the rare ability to appear to his new friends as their contemporary, although by age and experience, he was something of a transitional figure. He had been a student when Lowes Dickinson (who was in love with him) was a young don at King's, just four years older than he; a contemporary of his at King's was C. R. Ashbee. Ashbee, who became a disciple of William Morris, was influenced, as was E. M. Forster, by the philosopher of sexual liberation, particularly homosexual, Edward Carpenter.

Fry's wife, Helen Coombe, whom he married in 1897, was an artist affiliated—as was Ashbee—with the Arts and Crafts movement. Perhaps her best-known piece was a Dolmetsch harpsichord that she decorated in collaboration with Herbert Horne and Selwyn Image, which was displayed in the 1896 Arts and Crafts Exhibition. In fact, she had solicited Fry's advice on the decoration.[2] In 1913 Fry founded the Omega Workshop, which rejected any similarity to the ideas of William Morris. Yet with its belief in the relationship of the artist to design, and its interest in a move to simplicity, a seeking for underlying forms, there was more of a continuity than Fry might have wished or admitted. For Fry, the Arts and Crafts movement had become too English, soggy, moralist, and sentimental. Omega, as was more and more true of English design in the years to come, was profoundly influenced by the Post-Impressionist Exhibition, marking a dramatic break with Arts and Crafts.

Fry's initial interests as an art scholar were in the Renaissance, and he was a disciple and colleague of Bernard Berenson's. He, like Berenson, was influenced by the ideas of Morelli, the Italian critic, and his methods of attribution through a study of stylistic similarities. Fry, under the sway of Berenson, was moving in his ideas from an emphasis in art on beauty and representation to a greater emphasis on form. In a sense, he was a precursor of the revolution to come, distinguishing the true reality in the forms that organized the picture and that had an inherent power to transmit emotion. It was a sort of Platonic idealism which also corresponded to the belief of the Apostles in the differences between the apparent and the real world.

At the same time as he was pursuing his studies and work, as a painter, he wrote critical articles for the *Athenaeum* and the *Burlington Magazine,* a serious art journal, of which he had been one of the founders in 1903. Certainly there had been plenty of journals devoted to art in the nineteenth century, but at the turn of the century came a change in their style, with greater attention paid to the scholarly aspects of connoisseurship. Many of the painters of the Renaissance whom we now regard as canonical were actually being established in their modern reputation at this time, as in the critical study of Botticelli by Herbert Horne, an Arts and Crafts figure as well as a member of Berenson's circle. These critics were devoting themselves to the nature of art. Yet they found that questions of attribution proved to involve ever greater sums of money as the plutocrats of the period—British and American—became major purchasers of Renaissance paintings. Fry's first book was Berensonian, a short monograph on Giovanni Bellini, published in 1899.[3] In 1903 he was involved with the founding of the National Art Collections Fund, an organization that catered to his interests at the time with its emphasis on old masters, and also—ironically, considering what would be the next step in his career—to prevent the departure of works of art (not necessarily British) resident in Britain for the United States.

Thus, Fry pursued a multiple career as artist, scholar, and activist in the world of art. Though deeply serious about what he was doing, he was also in the English tradition of being adept and knowledgeable about many pursuits while running the risk of not reaching fulfillment in any one of them. Ultimately, the standard, perhaps overly severe opinion was that he was quite weak as a painter—the vocation which might have meant more to him than any other—but vindicated as a critic: the most important British art critic of this century. He became a prophet of modernism, an advocate of formal values in painting, a bridge away from representation toward abstraction (even though he himself was a representational painter). It was that critical commitment which took place in 1910.

Active as a painter as well as a critic, he was involved very early with the progressive artistic movements in England at the turn of the century. Charles Ricketts and Charles Shannon, late exponents of aestheticism, and other supporters of the more modern developments before 1910 were colleagues of Fry's: the art critics D. S. MacColl, who was devoted to Impressionism, and Robert Ross, who ran the Carfax Gallery and arranged, in 1903, for Fry's first exhibition there, which was a great success. Fry was in English terms one of the party of the advanced. But it is striking, as we shall see, that these critics, Ricketts, MacColl, Ross, broke with him over the new in French art. For them, Impressionism was as far as they were willing to go.

Fry was also a member of the New English Art Club (NEAC), founded in 1886, and very active in its affairs. It was part of the attempt in the 1880s to move British art forward and away from what was seen as the stultifying grip of the Royal Academy. The painters who were powerful in the NEAC at the beginning were George Clausen, Wilson Steer, and John Singer Sargent, admirers of the French *plein air* painters and very sympathetic to Impressionism. Some years later Walter Sickert became a dominant force, influenced by Degas and Monet, and by 1910 William Rothenstein was a leading figure in the Club as it settled into its own conventions. Meanwhile, various other small groups of like-minded artists came together, spurred by the example of the NEAC. In 1905 Vanessa Bell formed the Friday Club for gatherings, talks, and an annual exhibition. In 1907 Sickert organized what was known as the Fitzroy Street Group, and then in 1911 he founded the Camden Town Group, where he was joined by quite a few of the most interesting English painters of the day, such as Robert Bevan, Harold Gilman, and Spencer Gore. Yet Sickert recognized the importance of the earlier organization in a remark he made in February 1910. "I doubt if any unprejudiced student of modern painting will deny that the New English Art Club at the present day sets the standard of painting in England."[4] But its members would not follow their fellow member Fry into Post-Impressionism.

Fry did not make this commitment absolute until 1910. The year was one of great difficulty in his private life. His wife was mad, as had been feared since 1898, and could no longer be looked after at home. There was the further problem for him of raising their two children, Julian and Pamela, even though his sister Joan was helping. Fry had consulted with the same doctors who had treated Virginia Stephen—Sir George Savage and Sir Henry Head—and had solicited many other opinions. He designed a handsome house, Durbins, built in 1909 near Guildford, where he hoped his wife might function better, but he was being reluctantly forced to the conclusion that she needed to be institutionalized. The emotional as well as financial pressure was immense. Sympathetic women were important to him, notably at this time Lady Ottoline Morrell. As he wrote to her in 1910:

> I can't tell you how it helped me to have you, at such a difficult time, to help and advise. I don't think I could have done it without you with the feeling of anxiety about H[elen] going on all the time. . . . I've seen the Dr. and he thinks we can pull through the attack without sending her to the asylum. I do hope so. That is what I dread most. I know how utterly she wld. break up if she once found herself there, and I fear she would lose any chance of recovery, tho' I know how little that is anyhow. I shan't give her the hat [possibly a gift from Lady Ottoline] now—she would only tear it up. . . . Please remember I owe you a lot of money.[5]

He repaid the money in October and November.[6]

In the early years of the twentieth century, Fry, like Berenson and Horne, was tailoring his expertise to the need of American millionaires to acquire old masters, in Fry's case principally J. P. Morgan, but also Henry Clay Frick, and John G. Johnson of Philadelphia, for whom his most notable acquisition was some panels by Botticelli.

In 1904 Fry had traveled to New York in a successful effort to raise money for the *Burlington*. At that time, J. P. Morgan ran the Metropolitan Museum almost as a private fiefdom, having become its president that year, and offered Fry the assistant directorship. The salary was not sufficient, so the appointment fell through.

Two years later Morgan had the Metropolitan offer Fry the post of curator of painting, which he accepted. The salary was ample for his needs, and for a while his professional career would no longer be in danger of becoming a matter of bits and pieces. While at the Museum he was being absorbed into many aspects of its burgeoning collections, as well as responding as tactfully as he could to Morgan's eclectic and arbitrary tastes. (By great misfortune once he had committed himself to the Metropolitan, he had the offer of the directorship of the National Gallery, which might have suited him better.)*

Morgan did not want a firm line drawn between the Museum and his own collection, and Fry would find himself acting as a personal scout for Morgan when he thought he was acting for the Museum. In 1907 he resigned the post of curator to become an adviser on European painting with the understanding that it would require him to spend quite a bit of his time abroad. Fry was a mixed blessing for the Museum, especially when he supervised restoration, which he thought he understood but which, according to John Pope-Hennessy, perhaps he did not. He did buy a superb Bellini for the Museum and the impressive Renoir portrait of "Madame Charpentier and her children,"[7] and he arranged for the purchase of British paintings, by William Rothenstein and Wilson Steer, as well as others by Rossetti and Alphonse Legros.

Morgan and Fry had their most famous clash in June 1909, when Fry advised Morgan that a Fra Angelico (which it subsequently turned out not to be) was available from a dealer in Brussels. Fry had meant it for the Museum; Morgan bought it for himself. Fry wrote to Morgan on June 30: "I learned in Paris, where I was yesterday, that you had acquired that superb Fra Angelico from King Leopold's collection. I think I ought to tell you that I saw it a few days before you did, and considering it of the utmost importance to the Museum and also likely to be snapped up quickly I bought it." Morgan was not accustomed to be troubled by subordinates, and wrote on Fry's letter of protest, when returning it to Fry: "The most remarkable letter I ever received. I do not propose to answer it until I see you. Bring it back."[8]

The high tension in Fry's life, intensified by the worry and expense of his wife's illness, is evident in a letter to Edward Robinson, who was then the acting director of the Metropolitan. His state of mind also suggests a rising volatility, that he was ripe for a dramatic change and a redirection that would allow him to move on. For the moment, in the fall of 1909, he wanted to keep his position at the Museum.

> In my present situation with the crushing expenses which my wife's illness entails, it would be a very serious matter for me to have to look for a place here again when I gave up everything. . . . I had, when I first came over, as you know, the offer of the highest position here, and I think that some consideration ought to be shown on that score. . . . If Mr. Morgan feels so bitterly toward me that he cannot have me working for the museum in which he presides, he should in common decency recompense me for the loss of opportunities and work which I have done for him personally, entirely without payment. I might indeed have repaid myself many times over if I had listened to the siren voices of certain Israelites [the easy English anti-Semitism of the time]; that I haven't is precisely what puts me now in so painful a predicament.[9]

Just before Christmas the Board of the Metropolitan gave him six months' notice, Fry having declined to resign. The termination of his position and income put his career, and his finances, into a crisis. He certainly felt that he had been fired over the incident of the Fra Angelico. "Morgan could not forgive me for trying to get that picture for the Museum."[10] But his break with Morgan was not quite as absolute as one might expect, and he was still willing to act as Morgan's agent in Europe—perhaps it was easier now that there wasn't a conflict of interest in Fry's mind between being employed by the Museum and finding himself acting for Morgan without knowing it. (And his financial need must have helped him swallow his pride.) Just when he was being let go by the Museum, he sent Morgan information, on December 27, 1909, about a rare Persian astronomical treatise that could be purchased. Despite his great dislike of Morgan, he continued to scout for him, writing in July about a large group of Macaulay manuscripts, as well as a late sixteenth- or seventeenth-century Italian bronze door. In October he raised the possibility of some paintings Morgan might want, a possible Titian and a portrait of Elizabeth of France. Belle da Costa Greene, Morgan's librarian and art adviser, who got on well with Fry, wrote that Morgan wasn't interested in the bronze door or the paintings, but that Fry might "be able to do something with him when he comes to England."

The relationship was clearly not all that sour, as Fry wrote a pressing letter to Miss Greene at the end of the year. "I am very sorry that Mr. Morgan would not get the bronze door—it is a thing quite for him—I wonder whether he might not get it for the Museum. Meanwhile I have discovered a quite unknown & marvelous little bronze from an old Russian family with Imperial connections. I firmly believe it is by Benvenuto Cellini. . . . The man who owns it asks £12,000 twelve thousand pounds but I might get a slight reduction tho' not much for he knows what a treasure it is." She replied in January that Morgan had no interest in the Cellini but added: "Mr. Morgan is sailing for Europe very soon and I dare say you will see him in London before long."[11]

The year 1910 was marked by somewhat frantic behavior. As Fry wrote to his mother in July: "I don't think I told you of the ceiling that I have to paint for Sir Andrew Noble [at his house in Scotland], which is a vast work 20 feet long. . . . Then I have promised to restore one of the Mantegnas at Hampton Court. It was one of the last things that Edward VII decided on [before his death in May]. That will take me at least a fortnight & then numbers of people are clamouring for writings from me so I can't complain of want of occupation."[12]

Nevertheless, his financial need was still great, and he now made a best effort to be selected for the Slade professorship at Oxford, a distinguished rotating position in art history. On February 14 he wrote his father, "If that fails I must hope for some post as critic on the daily or weekly Press or else I must try the possibility of lecturing."[13] Then he wrote a few days later: "It would relieve me of great anxiety if I could [secure the post.]"[14] He asked his father to use his influence with the president of University College of the University of London, who was one of the electors, and he himself wrote to Berenson and D. S. Mac-Coll about their support. He secured testimonials from various eminent figures, including the outgoing director of the Metropolitan. Ironically, the Slade post went to Selwyn Image—a collaborator with Fry's wife on the Dolmetsch harpsichord—an artist sympathetic to progressive art work in England a decade before, but now profoundly critical of the new developments, particularly in French art.

He tried to put the best face on the defeat, writing to the poet R. C. Trevelyan: "I think I'm not made for titles and posts and honours, and really, if I can exist without them, I don't care a hang. It's their money I want, that's all." And to Clive Bell: "Also I really like Selwyn Image and am glad that he should have this consolation prize in his old age; it is all very English and perhaps rather admirable."[15]

Friends were eager to help him financially, and with typical diffidence E. M. Forster tried to assist. He wrote to their mutual friend Trevelyan: "I was at Lady Ottoline's yesterday, and met Fry: the children are away, and his wife is at home. He did not say how she was, but seemed in good spirits."[16] In August Forster was writing to Trevelyan about the possibility of Fry's doing the end papers for a book of his short stories to be published by Sidgwick and Jackson.

> Sidgwick & Jackson are nibbling, though feebly, at my short stories. They suggest illustrations. That I won't have but have no objection to "End Papers." To come to the point, would it vex Fry if they asked him to design one? Does he feel for the stories anything the least approaching enthusiasm? I know that he wants money, but would rather he went without it than that I procured it for him by means of uncongenial or "contemptuous" work. I think the stories good myself, so do not mind hearing the opinions of others. *If* Fry has had one, and

you know it, I should be very grateful. This idea has only just occurred to me. . . . I expect nothing will come of it.[17]

In fact, Fry did execute some rather pleasing end papers, illustrating the title story in *The Celestial Omnibus* but also suggestive of the "rainbow bridges" of *Howards End*. The book was published the following May.

No doubt in order to help his finances, but also because he was accustomed to such activities with Morgan, Fry also assisted Henry Clay Frick in the amassing of his considerable collection, as well as the Philadelphia collector, John G. Johnson. Old masters on the one side; modern art to become dominant at the end of the year. Such a view may be overly schematic, but it does serve as a model for the watershed aspect of the year.

It was in connection with Frick that Fry had perhaps his most dramatic adventure in the world of old masters and American million-aires. In the spring of 1910 he acquired for Frick one of his most famous paintings and now a favorite on display at the Frick museum in New York, Rembrandt's *The Polish Rider*. (The attribution of the painting to Rembrandt has recently been under dispute.)[18] It is not clear how it came to be known that the Polish owner of the picture was willing to part with it (Knoedler's Gallery in Paris was involved), but Fry was sent to Poland in April to acquire it. He wrote to his mother:

Just now I have to go to Poland to buy for Mr Frick a v[er]y important picture. . . . The owner is a rather stupid country gentleman who insists on selling the picture in his chateau, that's why I have to go & get it, as I must see it before buying. The picture costs £60,000 so it is an important affair. It's tiresome & rather hateful work but I couldn't refuse to do it. I hope Mr Frick will be more decent to me than his fellow millionaire. At all events I ought to get handsomely paid for all I have done & indeed it comes at a critical time for I am just at the end of my resources and have been feeling v[er]y anxious of late as to how I can possibly meet expenses. . . . I am anxious about Helen.[19]

At a later point Fry described to Osbert Sitwell the moment of discov-ery of the painting at the castle of the owner, Count Tarnowski. "He

[Fry] arrived at the most remote castle, full of second-rate French furniture and 1880 objects: he felt it was impossible that any real work of art could exist in such surroundings—and then, suddenly, a cord was pulled, a curtain was rolled back, and there, before his eyes, was revealed one of the world's masterpieces of painting."[20] Documentation on the picture only went back to 1791, when it had turned up in Lithuania; it had then entered Polish collections. It had been cleaned in 1877 in Vienna and in 1898 in Berlin. On its way to Frick's collection, it was exhibited at the Carfax Gallery in London (where Sickert wrote a favorable review of it). While in London, the picture was copied by Ambrose McEvoy for the former owner. Fry had been given the authority to buy it, after telegraphic consultation with Frick and Knoedler, if he felt that it was genuine and worth the high price. Clearly he did. The acquisition was sufficiently striking that it was mentioned in the *Annual Register* for the year as an example of the great sums paid for pictures at the time.[21]

On his way back from Poland, he wrote an interesting letter to his wife about his reactions to the trip. The letter is also revealing, indirectly, in its style, as if one were writing to a child. "The Poles still seem to dream of having their country back again and indeed it seems quite monstrous that they shouldn't. For they are quite a big people with a great deal of national feeling. However in Austrian Poland, where I was, they are fairly contented, for they have a great deal of Home Rule. I can't understand why one country ever should govern another, can you? Only we are rather bad offenders in that way."[22]

Fry felt the adventure had gone well, writing again to his mother in July: "Mr. Frick has bought another (quite small) picture through me so he is not displeased with my action in the Rembrandt matter."[23] Even at the height of the Post-Impressionist Exhibition he could still execute commissions for Frick, particularly as his finances were no better. He wrote to Lady Ottoline at the end of December, when he was just about to go off on a much needed holiday with Logan Pearsall Smith: "I've just discovered an unknown Rubens, & bought it for Frick."[24]

Morgan and Frick were his former life, of high finance and high connoisseurship. That had been the world of the Metropolitan and Berenson, and to a degree of the National Art Collections Fund. One of the events of 1910, leading up to the Post-Impressionist Exhibition but also involving those such as MacColl and Ross who would be unhappy with Post-Impressionist paintings, was the founding that year of the Contemporary Art Society, an organization that still flourishes and has as its brief the acquisition for the nation of contemporary works of art.[25] The story of how it came into being is a splendid example of how such things happen in England, where various members of the "army of the great and the good" come together in order to support a particular cause.

On April 9, 1909, Lady Ottoline had a luncheon at her house at 44 Bedford Square for, among others, Fry; D. S. MacColl, a prominent critic and at that time Keeper at the Tate; the painter C. J. Holmes, who was director of the National Portrait Gallery; Charles Aitken, director of the Whitechapel Art Gallery in the East End—an adventuresome Art Nouveau building that was attempting to bring art to the poor; as well as Lady Ottoline's husband, Philip Morrell. Fry had initiated the lunch the previous month with a letter he had sent to MacColl proposing a meeting of the two of them and Lady Ottoline. "Lady Ottoline Morrell is most anxious to meet you and I am most anxious to be the means of bringing it about because I think you will like each other as much as you ought. She has been very good to me and has a real feeling for art."[26] The premise was that private patronage was not sufficient as a support for living British artists.

The scheme the art critics were evolving—parallel to the National Art Collections Fund founded in 1903—was that private individuals were to collect funds to be used to buy works of art for the public. As with the state, collective action needed to replace individual funding. The plan, unlike the National Art Collections Fund, was primarily for living or recently deceased British painters. At the lunch the discussion was about the comparative merits of William Rothenstein and G. F. Watts. Rothenstein was favored, Fry arguing fervently on his behalf. It was decided that the organization should be separate from the older art collection scheme, as it would attempt to serve a different constituency of artists.[27]

A year later the group officially set itself up, and established a purchasing committee of Fry, MacColl, and Robert Ross. The new organization very consciously did not wish to be in competition with the National Art Collections Fund. It enunciated its purpose as "acquiring works of art by living or recently deceased artists, to be presented to London or provincial galleries or held by the association for the purpose of public exhibition."[28] Or as it stated more formally in its first annual report:

> From the conviction that some of the finer artistic talent of our time is imperfectly or not at all represented in the National and Municipal Galleries, the Contemporary Art Society was initiated in the year 1909. Its aim is to encourage by purchase and exhibition the more remarkable examples of painters who in any other country would enjoy a certain official patronage. . . . The Committee, on which are represented widely different opinions, believes that with the exercise of discrimination pictures by contemporary artists should be purchased in order to supply what may seem to posterity an inexcusable gap in our public museums and galleries, already overloaded with ephemeral work of the age preceding our own. The Scope of the Society is limited to Artists living or recently dead, and is chiefly concerned with British Art.

It also had as its mandate to make contemporary art better known outside of London. By the end of 1911 it had displayed modern works in Manchester, Leeds, Aberdeen, Bradford, and Newcastle.[29]

It would be a quiet and it hoped rich organization that would not seek publicity—perhaps aware that the most recent art might be the most controversial. The president of the organization was the immensely wealthy Lord Howard de Walden, who happened to be Lady Ottoline's cousin. The Century Art Society, the New Society, the Howard Society were suggested as names among other possibilities. On May 18 it became the Contemporary Art Society. At the same meeting—perhaps indicating trouble that was to come over Fry's exhibition and Robert Ross's attitude toward it—Ross moved that the artists purchased should have at least a British grandfather and should bear a British name. But rather nobly, that motion was defeated.

The early history of the Contemporary Art Society sheds light on the development of modernism in England, and also on Fry's influence at the time. The first works of art acquired were recorded at the meeting of October 19, 1910: a gift by Wilson Steer of Sickert's portrait of George Moore; an anonymous offer of a bronze statue by Ricketts; and the first purchase, for £225, of Augustus John's splendid *Woman Smiling*, a portrait of his second wife, Dorelia, painted in 1908–09, which was presented to the Tate in 1917. The organization decided to go public to a greater degree and announced to the press its acquisitions, and also appealed for funds. A further intent was to sponsor exhibitions so that British painters might become better known to the public. In this the organization was increasingly successful. By November there was the possibility of purchasing foreign paintings as the Society was interested in some work by Puvis de Chavannes. In December 1912 it contributed £50 toward the potential purchase of a painting by Matisse, demonstrating how rapidly the new art, now at the time of the second Post-Impressionist exhibition, was being accepted.[30] In 1913, over the issue of Post-Impressionism, MacColl would resign from the Society. By then, it had grown to 144 members.[31]

Despite their differences about the Post-Impressionists, Fry and Ross could cooperate over their purchases for the Society: in 1911 they bought two related bas-reliefs, a crucifixion and a provocatively posed naked woman by Eric Gill, the first sculptures acquired by the Society. They were also among Gill's first works in the medium and were on display in the exhibition he had at the Chenil Gallery in January. Fry was already a great admirer of Gill's, having asked him in 1910 to engrave a Christmas card for him, one of Gill's first ventures in that art form, and the only one he did that year, a scene of the nativity, with St. Joseph and a midwife.[32] Fry was thrilled with it: "It's absolutely new & fresh & alive and how *beautiful!* You see you've reduced the professional critic to impotent gasps of pleasure."[33]

Fry was the moving force behind the purchase of the sculptures but he was pessimistic about the reaction of his colleagues to their acquisition, although not about Lady Ottoline's. He was wrong on both counts. He wrote to Lady Ottoline: "I think you will like them immensely & I said you might be willing to let him put them in yr. all hospitable house for a time. They are reliefs about 3 ft. high. May he? I want to find him a purchaser. Our society ought to buy them but it won't of course."[34] In fact Lady Ottoline disliked them.[35] It is not recorded whether she gave them house room.

Both pieces were controversial, and the one of the woman was not presented to a national collection, that of Hull, until the 1950s.[36] Gill plays an interesting role in the history of modern art in Britain, and rather a counterpoint to Fry's activities, as he was less "international" in his view than Fry. The sculptures were comparatively expensive—£100 plus £10 commission—and were meant to stay together. Gill's working titles for them were *Schmerz*—"Grief" and "Joie," the latter a full frontal female nude standing in a provocative pose and adorned with a painted necklace (which Fry disliked),[37] red lips, and nipples. But otherwise, he thought the pieces were splendid, and felt that they should be publicly displayed but that they "can't be till we're much more civilized in the real sense."[38] The final title for the two was the odd "A Roland for an Oliver," a phrase indicating that that the works were a pair, "tit for tat," the nude being a contrast, a conflict, with the Christ figure. The two sculptures were ultimately, however, divided, the crucifixion going to the Tate in 1920, the first Gill to be in a national museum.[39]

Gill was a modernist in his commitment to sexuality and its indulgence, combined in his case with an intense religiosity that would lead him to Catholicism. In these two pieces he was, in effect, attacking religion for suppressing sex. The female figure had engraved around its border a quotation from Swinburne: "O Pale Galilean, but these thou shall not take: the laurel the palm & the paean the breasts of the nymphs in the brake." In contrast, the crucifixion is, in this case, depicted as life-denying, with Christ's minute genitalia, and the two inscriptions from the Bible being, one in Latin, from the Psalms, "He taketh no pleasure in the legs of a man," and one in Greek from St. Matthew about eunuchs.

Although not close to Bloomsbury, Gill was something of a touchstone for it. (The extraordinary sexual freedom of his own life went even beyond Bloomsbury permissiveness; I don't believe its members would have been comfortable with incest, no matter how intense the relationship between Vanessa and Virginia. And Virginia felt damaged by her half-brothers.)

John Knewstub of the Chenil Gallery had also on view, to be seen in a back room, even more sexually explicit works by Gill. One that is now in the Tate, given the title *Ecstasy* after Gill's death, depicts a standing couple having intercourse. The recent catalogue of Gill sculpture tells us that the sculpture was known as "They—(big)." It may have been influenced by Indian sculptures of couples copulating, perhaps a reflection of his correspondence with William Rothenstein, who at the time was traveling in India. Gill's biographer, Fiona MacCarthy, writes more succinctly that Gill called the piece *Fucking* and that the models for it were his sister Gladys, with whom he was having an affair, and her then husband, Ernest Laughton.[40] It was acquired in 1912 by the American collector, living in Lewes in Sussex, Edward Perry Warren. Gill did a companion piece, a bas-relief, known as "They—(little)," which depicted a copulating couple with the woman astride the man beneath her. The piece was inscribed "Votes for Women," invoking the campaign for women's suffrage which had reached a new level of violence and intensity in 1910. The object made clear the intertwining of sexuality and the struggle for the vote. But Gill, not a feminist, added to the slogan "IDT," standing for "I don't think."[41]

Keynes, who joined the Contemporary Art Society in 1910, was interested in this piece, but was uncomfortable with the political title. He was also drawn to a finished "Mother and Child" and an unfinished one. He bought the latter for £25. Knewstub wrote to Keynes about "They—(little)" that Gill had written to him: "I am willing to delete the title of the stone—'Votes for Women'—on condition that I am allowed to put another title in its place, a title which I shall put on record, as the present one is intended to do, the fact that I regard it—the stone—in the light of a joke and not as a serious contribution to the thought of the time—I am willing to discuss this with your client." Knewstub went on: "From an artistic point of view the composition and execution is unquestionably exquisite and full of Gill subtlety, and had Mr Gill avoided the title & not emphasized the sex I should unhesitantly have hung it in the exhibition as the pose is one that may be seen from time to time in acrobatic or trapeze displays, and some such title would have disarmed the super-sensitive."[42] One might say that if you believed that, you'd believe anything. Keynes finally bought the piece for five pounds in August 1912, Knewstub writing, "I've taken out the inscription (V for W) & otherwise made it more respectable."[43]

That progressive ideas could co-exist with an intensely class-conscious society before the First World War is suggested by an ironic exchange between Geoffrey Keynes and his brother about the bas-relief.

Votes for Women by Eric Gill.

He asked Maynard "What does your staff think of it?" Keynes's reply was "My staff are trained not to believe their eyes."[44] The sculpture is now lost; it is only known now by a photograph which has preserved the "Votes for Women" slogan, making it a far more relevant document of its time, despite Gill's dubious attitude toward the campaign. The Society was aware of the disputes that might ensue over the Gills it had acquired. At the meeting of March 16, 1911, a letter was read from Gill inquiring about the destination of his bas-reliefs. "It was decided to reply that the Society must reserve full liberty to deal with these as they thought best."

The founding of the Contemporary Art Society was noted in the *Annual Register*, which succinctly stated its aim of being a mediator between the official art world and the private patron who could follow his or her own taste. As with the National Art Collections Fund, it is and was a fine example of that special English style of combining the public and the private. "Its founders believe that among artists working to-day are some of great talent whose work for various reasons does not find favour with official purchasers, and is therefore rarely if ever to be found in national or municipal collections."[45] Fry's intense activity in this new organization was yet another indication of how his, as well as others', interests were changing in 1910 and were leading up to the central event, the first Post-Impressionist Exhibition.

———

Throughout 1910 connections were developed that would play an important role in the strengthening of Bloomsbury, such as the friendship between the Bells and Roger Fry that was at its most intense in the years from 1910 to 1914. There were also the continuing friendships between Lytton Strachey, Duncan Grant, and John Maynard Keynes. Although Strachey's relations with the sisters were slightly rocky during this year owing to Clive's antagonism, and he was away from London quite a bit, most notably in Sweden, he was still a pivotal figure in keeping up with the various figures of the group. He even kept Leonard Woolf, away in Ceylon governing 100,000 people as an Assistant Government Agent, informed about the activities of his friends.

Vanessa Bell wrote at the time of Roger Fry's death in 1934 a memoir of him which also would serve as a help to her sister when she came to write Fry's biography. (Bloomsbury, although it felt free to live its own life as it wished, nevertheless did not believe in publicly flouting the customs of the time, nor in hurting the feelings of the living. So Vanessa's intense affair with Fry from 1911 to 1914 was not included in the biography.) In it she recalls first seeing Fry in 1902 or 1903 in the Fellows' Garden at King's College, Cambridge, knowing of him as a brilliant art critic and lecturer but not having heard him as she hated going to lectures.

At this point she was in the midst of her own artistic training. Born in 1879, she had first studied drawing in 1896, then from 1901 to 1904 attended classes at the Royal Academy. In 1904 she studied briefly at the Slade, exhibiting for the first time the next year her first serious painting, a portrait of Lady Robert Cecil. The same year she helped form the Friday Club, founded to discuss art with an expanded group of her friends and young painters as well as to sponsor exhibitions.

She remembered next meeting Fry at a dinner, about the same time—in 1905—at Desmond MacCarthy's and being somewhat frightened of him as a forbidding older artistic figure, in a category similar to the artist and formidable Slade faculty member Henry Tonks. "In fact all members of the N-E A C [New English Art Club] seemed somehow to have the secret of the art universe within their grasp, a secret one was not worthy to learn, especially if one was that terribly low creature, a female painter." They argued about Sargent, whom Fry disliked intensely. (Sargent had taught Vanessa at the Royal Academy Schools.) "I had for long doubted, denied his merits, thought him vulgar, but had at last gone over with vehemence, overcome by what seemed such superb painting."[46] Shortly afterwards Vanessa visited the Frys in Hampstead; Helen Fry, as she had seemed at the MacCarthy dinner too, was quiet and apparently ill.

Their first common interest was as artists, Vanessa as a beginning one, Fry more established but not really successful as a painter although certainly quite well known already as an art critic. The places where more advanced art might be shown in London in the years before 1910 were comparatively few although in many ways the art scene was lively, and was moving away from its Victorian proprieties. Vanessa had exhibited regularly at the New English Art Club from 1907 to 1910, stopping that year. The Club was no longer as important or as vital an organization as it had been some years before. Its middle-of-the-road position can be seen, to anticipate somewhat, in the review in the *Times* of its annual exhibition in November 1910, where the work shown is explicitly contrasted to the Post-Impressionists. At the same time there is an awareness in the review of the tendency of any institution, perhaps particularly in England, to become more conservative. The *Times* wrote that the exhibition "is fairly representative of what may be called the modernist movement among our painters. While almost free from the anarchistic absurdities of the post-impressionists, it is, of course in flat opposition to the older academical canons, though, to be sure, the club includes one full-blown R.A. and one Associate [of the Royal Academy]."[47]

Frank Rutter, the art critic of the *Sunday Times,* had founded the Allied Artists' Association in 1907 to be more welcoming of new art. He had been an early proponent, by English standards, of the Impressionists, and Vanessa had overcome her dislike of lectures by going to one of his on the topic. The Allied Artists' Association wished to operate without a selecting, that is, "hanging," jury and hence avoid the elitism of the Royal Academy. But that decision meant that the exhibition was too huge and undiscriminating, democratic as it might be, to carry much weight, even if it provided a place to exhibit for those who were outside the art establishment through youth or being too unusual. It had its first display in July 1908 in the Royal Albert Hall, at which Vanessa exhibited.

There were some progressive galleries, such as Chenil's, run by Jack Knewstub, Orpen's and Rothenstein's brother-in-law, much associated with Augustus John; and the Carfax, with Robert Ross as one of those in charge. The Carfax had been founded in 1898, and Rothenstein was active in choosing the pictures shown there. In 1906 the leading London gallery Agnew had been very adventuresome and had a showing of

"Some Examples of the Independent Art of Today," which meant Steer, Orpen, Tonks, Conder, Rothenstein—"even Sickert [as Frank Rutter remarked years later] though in the result it proved that [his] contribution . . . was only hung on the staircase, as if to break modern painting gently to Messrs. Agnew's eminently respectable clientele."[48]

But even this presentation was too much for the traditional art public. Advanced opinion in England, with some opposition, was favorable to the Impressionists, but quite a few of the progressive figures dug in their heels at the Post-Impressionists. Henry Tonks had shown work in Agnew's show, and was a leading teacher of the young at the Slade. His biographer remarked: "When New English [Art Club] work was admitted to Agnew's in 1906, people spoke and wrote as if the barbarians had entered the Roman Senate House, whereas the fact was that painters like Steer and Tonks were already much more like Senators of the old nobility and all the time 'quite a different race of barbarians, the real thing, were growing up in Paris.'"[49]

Certainly in retrospect the exhibition at Agnew was far less adventuresome than the Post-Impressionist show. A sense of the importance of the market, and its relation to art, can be glimpsed in the obituary in the *Times* in November 1910 of Sir Thomas Agnew, the son of the founder of the gallery. The firm had begun in Manchester in order to provide pictures for the local businessmen who in the early days would buy contemporary paintings (a major reason why Victorian painters did so well) but had more recently turned to the old masters as these purchasers became grander and less apprehensive about forgeries. Perhaps Agnew was trying to educate its clients to be more sympathetic to work by contemporaries, one reason for its 1906 exhibition. As the obituary noted about the interest in older art: "The passion, as everyone knows, has now assumed dimensions disastrous to modern artists, who complain that nobody now buys their pictures as the Manchester men used to buy them forty years ago."[50]

The art world was caught up in the same paradoxes as the rest of society. This was the period of Edwardian luxe and vulgarity when the rich had a great deal of money to spend but might find it hard to decide whether to spend it on the new or the safe. At the same time, as reflected in the politics of the period, as in Old Age Pensions, there was a parallel need to cater to, as well as, some thought, a moral imperative to serve the needs of a wider public in the worlds of culture and art. This motive inspired such enterprises as the Medici Society, founded in 1908, which provided, on a large scale, cheap reproductions of famous pictures; and in the world of books series of inexpensive printings of standard works or what should be so considered, such as the World Classics and Everyman series, and in design such shops as Heals and Liberty. A larger public existed for such works.[51]

But an elite is always likely to have mixed feelings about a popular development of that sort, even the political liberals among them. The diffusion of culture is an obvious good, but how high a price is paid for its dilution? Taste was changing in the Edwardian period, and painting was becoming more domestic and less pretentious. The way was being prepared for the modernism of the Post-Impressionists, even if the actual exhibition itself would be, for many, a shock.

One of the more fascinating aspects of English society and politics, I believe, is its relation to the Continent of Europe which has continued to our day, as reflected in the debates about the Common Market and the European Community, to have a rather love-hate quality. (Of course this is frequently characteristic of any major nation's relation to others. For instance, while the English had a sense of inferiority about many of the more sophisticated aspects of European life, at the same time English taste was frequently viewed as very sophisticated on the Continent.) In the political world of international relations, England could no longer afford to pursue its policy of trying to remain as independent as possible and had concluded treaties, with limited commitments, with Japan, France, and Russia. (The alliance with Japan was celebrated, in 1910, with the Japan-British Exhibition which ran from May to October in White City; the Entente with France had been marked by a similar exhibition in 1908.)

The Impressionists were exhibited in London in the early years of the century, most notably at a show at the Grafton Gallery in 1905, sponsored by the Paris dealer Durand-Ruel, showing more than three hundred pictures, including among them works by Degas, Renoir, Manet, and ten unremarked-upon Cézannes.[52] Cézanne had already been shown as early as 1898 at the International Society in London without being noticed; also in 1906, at an exhibition which Fry had favorably reviewed; and in 1908 at the New Gallery, when he received some attention.[53] In 1906, in the *Athenaeum*, Fry had been praising but muted about the two Cézannes on display. "We confess to having been hitherto sceptical about Cézanne's genius, but these two pieces reveal a power which is entirely distinct and personal, and though the artist's appeal is limited, and touches none of the finer issues of the imaginative life, it is none the less complete."[54]

The anonymous review in the *Burlington* of the 1908 show attacked the paintings of Denis, Signac, Matisse, and Gauguin as "trivial," "infantile," and showing "positive disintegration." The reviewer, aware of the risks of attacking young painters and hence being regarded as wrong in later years, nonetheless felt that these painters were followers of Impressionism rather than innovators. "Now if history proves that revolting youth is generally right and conservative old age is generally wrong, it proves with equal certainty that the best work done by any movement is done by its pioneers. In the hands of their immediate followers the revolt loses its freshness: in the hands of the next generation it sinks into callous imitation or empty caprice."[55]

The following month the *Burlington* published a letter by Fry criticizing this review and coming to the defense of the painters attacked, including Cézanne, who had not been mentioned. Fry maintained that such painters as Gauguin and Cézanne were a new strong development, demonstrating an emphasis on form, a sort of proto-Byzantinism, a movement on from Impressionism, which might be compared to the art of the Roman empire. "MM. Cézanne and Paul Gauguin are not really Impressionists at all. They are proto-Byzantines rather than neo-Impressionists. . . . There is no need for me to praise Cézanne—his position is already assured."[56] But these new painters would not make a real impress upon the English art scene until two years later.

Even in the appreciation of the Impressionists, there was a rather slow catching up in England. Frank Rutter attempted to interest the National Gallery in purchasing Impressionist pictures, but with very limited success. He did raise a comparatively small fund of £160, but the Gallery wouldn't buy Monet, Renoir, or Degas as being against its policy of purchasing work from artists who were still alive, and found Manet, Sisley, and Pissarro too advanced; so Boudin was bought as a compromise.[57]

In its insular way, English art did change and become somewhat more "modern." Many painters were of course influenced by the 1910 exhibition itself; for instance Henry Lamb, who had not seen much Gauguin before, modified his style under Gauguin's influence after the Grafton exhibition. But apart from the exhibition, English painting was changing. In 1911 Sickert, increasingly well known and admired outside the Academy, helped form the Camden Town Group. Though heavily influenced by French painting, particularly Degas, he was not a supporter of the Post-Impressionists, and his group included younger painters who gathered around him when he came back to live in England in 1905: most notably Spencer Gore, Harold Gilman, Charles Ginner, and Malcolm Drummond. Duncan Grant was briefly a member—but he and Vanessa Bell were really developing in a different direction, and were much more influenced by the Post-Impressionists. (In any case, the Group would not admit women.) Nevertheless, some of the Camden Town Group exhibited in the second Post-Impressionist Exhibition in 1912.

In the Camden Town Group, there was an emphasis on the domestic and the smaller scaled, to get more at the essence of life than Victorian painting had done, but not in the direction of the more "extreme" forms of art shown in the Grafton Gallery in 1910. The most famous statement of Camden's direction, not necessarily followed in the more lyrical paintings of some of the group, was made by Sickert in May 1910, in a short piece in the *Art News,* a publication started in 1909 and edited by Frank Rutter. "The more our art is serious, the more it will tend to avoid the drawing-room and stick to the kitchen. The plastic arts are gross arts, dealing joyously with gross material facts. They call, in their servants, for a robust stomach and a great power of endurance, and while they will flourish in the scullery, or on the dunghill, they fade at a breath from the drawing-room."[58]

Despite this brave statement, England seems incapable of producing a genuine avant-garde—revolt itself is domesticated, or is presented in domesticated forms. One might argue that the great strength and weakness of England is the domestication of the extreme. In the past, William Morris had been in many ways a revolutionary artist, and particularly of the domestic, but his most modern legacy was realized on the Continent, as Nikolaus Pevsner has controversially argued in *Pioneers of Modern Design*.[59] In 1910 Marinetti visited England and preached Futurism; some years later Pound and Wyndham Lewis formed the Rebel Art Centre. But, in England, such movements seem either to evaporate or be domesticated.

The Bloomsbury artists developed in a third direction: neither Victorian realism nor the "robust" new style of Sickert. Rather, they responded to a new aesthetic that emphasized the role of form, the abstract, as in the rhythm of the line, mass, space, light and shade, qualities potentially separated from content, as Fry discussed in "An Essay in Aesthetics" published in the *New Quarterly,* edited by Desmond MacCarthy, in 1909.[60] There, drawing on his scientific and Apostolic background, Fry made clear his belief in the need to reach what he regarded as essentials, as qualities beyond representation. Nevertheless, as Ian Dunlop has remarked: "The spirit of revolt, of defiance of authority, of change for change's sake, of anarchy and restlessness that had affected every major city in Europe—Munich, Dresden, Berlin, Brussels, Paris and Moscow, in particular—is almost totally absent from the London artistic world. There was an underworld in London, made up from immense poverty and lawlessness and spiced with petty villainy, but never a Bohemia."[61]

Bell's and Grant's pictures were more decorative than Sickert's, what one might call a modernism of the drawing room. One of Grant's earliest pictures is of a kitchen, but a far cleaner one than Sickert probably had in mind.[62] Christopher Reed has commented on the lines from Sickert quoted above that Bell's modernism "was inextricably linked with the drawing room domesticity she had created at 46 Gordon Square."[63] As Reed goes on to argue, Fry could lead her into a form of modernism that she would find compatible. Virginia came to admire Sickert, as she celebrated years later, in 1934, in her Hogarth pamphlet *Walter Sickert: A Conversation.* It had on its cover a drawing by Vanessa of a dining room table, close to but not quite the kitchen, presumably celebrating the meal Sickert and Virginia had together at the time of the writing. Virginia Woolf loved teasing, and enjoyed claiming to take, in the pamphlet, Sickert's side against Fry and Bell, and she even compares him to the early Arnold Bennett; his pictures tell stories.[64]

Fry had been changing his views somewhat in the years before 1910, as is suggested in the contrast between the National Art Collections Fund, which he had helped to found in 1903, and the Contemporary Art Society of 1910. The former had a greater emphasis on older art than the latter. So too in his involvement with the *Burlington Magazine,* also founded in 1903, with Fry, Bernard Berenson, and Herbert Horne as dominant figures and Fry becoming an editor in 1909.

Then, too, in early 1910 he translated and published in the *Burlington* Maurice Denis's articles on Cézanne. In June of that year there was an exhibition in Brighton, organized by Robert Dell (the *Burlington*'s correspondent in France) that included works by Gauguin, Cézanne, Matisse, and other French modernists which received some attention, mostly hostile. But perhaps because it was in Brighton and not London and lacked Fry's flair, it was barely noticed as compared to the later show. It did have a favorable notice in the *Times* that might have been written by Fry. The reviewer remarked of the one picture by Cézanne, a portrait of Albin Valabrègue:

> At first sight this portrait looks botchy in execution and wooden in pose; but forget your ideas of what execution and pose ought to be, and you will become aware of a peculiar intensity in the picture as you look at it. The artist seems determined to keep free of rhetoric and

commonplace. He will say nothing about his subject merely because other artists would have said it. He will paint only his own idea of the man as simply as possible.

Discussing the two minor still lifes by Matisse in the exhibition, the reviewer remarked: "The painters who have most to express sacrifice more and more of representation to expression. And that is the reason why they are so unintelligible to the public, who miss in their works those facts which they expect to find in a picture."[65]

Fry himself was unaware of how much the art story in England was going to change, thanks in large part to the exhibition he would soon organize. As late as a few days before the Post-Impressionist Exhibition opened, he wrote to Duncan Grant: "It struck me that you might care to exhibit at the New English so I have got you an invitation. As you know I am by no means enthusiastic about the society but still it is so far the only one that offers much chance & perhaps you should make use of it."[66] Fry was now moving toward a more radical stance, perhaps partially driven to it by the exigencies of his personal situation. He had a need to strike out in new directions; his personal life was making new demands, financial and emotional. There was also the newfound excitement, personal and intellectual, of his becoming friends with Clive and Vanessa Bell and through them with the other figures of Bloomsbury.

———

Let's return to the earlier months of 1910. The meeting of Vanessa Bell and Fry was at the railway platform in Cambridge; she wrote in what was probably a slip of the pen (or of the transcriber of the typescript) that it was early in 1908 but it was most likely January 1910. Clive was with her, and he would be the writer who did so much to make his version of Fry's ideas much better known. "'There's Roger Fry—But I dont think he remembers me'. We went up to him however & whether he remembered me or not, a question we disputed later, I introduced Clive and we entered the same carriage. He had brought a MS of course & intended to write an article or lecture on the way to London. But talk began and continued unceasingly."[67] The last two words are suggestive of what would happen for the next twenty-four years, until Roger Fry's death in 1934. In his later reminiscences, Bell remembers that Fry mentioned to him during this conversation that he meant to show the public the work of the newest French painters, but one suspects that the idea came to him later.[68]

Fry suggested the Bells visit him in Guildford, where he had built his house Durbins that year, and Vanessa wrote they did so in the spring. In any case, they met earlier when Fry talked to the Friday Club in February on "Representation as a Means of Expression." On the visit to Durbins, it was clear to Vanessa that Helen was seriously mentally ill, and indeed it was that year that she was declared incurable. Fry, with his scientific background, had a commitment to rationality, and, in the English manner, he urged his wife to apply rationality to her problems. It is ironic as well as sad that in his personal life he had to cope with the interplay of rationality and madness while being accused, at the time of the exhibition, of espousing the cause of the mad in art.[69] (Quite a few critics of the exhibition claimed that the artists were insane and presumably quite a few of them knew that Fry's wife was so as well. But I have not discovered any critic who was cruel enough to make that connection in print.) Fry would move toward a theory that a greater reality was expressed in the abstract aspects of a painting than in any apparent realism. It was also an Apostolic position that the real in the world was not the apparent. So too in Virginia Woolf's art, and in the argument she would have with Arnold Bennett fourteen years later about Mrs Brown.

In the early 1920s, in her essay "Old Bloomsbury," Virginia Woolf captured the excitement of Roger Fry's entering the circle:

It must have been in 1910 I suppose that Clive one evening rushed upstairs in a state of the highest excitement. He had just had one of the most interesting conversations of his life. It was with Roger Fry. They were discussing the theory of art for hours. He thought Roger Fry the most interesting person he had met since Cambridge days. So Roger appeared. . . . He had more knowledge and experience than the rest of us put together. . . . The old skeleton arguments of primitive Bloomsbury about art and beauty put on flesh and blood.[70]

In her biography of Fry, Virginia combines her own and her sister's impressions of him at this time.

> To a stranger meeting him then for the first time (1910) he looked much older than his age. He was only forty-four, but he gave the impression of a man with a great weight of experience behind him. He looked worn and seasoned, ascetic yet tough. . . . He talked that spring day in a room looking over the trees of a London square, in a deep voice like a harmonious growl,—"his and Forbes Robertson's were the only voices one could listen to for their own sakes" says Bernard Shaw—and he laughed spontaneously, thoroughly, with the whole of him. . . . There was something stable underneath his mobility. Mobile he was. He was just off—was it to Paris or to Poland?[71]

We've seen that much of Vanessa's time in 1910 was taken up with looking after her sons, Julian and the finally named Quentin, and with worrying about Virginia. She was continuing her painting career, about to be given an aesthetic jolt by the Post-Impressionist Exhibition. But she was not as active as she might have been otherwise in the actual making of the exhibition, and did not accompany Fry and Clive Bell to Paris to select the pictures. To a degree, that more active role was taken by a figure who was becoming closer to the Bloomsbury group, although never really a member of it: Lady Ottoline Morrell.

Bloomsbury never pretended to be generous in its judgments, and it could hardly have expected that so much of its private writings would be published. In those writings Bloomsbury was certainly ungenerous to Lady Ottoline. But writers and artists are famously unkind to their patrons—it is part of the relationship—and Lady Ottoline made herself somewhat of a figure of fantasy and jest with her great height, red hair, and extravagant way of dressing. To attack Bloomsbury excessively for its nastiness is rather unfair. It is a truth universally admitted that we all speak badly of others, even of those of whom we may in fact be quite fond. The more intelligent can also frequently be the meaner, and there was much in Ottoline to make mock of. But the generous remarks have to be noted as well. She was seen both as somewhat grotesque and as striking, or so Virginia Woolf recorded when she wrote about her in the *Times* at the time of her death in 1938. Lady Ottoline

> brought together at Bedford Square and then at Garsington, Prime Ministers and painters, Bishops and freethinkers, the famous and the obscure! Whether she sat at the head of her table against a background of pale yellow and pomegranate, or mused at Garsington with her embroidery on her lap and undergraduates at her feet, or held on her way down the Tottenham Court Road like a Renaissance princess listening to inaudible music while the passers by stared, she created her own world. And it was a world in which conflicts and collisions were inevitable; nor did she escape the ridicule of those whom she befriended.[72]

Born in 1873, a half-sister of the Duke of Portland, Ottoline Morrell was very conscious of being an aristocrat. In a well-known but probably apocryphal story which Bloomsbury circulated, perhaps based on a passing remark she made to one of them, she allegedly told a meeting of mill workers during the second election of 1910, "I *love* the people—I married into the people."[73] This was in 1902 to Philip Morrell, a not particularly well off member of a respectable middle-class Oxfordshire family who had been the solicitors for Oxford University since the eighteenth century—not the better-off brewers of the same name, though related to them. His mother lived in a house in Oxford that housed a collection that some have claimed was the model for Henry James's *The Spoils of Poynton*. Ottoline was a collector of famous people, most notably, other than the Bloomsbury figures, Aldous Huxley and D. H. Lawrence, who used her, not favorably, as a model for characters in their novels. Philip was a radical Liberal (to the scandal of his family) member of Parliament who lost his seat, in the Henley constituency of Oxfordshire, in the first election of January 1910 but regained another seat in December for the Lancashire constituency of Burnley. (He would hold his seat until 1918. He became increasingly unpopular during the First World War, which he firmly opposed.)

Ottoline loved to entertain artists and intellectuals, and had affairs with Augustus John, Henry Lamb, very briefly with Roger Fry, and most famously and longest, starting in March 1911, with Bertrand Russell. She would have several of these affairs going on at the same time; perhaps that was one reason that they generally seemed to be an amalgam of passion and lack of sexual satisfaction. In July Lady Ottoline had had a heart-to-heart conversation with Vanessa Bell about her marriage: "She had never been in love with Philip. She was passionately in love with someone else for a long time & then married Philip only because she found him a pleasant & soothing companion. They now have little or no physical feeling for each other & lead a most celibate existence. She is I think more or less in love with Henry Lamb."[74]

Lady Ottoline too entertained on Thursdays in Bloomsbury at her house in Bedford Square, a more worldly and older crowd than attended the more austere gatherings in Gordon Square or Fitzroy Square. She became an even greater hostess when she moved to her most famous house, Garsington Manor, outside Oxford in 1915 (the Morrells had purchased it in 1913). It provided a mecca for literary figures—most notably D. H. Lawrence, T. S. Eliot, Siegfried Sassoon, Aldous Huxley as well as the members of Bloomsbury—and a place for conscientious objectors among her friends to work on the land during the First World War, Philip Morrell putting his beliefs into practice. She was not as rich as those who exploited her hospitality thought, and the Morrells were forced to sell Garsington in 1928, not having run the estate well in agricultural terms and having spent more than they should have on improving it.

Much could be made of the importance of entertaining in English society. In many ways, the English were very formal. Yet "at homes," originally part of a highly ritualized system of visiting in the afternoon and the leaving of calling cards, might also be used as a less formal way of entertaining in the evening after dinner when the expense need not be great. Bloomsbury made its gatherings even more informal, but it was building on a well-established tradition. For instance Charles Sanger, a slightly older Apostle, and his wife had a weekly at home where they entertained Bloomsbury figures as well as friends of Lady Ottoline's. It was there that Lytton and Ottoline met for the first time in the autumn of 1910.

Before Garsington the Morrells had had a smaller house, Peppard Cottage, also in the Oxfordshire countryside, near Henley, in the village of Peppard Common.[75] They acquired it in 1907 as a place to raise their daughter, Julian. (Lady Ottoline had had twins in 1906 but the boy, Hugh, had died when only a few days old.) It also had the advantage of being in Philip's constituency. Julian was sent there with a nurse to have a quieter life than was possible in London but also to be less trouble to her mother, a nursery at a distance. At the same time, Lady Ottoline let friends use the house, most notably in 1910 Henry Lamb, with whom she was then having an affair (and who painted her as a nude dryad in the neighboring woods)[76] and Lytton Strachey, who was lusting after Lamb. Or rather Lamb used the house as a base; he stayed at the inn, the Dog, close by, and had his studio in a nearby coach house.

Lamb would be able to maintain his friendship with both Strachey and Lady Ottoline, although it is extremely unlikely that he went to bed with Lytton. In a fragmentary diary that Lytton kept in 1910 he recorded his affection for Lamb. Once, on March 19, when he went to be drawn by Lamb, he recorded: "I tried to embrace him. Extreme severity. 'Absolutely out of the question, impossible'. I was bitterly disappointed. Managed at last to discuss. 'Not enraged in the least—but only wanted to draw me.' I said, 'You knew I was a dangerous character'. He said 'I hoped to draw you first'. Eventually he admitted he'd perhaps been brutal. Should I come again? At last I said I would. As I went he said 'It's just like Ottoline.'"[77] In April Strachey wrote Duncan Grant about a party he had attended:

My last view of her [Ottoline] was at a dim evening party full of virgins given by the Russells in a furnished flat. I was feeling dreadfully bored when I suddenly looked up and saw her entering with Henry. I was never so astonished, and didn't know which I was in love with most.

Henry Lamb at Peppard Cottage, 1911. Taken by Lady Ottoline Morrell.

As to her, though, there seems very little doubt. She carried him off to the country with her under my very nose, and I was left wishing Dutch William [William III] and his friends [including his alleged lover Bentinck, Ottoline's ancestor] had never come to England.[78]

Lamb had known the Bloomsbury figures for some time through his slightly older brother Walter, who was their contemporary at Trinity and was one of the young men of the circle who thought himself in love with Virginia (at the same time that he rather flirted with Lytton).

Ottoline by Henry Lamb, 1911

Lytton met Henry probably in 1905, but it was not until 1910 that their relationship became closer, culminating in Lamb's portrait of him, started in 1912 and finished in 1914, probably Lamb's best-known picture, now in the Tate Gallery. Lamb visited Strachey in Cambridge but did not enjoy the academic atmosphere, perhaps in part because his father was a professor of mathematics. As he wrote about Cambridge: "Ugh! How I loathe those timid, well-mannered unambitious & unlovely existences."[79]

Shortly after this visit Strachey went to a sanatorium in Sweden for ten weeks for the sake of his health with his sister Pernal and Jane Harrison, the eminent classicist. Keynes wrote sympathetically in July: "I hope Sweden will make up to the body for the horrors it must inflict on the mind."[80] Strachey wrote Keynes at the end of September just before he was to leave to return to England. "I've stayed on here week after week, lured by the hope of attaining eternal health. . . . I feel that this has been a wasted Summer for me, except that I've put on a few kilograms of flesh, which I suppose is something. But no English country life, no conversation, and—ah!—no Eric!" He wrote that he was having erections at the thought of the Swedish bath attendants and of George Mallory, the beautiful predominantly heterosexual young man much admired by Strachey and others (Duncan Grant had an affair with him and also persuaded him to pose for him in the nude) and who would die on Mt. Everest in 1924. Having introduced the sexual, the letter went on jokingly: "Is it true that young Clarke discovered the Chancellor of the Exchequer buggering the President of the Board of Trade? That he then asked for the Viceroyalty, and that, after some negotiations, he agreed to take a seat in the Council? It seems the most probable explanation."[81]

Strachey had also spent time in Sweden the previous year in an attempt to improve his precarious health. While there he worked on a humorous piece on the suffrage movement (with which some of his sisters and his about-to-be sister-in-law, Ray, were so involved), and yet again tried to make a book of his dissertation on Warren Hastings, which had failed to secure him a fellowship at Trinity five years before.

At Peppard in the autumn after Strachey's return from Sweden, Lamb found Strachey interesting to be with, and reported enthusiastically to Lady Ottoline about their time together while she was away campaigning for her husband. His letter must have made her jealous to a degree. Lamb wrote, "We remain apparently the best of friends in spite of some severish tests. At the same time I feel vaguely guilty because I know I should be working harder alone. But the experience is worth much sacrifice. I have not had such stirring conversations since the early days when I had just left school & it is good so to be stirred to one's mind's depths occasionally."[82] Strachey told his mother that the visit was good for his health. "Lady Ottoline is in Lancashire electioneering. Henry Lamb (artist) is my only companion. He is painting my portrait, and in the intervals plays divinely on the piano. We also go out for enormous walks and eat enormous meals."[83]

At around the same time, Lamb wrote to Ottoline that he missed her a great deal and that his relationship with Lytton had elements of strain: "You will certainly expire if you stay longer in Burnley at that idiotic game. Are you really as necessary to Philip up there as he imagines? & does liberal Burnley demand your immolation? . . . Strachey & I are stranded without you. I was in fearful dread that we should be unable to keep up a pretence of even civility to each other: though we are beginning to associate reasonably & perhaps graciously."[84]

Lytton felt that the way to keep everyone happy was to radiate contentment, although perhaps he was also interested in rousing Ottoline's jealousy. While London was having the excitement of the Post-Impressionist Exhibition, Lytton was at Peppard. Ottoline was away with Philip in Burnley campaigning for his return to Parliament, as a member of the people. As he wrote in his thank you note to Ottoline: "My fortnight at Peppard was perfect bliss—an interlude from the Arabian Nights, and the ordinary world seems sordid and stupid after it. I am very grateful to you for the great enjoyment. . . . Henry quite overcame me. It was a tonic to be with him, and I don't think anyone has ever treated me so kindly. . . . I find that I liked his work more and more the more I saw of it." He also felt it necessary to urge Ottoline to take strong stands on her husband's behalf: "The Burnley news was splendid. I hope now that the general position is safe. I believe the great fault of the English nation is its hankering after compromise—and it's quite a new thing too: it was not compromise that repealed the Corn Laws and cut off Charles the First's head."[85]

Roger Fry too was part of the traffic to Peppard, visiting in November. In his thank-you note he said: "It is very strange that just as my inner life which was all bound up in Helen seems definitely crumbling to pieces the general life seems to have suddenly become so immensely more worth while, and in all that you know how much you have counted."[86] The next week he commented on the political scene, but one senses the somewhat diffident attitude that much of Bloomsbury took toward politics. "I've got to begin political meetings to-morrow. How I hate it, & I am no good at it either."[87] Also it didn't help, as the Tory candidate won in Guildford.

Then on December 7, when Philip's victory in Burnley was known, Fry wrote:

> I meant to write my congratulations but was distracted by many things. And now the first flush of gladness has got tempered by many thoughts of what it will mean. Still on the whole I am glad, just that you have brought off a difficult victory. It's good for the country if not for you & so I suppose one's best self rejoices. I wonder what you feel. I can't quite guess. Of course it is good to do one's "job" well so I expect you are happy & this will sound horribly lukewarm. Well I can only say that if you are glad I will be glad too tho' I know it'll mean such a lot of squalid things to do later on which we shall all want you not to be doing.[88]

On New Year's Day, 1911, Virginia wrote a letter of congratulation, with a similar sense of diffidence. She had participated in the election to the extent of going to a political meeting and sitting on the platform, even if she is hardly flattering about the unnamed candidate. "It must be delightful [for Philip] to be in [Parliament], so triumphantly—and what a mercy to have it over—only aren't you worked to the bone? We went to one meeting only, and that, what with cheering and stamping and emotions of all kinds, was very exhausting. The candidate was a loathsome Portuguese Jew. But the crowd was far more exciting than anything else, and makes it almost impossible to sit down and read in ones room again."[89]

After Strachey left Peppard, Lamb wrote again to Ottoline in December: "I shall certainly miss G.L.S: he was a charming companion: & so well instructed, but I am also glad he is gone, because I can turn him to still better account now in retrospect, & shall have time to sift out what of our frothy gabble may be worth assimilating. I feel I have been laughing too much & have grown too fat."[90] Strachey appeared to enjoy the more raffish world of artists, a more relaxed ambience than Bloomsbury that perhaps compensated for his temporary exclusion from Gordon Square. This sort of connection would climax in 1915 when he began his very close if asexual companionship with the artist Dora Carrington, one of the bright young students at the Slade in 1910, which lasted until his death in 1932.

In this letter Lamb also, inadvertently or deliberately, turned up the sexual heat by informing Ottoline that Helen Maitland, also a lover of his, was coming to visit at Peppard. Helen Maitland, of Scottish descent, had been born in 1885 in California, where her father attempted, unsuccessfully, to start a winery in Napa. He then disappeared, and Helen's mother, Louise, worked in 1894–95 as a cataloger at the Library at Stanford, living on the campus, before mother and daughter moved to New York and then to Europe. In Paris, Helen met Lamb and became romantically involved with him. Through him she met Boris Anrep, whom she married in 1918 after having two children by him. In 1926 she left Anrep for Roger Fry.

She had never received much of an education; she wrote a rather incoherent thank-you letter to Lady Ottoline, who had been at Peppard some of the time that she was there:

I was perfectly mystified by things you said at Peppard, so much so that I can't even quote them. Do you think I am really just such another being as Strachey, a sort of snobbish vampire who battens on distructive [*sic*] criticism? You have probably never thought anything so vindictive of anyone, but that's what it would be if it were translated into my thought. . . . H. L[amb]. seems to me to recognize essential things parts [?] more than he ever did which I am sure is due to you. . . . My brother has fired me with a desire to go back to California. Will you come and sojourn under a redwood tree with me?[91]

Strachey took a certain amusement in the complicated sexual situation; in 1912 he made a caricature of Lamb holding himself and Ottoline in nooses, with Strachey and Ottoline holding hands and saying "When will he realize what he makes us SUFFER."[92]

———

During 1910 Lytton Strachey was continuing to build his literary reputation. While in London, he had lived in Lancaster Gate with his parents. They left Lancaster Gate in 1907 for a small house in Hampstead; his father, more than twenty years older than his mother, died in 1908. Lytton found living with his parents depressing and didn't enjoy being in London, particularly as at this moment he wasn't very welcome in Gordon Square. He liked to travel about, either renting a place or staying with friends. During 1910 he was with Rupert Brooke at West Lulworth, near Studland; with Keynes at Burford; with Mollie MacCarthy at Eton; with George Mallory at Charterhouse; and in Cambridge. He had been there at the time of Edward VII's death in May and wrote to his mother about it: "I fled from Cambridge to Rupert at Grantchester for the day, as all the Colleges were draped in black, and all the fellows walking to & fro in funeral processions. The lodging-house keepers are ruined, as the May Week balls have been abolished, and no ladies are expected in consequence."[93]

Not yet having really established his career outside the University, he spent more time at the scenes of earlier student triumphs perhaps than he should have. In June he invited Desmond MacCarthy to visit him. "I'm rather délabré, but breathing and happy. . . . He [G. E. Moore] was superb on the hearthrug [the obligatory comment at a meeting of the Apostles]—the lava stream pouring out in full flow. . . . Cambridge is pleasant but more sterile than can be conceived. I lie in a punt on the river all day, surrounded by about half a dozen infants in arms, and wondering when I shall write a masterpiece."[94]

Lytton's formidable mother was intensely literary and political, as were quite a few of his twelve siblings. Several of them were almost as involved with early Bloomsbury as Lytton. He had not yet managed to complete the transition from precocious undergraduate to independent man of letters. He had had a brilliant career while an undergraduate, securing various prizes, and certainly, as a member of the Apostles, he had been at the center of Cambridge's undergraduate intellectual life. But he did not receive a first on the Tripos, the culminating examinations; and then his two years of work on Warren Hastings ended in disappointment as he did not secure a fellowship at Trinity. He maintained close contacts with his Cambridge friends in London, as well as spending much time in Cambridge itself—frequently a sign of a failure to grow up on the part of someone who no longer has a present role to play at the university.

In these years, Lytton was leading an active but not particularly distinguished literary life, writing frequent reviews, most often for the "family" weekly, the *Spectator*, edited and owned by his cousin St. Loe Strachey. James Strachey, Lytton's younger brother, who became their cousin's assistant, wrote about the publication:

> It was at that time far the most widely read of the political weeklies, with a circulation in the neigbourhood of twenty thousand copies, almost three times as large as that of any of its rivals. . . . *The Spectator* was in fact something of a laughing-stock among the intelligentsia of the period, and, indeed, among the younger members of our own family, who applied the term "spectatorial" to any particularly pompous and respectable pronouncement. At the same time we were very fond of St Loe, who was the kindest of friends and a most entertaining companion and was in many ways far from spectatorial in real life.[95]

St. Loe asked Lytton to write for him in 1904, and from the fall of 1907 to April 1909 Lytton contributed a review a week while on an annual salary of £150, becoming, somewhat reluctantly, a regular member of the staff. He wrote eighty articles for the *Spectator* in total, ending in 1914, the bulk of his journalism.

James Strachey notes in his preface to a collection of Lytton's pieces from the *Spectator* that he had been reluctant to republish them, feeling that the work was more ordinary than most of what Lytton wrote, as he generally conformed to the attitudes of his cousin, a sort of pre-censorship. St. Loe did give Lytton slightly more freedom as a theater critic—those pieces were signed by a nom-de-plume, "Ignotus." His other contributions were unsigned which in effect meant they had the approval of the editor, who had shaped them in conversation beforehand and who would edit them heavily if necessary. The *Spectator* had broken with the Liberal party in 1886 over the issue of Home Rule in Ireland and had become more noticeably conservative; its alleged typical reader was a vicar in a country parsonage. At the same time, Lytton was becoming increasingly radical in his own thinking, turning on the Tory party and the House of Lords in their attempts to thwart the Liberal party. In a way, he was preparing himself in these years for his assault on the Victorian age in *Eminent Victorians*. As another indication of his increased political awareness he supported his sisters in the suffrage movement. As he wrote to Keynes in July: "I hope to get a seat in the House for Tuesday, and if I do, of course, I shall have to shriek and be torn to pieces. An uncomfortable, but no doubt noble death."[96]

In 1910 he wrote only one review, quite a contrast to previous years, for the *Spectator,* perhaps pleased to be released from his weekly obligation. He clearly had great latitude there in choosing what to review, for it was unlikely that the two volumes on Warren Hastings from the *Selections from the State Papers of the Governors-General of India* edited by G. W. Forrest were of great general interest. He pointed out the inadequacies of the work and its failure to take note of sources, both published and unpublished. There is a certain irony here, looking to the future when Strachey himself would be attacked for not doing enough original research for his masterpiece of 1918, *Eminent Victorians*. His complaints in 1910 are similar to those that would be made in subsequent years about himself. "It is not only in matters of detail that Mr Forrest's exposition might be improved upon; his whole view of the incident lacks breadth and proportion."[97]

In a sense, the review was a farewell to the topic, for after many years he was abandoning his attempt to turn his dissertation into a book. His earlier work had been a defense of Warren Hastings, and the effort seemed weighted down by some sort of family obligation to India, so identified with both his parents and the parental tradition. He was even named after a Viceroy, who also served as his godfather: the Earl of Lytton, a poet and son of the novelist Edward Bulwer-Lytton. The Lyttons at this time, like the Stracheys, were much involved with the campaign for votes for women. Lord Lytton, the Viceroy's son, was a prominent supporter, chairing the Conciliation Committee, and his sister, Lady Constance Lytton, had made a point about the English class system when she had been badly treated when arrested in January 1910 for militancy under the assumed working-class name of Jane Warton.

Strachey published just one other piece that year, in the *New Quarterly*. But he had written it in 1907, just when the journal had been founded with Desmond MacCarthy as literary editor. For whatever reason, the piece—a long negative review of a defense of Rousseau against Diderot and Grimm published in 1906—was not printed until 1910.

He was now less interested in reviewing as he was about to embark upon his first book, *Landmarks in French Literature,* a fifty-thousand-word survey of French writing. At this time his preferred area of interest was the eighteenth century, in both England and France. H. A. L. Fisher, Virginia's first cousin (but not very close to her) and brother of the officer on the *Dreadnought,* had written to Lytton in Sweden that he and the classicist Gilbert Murray were editing for the Home University Library a series designed to serve as intelligent handbooks for the general reader in literature, politics, and history. As Lytton wrote to his mother from Sweden: "The only news is that I have been asked by Herbert Fisher (Oxford) to write a sketch of French Literature for a new series he is editing! I have accepted. I think it will be rather fun, but very difficult, as it has to be very short."[98] Both Virginia and Lytton thought Fisher was something of a fake, but he fortunately maintained his high opinion of Lytton when they met in October, and terms were agreed: he would be paid a fee of £50, and a penny on each volume sold.[99] The study, the thirty-fifth volume in the series, was published in 1912. In later years Lytton chose not to list it among his books.

Michael Holroyd, in his magisterial biography of Strachey, ends the first volume here:

> With the commission of this first book, his years of obscurity and pessimism had reached their end, and to coincide with the new emergent phase, his social and emotional life were also about to undergo some dramatically involved variations of pattern. The composition of *Landmarks in French Literature* injected into him a rejuvenated, long-sought-after burst of self-confidence which, like an expanding spring, released him from the lugubrious routine of the past, its frustrations and lethargic aimlessness, and led on to what he himself described as his "Spiritual Revolution."
>
> So that now, in the autumn of 1910, he stood on the perimeter of a new and ultimately happier world.[100]

Holroyd, in the first version of his biography, picks up the rest of the story of 1910 as the first chapter of volume 2, not surprisingly using as its epigraph Woolf's aphorism. In late December Strachey left to spend four months at the house of his sister Dorothy Bussy in the south of France to start work on *Landmarks*. For him, 1910 marked the beginning of an important stage in his career, a stage that would culminate eight years later in his second book, *Eminent Victorians*, which would make him one of the best-known writers of his time and a revolutionary force in biography. Debunking biographies had not been totally unknown before, but Strachey's work was modern in its selectivity, its attempt to get at the essence of the character, its "significant form."[101]

Quite a few of the younger men in Bloomsbury, as well as Virginia Woolf, were also busy writing, and through their reviews and short pieces had become somewhat-known names in the literary world of the time. However, the tradition of unsigned pieces in the periodical press would have prevented their names from having wider recognition. That tradition had, as far as I understand it, two intriguing bases. An unsigned piece might acquire a certain magisterial tone by not being associated with an individual writer but instead, as in the *Spectator,* with a common editorial stance. But particularly in periodicals other than newspapers, anonymity also helped sustain the myth of the gentleman who was writing, it might be assumed, not for anything so vulgar as pay, but to share opinions with the world that counted on important issues.

The financial status of the members of Bloomsbury varied quite a bit, but in most cases their needs were modest. A small private income, such as the Stephens and Forster had, would provide an essential "golden island" that would allow one freedom to make one's own choices independent of the dictates of the marketplace. They assumed that they would live with a certain level of comfort and with help from servants. But with or without such a "golden island," all of Bloomsbury belonged to the "gentle" classes.

By 1910, only E. M. Forster and to a lesser extent Roger Fry had made anything approaching a significant mark on the literature and intellectual life of their day. The others were aspiring writers and busy talkers at the weekly "at homes" and other gatherings they attended . They moved around England (and on the Continent) and took short vacations at various times in the year, in Virginia's case for the sake of her mental health. Fry of course had been in Poland, and he, Clive Bell, Desmond MacCarthy, and Ottoline Morrell would be in Paris in the fall selecting pictures for the exhibition. Leonard Woolf was still ruling the empire in Ceylon.

Of those who came to the Thursday evenings, who would be remembered, ultimately, for their achievements? Some of the names are now preserved primarily because they were there, perhaps most prominently Saxon Sydney-Turner, a central Bloomsbury figure, part of the original group of friends at Trinity College, who spent his life in the obscurity of the civil service. While at Cambridge he had done brilliantly in classics and also distinguished himself in mathematics. He was famous for his silences, although he would talk more after midnight; and he would generally be the last to leave the weekly gatherings, perhaps as late as three in the morning. (He, presumably, had to turn up to work in Whitehall the next day; the others did not have specific obligations in terms of employment.) He was devoted to music, opera in particular. In 1908 Vanessa had painted a fine portrait of him at the piano. In 1909 he, Virginia, and Adrian had gone together to Bayreuth. Adrian shared his interests, and much of their correspondence in 1910 was devoted to arranging to go to concerts or operas.

At this time the Thursday evenings, starting at ten and possibly going on into the morning hours, were held in the "bachelor" quarters of Virginia and Adrian in Fitzroy Square. Some would attend who are now virtually forgotten or certainly less well known: Charles Sanger, Theodore Llewelyn Davies, Hilton Young, Charles Tennyson, Harry Norton —most but not all contemporaries of Thoby Stephen's from Cambridge—and some of Lytton's siblings, most notably Marjorie and James. Duncan Grant described the evenings as follows: "About 10 o'clock in the evening people used to appear and continue to come at intervals till 12 o'clock at night, and it was seldom that the last guest left before two or three in the morning. Whisky, buns, and cocoa were the diet, and people talked to each other. If someone had lit a pipe he would sometimes hold out the lighted match to Hans the dog, who would snap at it and put it out. Conversation; that was all."[102]

Those with lasting fame whom we haven't discussed much as yet, and who were certainly central figures, were Duncan Grant and John Maynard Keynes, and to a somewhat lesser extent, Desmond MacCarthy. Leonard Woolf was offstage in Ceylon. In terms of centrality and lasting interest, those members of Bloomsbury who made the greatest contributions were Virginia and Leonard Woolf, Vanessa and Clive Bell, Duncan Grant, Roger Fry, Lytton Strachey, John Maynard Keynes, and, in his slightly off-center way, E. M. Forster.

Perhaps because of the smallness of the country, the English young of the upper-middle class, some with private incomes but others in any case without occupations that demanded that they be in offices daily, did spend quite a bit of time moving from place to place, alighting at their parents' homes—after all most of these individuals were still in their late twenties—or taking rooms at one location or another. To a degree it was the restlessness of youth. Only Vanessa and Clive had apparently settled down to family life, with two sons. Clive had been flirting with Virginia and taking up again with his mistress. Yet their family home, 46 Gordon Square, was one center of Bloomsbury, along with 29 Fitzroy Square, where Virginia and Adrian lived from the time of Vanessa's marriage until they moved to 38 Brunswick Square in 1911.

Duncan Grant had a flat in 21 Fitzroy Square from 1909 to 1911, and Maynard Keynes had a room there as his London pied-à-terre until they joined forces with the Stephens at 38 Brunswick Square. Virginia and Adrian were at the more Bohemian end of Bloomsbury, also known as Fitzrovia. Sickert had his studio in the Square and Henry Lamb had his in Fitzroy Street. Keynes's final home in Bloomsbury was the first Bloomsbury house, 46 Gordon Square, which became his London base in 1916.

From 1906 to 1908 Keynes had been a civil servant in the India Office. From then on his main professional identification would be as an economist, becoming a member of that faculty at Cambridge in 1908 and a Fellow of his old college, King's, from 1909 until his death in 1946. So in these years Keynes's life, too, took its definitive shape. Keynes was making his way, and doing quite well financially through his fellowship, some income from his father, the philosopher who became that year registrary of the university, as well as from speculations. He was working on his study on probability, which would not be published until 1921. He was pleased with his progress, slow though it was. He wrote to Grant on July 10: "I spend most of my time writing logic. . . . My final account of the nature of scientific argument is better than anyone else's."[103] He had failed to be elected as a Fellow in 1908 but was so elected in March 1909. He was establishing himself as a teacher, reporting to his father in January 1910: "My Stock Exchange class yesterday numbered 52! and there wasn't even standing room."[104] The previous October he had written to Duncan that "the work of the

Duncan Grant and Maynard Keynes at Asheham House, 1911. Photograph by
Vanessa Bell.

don is the hardest work in the world" and, a few days later: "The day before yesterday I founded a Political Economy Club for the undergraduates and am to give an opening presidential address on Wednesday week. . . . My private pupils have now risen to 24 in number. So work lies heavy on me."[105]

He managed to find the time to do quite a bit of other writing as well, articles and reviews. He was caught up in the two elections of the year, and wrote articles in favor of free trade, most notably one entitled "Great Britain's Foreign Investments," arguing that free trade did not hurt investment at home, which was published in February 1910 in Desmond MacCarthy's *New Quarterly*.[106] He would also engage in polemics at a more popular level, and on January 13 in the *Cambridge Daily News* he defended free trade against the attacks of Archdeacon Cunningham. Since June 1909 he had been secretary of the Free Trade Union in Cambridge. At the same time, along with his teaching, in the course of the year he was engaged in a dispute over statistics with Karl Pearson, was preparing a memorandum on a currency system for China, and was studying the question of gold reserves.

In his particularity and exactness one can see one reason why he was such a good economist, and why others in Bloomsbury felt that, despite his extraordinarily wide interests, there was a touch of the Philistine about him. He kept a meticulous weekly account of his expenses, his income, and his small loans to Duncan. In his papers are preserved his check stubs, including his guinea to the Contemporary Art Society. He was, however, well aware of the power and organization of his mind. In October he wrote to his father, asking him to congratulate for him his brother Geoffrey at a fine result on an examination. "We're really a wonderful family, take us all round, at examinations. Probably the finest in the Kingdom, I expect. If only the examination system lasts another two or three hundred years, we shall end, I'm sure, by becoming the Royal Family."[107]

Strachey and Keynes were still a little uneasy with one another about Duncan. In earlier years they had enjoyed their discussion, and pursuit, of the "higher sodomy." In 1908, when in effect Keynes had taken

Grant away from Strachey, Duncan had been an issue between them, but now, with Duncan falling in love with Adrian, Strachey and Keynes were on better terms. Duncan was a sort of holy innocent whom everyone loved, but such figures, lovable as they are, may cause a certain amount of trouble. Eventually Vanessa would fall completely in love with him, and they would have a child together, Angelica, in 1918. But Duncan's primary commitment was homosexual, and he had as his lovers, among others, over the years, Adrian Stephen, who would marry Karin Costelloe in 1914, and David Garnett, who would marry, as his second wife, Angelica in 1942.

Although Keynes was not as close to Duncan as he had been before, they were still much in touch with one another, and Keynes helped support Duncan, sending him small sums from time to time. For the rest of Keynes's life, there is little question that Duncan remained his closest male friend, as Lydia Lopokova, his wife, became the woman closest to him. Keynes and Grant took a long trip together during 1910, having a splendid time in Greece and Turkey. But the mood of the trip was of two close friends rather than lovers. Keynes wrote to Grant after he had finally decided to go on the trip: "It is a great weight off my mind too, that you have made up your mind. I am sure it will be delightful and I don't see why we should lose our tempers with one another. . . . I wonder what your Adrian affair is like now. When you last wrote it sounded perfect from the point of view of pleasure."[108] Duncan wrote enthusiastically to Lytton about the trip: "O, Lytton! the camels, the cries, the colours, the mysteries. . . . The beauties d'un tout autre genre même . . . I wish you could have come with me yesterday through the bazaar at Smyrna. . . . I hope your seaside party was a success."[109]

Keynes wrote to Duncan in the autumn: "I had a dreadful conversation on Sunday with my mother and Margaret [his sister] about marriage, and had practically to admit to them what I was! . . . I must try, if I can, to fall in love with someone else besides you."[110] He also remarked: "The sooner we can become womanizers the better, I am sure." In his letters during the year to Duncan he commented upon the attractiveness of the freshmen, his discussions about homosexuality with

Lowes Dickinson, his sexual feelings for an Indian student whom he had assisted in gaining admission to Clare College at Cambridge. He also told Duncan, in part a reflection of his state of tension about the Indian student: "I did in the end stroll out on Tuesday night and bring a boy back."[111] He was clearly quite unhappy about the loss of Duncan's love, as reflected in a comment Duncan made to him in December. "I certainly was not always wishing to be with Adrian when I am with you. For one thing it is not always possible to be with him & when I am as certain as I am of Adrian's affection for me, I can afford to be much 'kinder' as you call it than was the case when I was uncertain about it."[112]

Keynes also commented on less directly personal matters, such as sexual hypocrisy in the heterosexual world. He wrote to Duncan about the resignation of a Cambridge professor "because he has committed adultery. Can you conceive of a worse reason for resigning one's professorship of pure mathematics. Do you think I ought to resign my lectureship." He added two days later: "A society, in which a man is ruined for such a thing, is one to be ashamed of—but I don't make much headway."[113]

One of the most unusual cultural events of the year was the Japan-British Exhibition that was open at White City from May to October. As with the Franco-British Exhibition two years before, it marked Britain's new allies, and its need to have them. It was also a celebration of Japan's industrial progress and aesthetic contributions. Grant wrote to Keynes: "I went this afternoon to see the Japanese pictures at the Exhibition. Some of them are among the finest works of art I have ever seen. The statues are marvellous too." He went on to comment on another phenomenon of the year: Halley's Comet. "The comet's tail last night produced a very odd state of affairs in the air here. It was oppressive & electric & rather exciting."[114] Keynes fitted the fair into other activities: "Dined with Strachey & Macmillans—visited M's office. It is the grandest and most pompous office I've ever set eyes on. They promised to make my fortune if I would write a text book on economics for them. I went also to the Japanese exhibition, which is well worth a visit, to a Mozart opera, and to 'The Speckled Band' at the Adelphi.

This is the latest Sherlock Holmes play and very good I thought."[115] When the Exhibition ended in October Grant purchased some prints and dwarf trees.

Keynes's general meticulousness about his life is suggested in two quite extraordinary documents he wrote out in 1915 tabulating his sexual activity since 1906 and his sexual partners since 1901. It is unclear why he compiled such a list, perhaps it was some sort of reaction to the death of young men in the war, perhaps it was a reaction to his own sexual situation then when he was part of a *menage-à-trois* with Duncan and David Garnett. In any case, he records his Eton experiments in 1901 and 1902, no sexual partners his first years at Cambridge, 1903–1905, but then for the next three years both Lytton and James Strachey were his lovers. Duncan became the chief love of his life—holding a position comparable in many ways to that of Lydia Lopokova—from 1908 on, although the love became less intense quite soon. In 1910 he also had sexual relations with Francis Birrell, at the time a King's undergraduate, the son of the Liberal politician and literary figure Augustine Birrell, and with a young working-class actor, St. George Nelson, whom Keynes had to aid financially from time to time. He seemed rather to enjoy it, writing Duncan on Christmas Eve, 1910, from Ramsgate, where he had gone to help Nelson, that he spent his "evenings in the basement of a lodging house chatting with low comedians—whose chief characteristic seems to be their extraordinary kindness. . . . This is a most remarkable place. Lodging houses and hotels tower one above another to an incredible height against a lurid sky, and below long empty esplanades above chalk cliffs and a muddy sea. The streets are full of sailors home for Christmas. Everything is second or third class."[116]

He made mathematical his dictum that economics was the most fascinating pursuit except copulation. He noted, dividing the year into quarters, running from February 1910 to February 1911, that he had copulated twenty-six times, a rather modest figure for a young man of twenty-seven. He also recorded that he had masturbated twenty-seven times and had had fifteen wet dreams. Such was an economist's exactness.[117]

The life could be a little louche, and from time to time there was some apparent danger from blackmailing servants. But he enjoyed himself. In September he had a bicycle trip which despite lots of punctures was, as he wrote to James Strachey: "a very happy four days on the North Downs, full of flirtations with shepherds and young farmers. They are charming people on the uplands."[118]

Some of the change in the sexual tension at this time can be seen in a letter Keynes sent to Lytton about the possibility of Strachey's visiting Duncan and himself in Burford in the Cotswolds, where Keynes had taken a house in September 1909. Keynes wrote "I at any rate would not feel altogether at ease alone with you and Duncan. All the feelings would be too uncertain. Perhaps I am absurd."[119] But a year later he felt more relaxed, as by then neither was Duncan's major interest, and asked Strachey to stay when they were at Burford again.[120] Duncan came to Burford for far less time than expected, having been with Adrian at Skegness.[121]

Keynes teased Grant about the time in Burford: "when I'm at Burford everyone who stays with me will be forced to have their photographs taken naked—and the best will be published in the special issue of the Sketch."[122] There seemed to be limits to Duncan's liberation, as, in reply, presumably referring to some other photograph, he wrote, "I cannot on any account allow it [a nude front view] to be shown to anyone."[123]

Duncan Grant was increasingly becoming a part of the Bloomsbury circle, and was bringing Keynes more into it, spending a lot of time with Keynes, in London, in the country, on trips abroad, and in Cambridge, where he designed costumes for an undergraduate production of Aristophanes' The Birds. During this period he painted a powerful portrait of himself in a turban as well as a charming picture of Keynes's shoes, hat, and pipe.

Grant was born in 1885 in Scotland, a grandson of the Laird of Rothiemurchus, destined to follow his father's career in the army. At nine he was sent home from India, where his parents were, to a prep school in Rugby, where he came to know his cousin James Strachey; he then went to St. Paul's in London. After being a boarder for two terms, he left to live with his aunt, Lady Strachey. She persuaded her brother, his father, to let him study art in London and Paris, which he did in 1906 and 1907. He exhibited at the Friday Club and at the New English Art Club. He was interested in the more formal values in painting, being a great admirer of Masaccio, Piero della Francesca, and Poussin, among others. He was well situated, in his painterly values, to become a subscriber to the idea of "significant form."

But it was not until 1909–10 that he became a frequent visitor to the Thursday evenings, and he was one reason Keynes, who of course had been so close to the male part of early Bloomsbury in Cambridge, played an increasing role in its London life. It was painful for Keynes, who wrote to Duncan on December 17: "You're married to Adrian now, which you weren't before. . . . I'm feeling very wretched and don't know what I ought to do."[124] Duncan painted that year a splendid portrait of Adrian. In February he was part of the *Dreadnought* hoax. In June there was a successful exhibition at the Friday Club at which Vanessa thought his *Lemon Gatherers,* which she bought, was much better than the Puvis de Chavannes she had been particularly interested in seeing:

> In the principal place of honour, is hung a sketch by Duncan which I thought far better than anything else, including the Puvis's. It is really very good indeed, very well drawn and a beautiful composition, of women carrying loads on their heads. I was very much impressed by it and really think that he may be going to be a great painter. There seems to me to be something remarkably fine in his work, and in the grand manner. He is certainly much the most interesting of the young painters.[125]

She was also impressed by two paintings by Mark Gertler, then only seventeen years old.

So here were a group of young people making their way in the world in the year 1910. Their correspondence, and their lives, were mostly concerned with the day-to-day events that make up everyone's lives. (No doubt there was more openness about sexual activity than was likely to be true in other correspondences of the time.) In terms of the public world, Virginia was rather marginally involved with the suffrage movement, and they had entered the great world of the navy as a footnote through the *Dreadnought* hoax.

But the year was one of extraordinary political turmoil. Perhaps, with the memory of the shattering effect of the First World War, we forget how much English society was changing in the years before 1914 and the outbreak of the war. Arguments can always be made about the significance of one date or another, but politically a strong case can be made that English society began to take on its twentieth-century guise, began to change in character, during the year 1910. This was the political background for the lives lived by the young members of Bloomsbury.

5

E. M. Forster

It was toward the end of the year 1910 that E. M. Forster began a long relationship with Bloomsbury. In many ways Forster was a Victorian inside out. The abiding sin of the Victorians, at least as seen by members of Bloomsbury, most notably by Strachey in *Eminent Victorians,* was their willingness to allow public values to intrude upon and determine the private values by which they lived. With Forster's emphasis upon personal relations, and his overly quoted remark about choosing, if one had the courage, friendship over country, it is easy to misunderstand the position of Forster and his friends. Thus, although they believed in a freer sexual life—Forster himself would not put theory into practice until his mid-thirties—they were far from self-indulgent or unreflective in their thoughts and actions. They did not deny themselves the obligation (also a pleasure?) to judge others: Forster could be severe with his friends if he felt they had lapsed. There is that tendency to moralism (very English) which has survived the Victorian age, and which for Forster was a true testimony of friendship. But what was different for him and his friends from the thoughts and actions of their Victorian forebears was that such feelings and actions were on behalf of private values. In that sense they were quite contrary to the age in which Forster had been born in 1879.

The Victorians did not make a distinction between private conscience and public duty. Forster did. But he accepted the obligation to speak out in public (within realistic limits) on behalf of what one believed. This is not to transform him into a premature activist—he valued the privacy of private life and he was not deeply upset that his homosexual novel, *Maurice,* begun in 1913, finished in 1914, and "dedicated to a happier year," could not be published during his lifetime. Decade by decade manners and mores were changing in England, and that novel (not among his best work) probably could have appeared there before he died in 1970. By then, however, he had grown accustomed to assuming that it was not to come out until after his death, though he had circulated it to chosen friends earlier. His unwillingness publicly to reveal his homosexuality—illegal in England until 1967—had nevertheless an important effect upon him: it was a contributing factor in his stopping writing fiction after the publication of *A Passage to India* in 1924.

In his masterly biography of Forster, P. N. Furbank uses as an epigraph a quotation from a letter Forster wrote to T. E. Lawrence in 1928: "But when I die and they write my life they can say everything." Bloomsbury did not believe, during its lifetime, in the revelation in public of its private life. It is a nice touch that it was Michael Holroyd's biography of Lytton Strachey (1967–68) that heralded the arrival of the nothing-held-back biography. Forster was not uncomfortable with the English compromise which provided personal liberty at the price of a certain measure of public conformity. Yet he did not hesitate to use his considerable authority to speak out on controversial issues of the day, particularly against censorship for sexual reasons, as in the cases of *The Well of Loneliness* and *Lady Chatterly's Lover.*

Roger Fry was to paint a "Post-Impressionist" portrait of Forster in 1911. Although not too pleased with it, Forster did purchase the portrait and hang it for a short period in the house he shared with his widowed mother. While it was still being painted, in December 1911, he wrote to his great friend and confidante Florence Barger: "It is too like me at present, but he [Fry] is confident he will be able to alter that. Post-Im-

E. M. Forster by Roger Fry, 1911.

pressionism is at present confined to my lower lip which is rendered thus
. . . and to my chin, on which soup has apparently dribbled. For the rest
you have a bright healthy young man, without one hand it is true, and very
queer legs, perhaps the result of an aeroplane accident, as he seems to
have fallen from an immense height on to a sofa."[1]

Forster was not especially sympathetic to the artistic convulsion that
Fry had orchestrated only the year before in his landmark exhibition.
But Forster's remark demonstrates how easily the term coined by Fry
for the exhibition, "Post-Impressionism," had already entered the language. And whatever his feelings about Post-impressionism, Forster's
lack of ease about his sexuality is suggested by the fact that he gave the
portrait to Florence Barger when a clergyman friend of his mother's
remarked to her after looking at the portrait that he hoped her son
wasn't "queer" (although the word lacked its modern meaning).[2]

The portrait of Forster, to my mind, delineates an "arrived" person:
a young man in his early thirties who had, in 1910, with the publication
of *Howards End,* been recognized as a major novelist. But that year was
important to him also for a number of reasons apart from the novel. It
was then that he had declared to his young Indian friend, Syed Ross
Masood, his great passion for him. Even though that declaration was
rebuffed, it represented a significant step toward the resolution of his
sexual identity. However painful, his continuing affectionate friendship
with Masood set him on the course that led ultimately to his writing *A
Passage to India.*

It was in 1910, also, that he had come closer to Bloomsbury, although
his relation with the group would always be characteristically tangential—a meeting of cool congenial spirits, one might say, in contrast to
the passion for Masood. All these events—the publication of *Howards
End,* the declaration to Masood, the association with
Bloomsbury—were to have lasting effects upon him and mark the year
as one of the most important in his life.

———

By 1910 Forster was already a fairly well-known writer, but it was
Howards End which established him in the front rank of his generation.

Where Angels Fear to Tread was published in 1905, *The Longest Journey* in 1907, and *A Room with a View* in 1908. In 1906 he had met Masood through a friend of his mother's, Sir Theodore Morison, who was Masood's guardian as both his father and grandfather were dead. A strikingly handsome Muslim, ten years Forster's junior, Masood was the grandson of Sayyid Ahmad Kahn, the founder of the well-known college at Aligarh in India which had played a major part in the Muslim "Awakening." At the celebration at the college of Masood's fourth birthday, the *bi'sm'lläh* ceremony (held as part of a conference on Muslim education), his grandfather had used the money ordinarily spent on the celebration to help build Strachey Hall at the college, named for Lytton's uncle John Strachey, an Indian administrator. Theodore Morison had been principal of the college, but had returned to England in 1905.[3] He was a respected scholar, and in September 1911 Keynes favorably reviewed his *The Economic Transition in India.* In December Morison wrote to Keynes from Old Avenue Lodge, Weybridge, that it was "the only review of any interest & value wh. I had, unless one exempts from the general condemnation one by Kennedy in the Asiatic Quarterly which deals with the future not the past or present."[4]

Masood had come to England to be educated, and it was arranged by Morison that Forster should be the young man's tutor in Latin to help prepare him for Oxford. Thus began the most influential friendship in Forster's life. Largely thanks to Masood, he would develop a life-long interest in India, where Masood would be his guide for a good part of his first visit there in 1912. Masood was thereafter a continuing focus of Forster's deepest feelings, though the two would see each other only infrequently over the years between Masood's return to India and his comparatively early death in 1937.

To judge by his letters, Masood was all expansiveness, charm, and unrestrained affection. His teasing about the English unwillingness to express emotion helped to liberate Forster, unlocked the "undeveloped heart" which Forster himself saw as the besetting English sin. His own letters to Masood at first were rather jokey. But he became increasingly fond of him, and Masood, in his warmhearted way, reciprocated. In late

1909 they went to Paris together, Forster's first visit. When he returned to London ahead of Masood, his young friend chided him (in a letter) for the coldness of his farewell at the Paris train station. Forster replied on December 30: "We mustn't quarrel about sentiment. We agree that it is the greatest thing in the world and only differ as to how it's to be made most of."[5] The next day he wrote in his diary: "I love you, Syed Ross Masood; love."[6] In March 1910 in his diary he commented: "Falling in love puts daily life out of gear, and makes us irritable, deceitful, and irrational in our judgment. Love—and affection too—must be opposed to reason if they are genuine. One sees the faults of the beloved, but cannot register them, and resent their mention by others. Let my own vexations teach me sympathy."[7]

The two were in frequent correspondence and had seen one another regularly while Masood was a student at Oxford.[8] He finished at Oxford that summer, receiving a second in History, where his tutor was H. A. L. Fisher, Virginia's cousin. He then moved to London to study law. In the early spring of 1910, Forster had gone to Italy with his mother, where he finished the manuscript of *Howards End*. In a letter to Masood commenting about the death of Edward VII and the English ladies buying mourning in Florence, he burst out: "Masood, I am sick of all these formalities: they are stifling all the heart out of life. Nothing but gossip & millinery, and all real feeling crushed into the background. Well, I suppose the Purdah is worse. Women are a bad drag on civilisation up to now."[9] Despite this disparaging comment, Forster was aware of women's aspirations for the future. The suffrage campaign was becoming ever more exigent, and the role for women was, in a sense, very much a theme of *Howards End*. But he was more a cautious supporter than an enthusiast, which disappointed Florence Barger, whose commitment to the cause was ardent.

With the publication of *Howards End*, worldly success, about which Forster would always have ambivalent feelings, appeared to be coming his way—another problem to be dealt with. But the Masood problem was much more disturbing. For there was Masood proclaiming his love for him, and at the same time confiding the difficulties that beset his evidently active heterosexual life. It would appear that Forster was finding it somewhat hard to cope, but he was improving in coming to terms with this most un-English effusiveness. By now, he fully understood the nature of his own sexual urges—very different from Masood's—but he had not brought them to a physical resolution, despite some kissing and hugging one evening on a sofa with an old friend, the married H. O. Meredith. (He was not to have a lover in the physical sense until his affair with Mohammed el Adl in Alexandria during the war.)

Masood wrote in mid-November, urging that they should travel together to Turkey.

What a dear fellow you are, & your letter shows me that you love me as much as I love you. . . . Whatever happens, don't let us give up Constantinople. I shall go alone with you. . . . Dearest boy if you knew how much I loved you & how I long to be alone with you in that romantic part of the world, you would never dream of changing our original plans. England is all right but it does not possess a romantic or even a pathetic atmosphere. . . . But this next time we will be alone, for I want to have you as much to myself as ever I can. . . . I only wish that you & I could live together for ever & though that is a selfish wish yet I feel sorry that it will never come to anything. . . . And now I have nothing more to tell you except the old fact that I love you more than almost any other man friend of mine & so kiss you au revoir.[10]

In Forster's rather "tutorial" letter to Masood on November 21 he seemed to be replying to an issue involving some woman, although what he meant precisely by the word "it" is not clear:

It is such a difficult subject and we shall not make anything of it until we talk together even more freely than we have before. There are two sides to it—firstly it is an experience for you; secondly, you may do good to her. Now, in this latter side I don't think there is any point at all. You will not do any good to her. I am absolutely certain of it. It is not your fault, or hers; but because you are the age you are, you will always be arousing hopes of another kind in her. This is natural. The only good you do is indirectly—through men. Vice can only be suppressed through men. Tell every one you know that it is a horrible, disgusting notion that love can be bought for money. The more men believe this, the fewer poor women will be forced into a life of debauchery and disease.

No doubt his own feelings were mixed into this letter. The previous week in his diary he had given himself something of a lecture, but did he really believe either statement? "Lust, whether strong or weak, is akin to romance. The human being of our dreamings is impossible. Lust idealises. Love is passion for an actual person, & the purer the closer it keeps to the fact. Both are good. Lust too can be pure, & dream of unity of souls instead of bodies. But in action it is disillusion & vanity, for souls like bodies can never merge."[11]

But the minatory tone of Forster's letter lightens with news of *Howards End:* "My book is selling so well that I shall probably make enough money by it to come to India. There will not only be an American edition, but a Canadian, and perhaps a translation into French."[12] Even before he knew that the novel would be a financial success he had a firm sense of what money might accomplish, for of course he already had a small private income, to allow him to visit India and to be generous to friends. He had noted in his diary on February 14: "It is a blessing to have money. I want to give the Bargers £50 to go to Greece, and then I shall save up for India."[13]

On December 20, Masood was urging him not only to visit India but to write about it: "You are about the only Englishman in whom I have come across true sentiment & that, too, real sentiment even from the oriental point of view. So you know what it is that makes me love you so much, it is the fact that in you I see an oriental with an oriental view of life *on most things.*"[14]

Emotions frequently run high at holiday times; perhaps they were even more intensified for Forster as his birthday fell on January 1. He and Masood had arranged to go together to see Richard Strauss's *Salome*, an opera that throbbed with sexuality. Although it had had its premiere in Germany in 1905, it was not performed in London until December 1910, as part of a season of two Strauss operas being conducted at Covent Garden by Thomas Beecham—the other was *Elektra*, which had had its world premiere in Germany the year before. The first performance of *Salome* was on December 8, and it aroused great advance interest: potential ticket buyers had started to queue at 6:30 A.M., hours early, and once the box office was open, tickets had sold out in an hour and twenty minutes.

The *Times* delivered itself of a burst of wonderment at the fashionable audience assembled for the opening performance: "During the progress of a General Election and at a time when the London season is not in existence [it is surprising that] an audience so distinguished and representative should have gathered together. Among those in the audience: the French Ambassador, the Duchess of Rutland and [her daughters] the Ladies Violet and Diana Manners, the Duchess of Manchester, the Ranee of Sarawak, Lord Ribblesdale, Lady Cunard, Lady Jekyll, Mrs George Cornwallis-West, Mrs. Willie James." It was the height of Edwardian luxe. For the next performance, the audience was equally grand: "Princess of Monaco, Duchess of Westminster, Colonel Sir Herbert Jekyll, Duke of Rutland, with Ladies Marjorie and Diana Manners, Lord Robert Manners, Baron and Baroness de Meyer, Lady Lytton." The review itself was rather grudging: "Between the prudes, who will raise an outcry at every gesture of Salome, and the prurient, who will insist on each revolting detail as an instance of 'courage,' the average clean-minded student of operatic development will have his work cut out for him if he tries to gauge the value of Salome as a work of art."[15] Vanessa Bell's reaction was rather similar, as she reported to Clive: "I went to Salome with Adrian. It was exciting in places I thought & horrid in others."[16]

These new operas, powerful as they were, being performed in December of that year, might well provide further evidence to support Virginia Woolf's comment that human character had changed in December 1910. Certainly they had a violence and sensuality quite different from the genteel tradition of well-bred art in post-Victorian England. There was also a quite characteristic English aspect of the performance: the peculiar relation of the state to the theater through the role of the Lord Chamberlain. In 1892 Wilde's play (the text for the opera) had been banned. There had been some advance since then in what was or was not deemed permissible for the English to see in the theater, but England was still behind the Continent in its artistic sophistication. Harley Granville-Barker, the great theatrical figure, wrote to the *Times* on December 17: "If in his [the Lord Chamberlain's] precious opinion, *Salome* is a noxious thing, is it not his duty to use his autocratic power to crush it? If he has come to his senses on the subject, then let him set the play free." The Lord Chamberlain had insisted that John the Baptist be called the Prophet instead;

> and what is this foolishness—and worse than foolishness—of forbidding the use of the severed head, compelling Mme. Ackté to make dramatic nonsense of the most poignant passages of the tragedy by addressing them to a bedaubed tea-tray? . . . It is an insult to the public, an insult to the work of Oscar Wilde, and an insult to a great composer. How much longer is this inept official to make our theatre the laughing stock of Europe?[17]

The *Annual Register* was moved to comment that the opera was "so maltreated by the direction of the censorial authorities as to have stultified the British opera-goer."[18] The censorship of plays was becoming increasingly ludicrous as earlier in the year the Lord Chamberlain had refused to license Laurence Housman's *Pains and Penalties*, a play about Queen Caroline, George IV's wife. Royalty was not supposed to be depicted on the stage, and the Lord Chamberlain remarked that the play could not be put on as it "dealt with a sad historical episode of recent date in the life of an unhappy lady," although the events depicted had taken place eighty years before.[19] No wonder many found English culture rather stultified, even though a play that received a great deal of attention that year, John Galsworthy's *Justice*, dealt with the problems of prisoners and allegedly led Churchill to modify the rules about solitary confinement. It was a triumph of the realism Woolf was later to decry. As the *Annual Register* commented: "In the unrelieved gloom of the subject, the sordidness of the surroundings, and the appearance of detailed realism, Mr. Galsworthy has surpassed himself."[20]

Forster and Masood went to *Salome* on December 28. Forster found the opera disappointing, but its passionate music was likely to have added to the intensity of his feelings. The year, after all, had been one of great tension in his and Masood's relations. As early as the previous January 15 he had written in his diary: "Joyful but inconclusive evening with him. I figured an unbearable crisis, but we only care for each other more than before, each in his own way." There had been a somewhat odd note of sublimation on July 21: "However gross my desires, I find that I shall never satisfy them for the fear of annoying others. I am glad to come across this much good in me. It serves instead of purity." But then the climax came on December 28:

Yesterday, in the O[xford] & C[ambridge] Musical Club, I spoke. He had been praising my insight into Oriental things, & I could bear no more. He answered "I know" easily. Today I posted a note to him, still anxious. I feel it will be all right, that nothing can be wrong. Yet have been irritable with Mother all day. Salome disappointing—when the music grew beautiful at the end it only demonstrated the baseness of the subject. Lust *or* vengeance are *both* heroic, but conjoined they make squalor.[21]

Afterward, there were days of misery for Forster at home in Weybridge. He wrote in his diary on December 31: "Brought this book [the diary] to review a remarkable year. But have not the spirits. Non respondit [that is, no letter from Masood], but though I believe it is all right, my breast burns suddenly & I have felt ill. He has sent me such a horrid ugly birthday present—!—tray with candlestick match box and sealing wax rest, colourless message inside: probably posted before my letter reached. (Love, Love)" Then Forster drew a large question mark. On January 1 he wrote in his diary: "We always think we would bear some other sorrow better. I ask for enlightenment. Soon I may ask for what I am bearing now. Yet there is one bitterest of all—to have loved unworthiness. I shall be spared that. If he goes away it will be with glory. It shall be my aim not to belittle him, or pretend that I was well rid. . . . After the morning post I feel I shall never get through the day, & the evenings are awful." Nevertheless that day he wrote Masood to thank him for the present but went on: "My real need is a letter. If you will use your imagination, you will see that I am not having much of a time."[22]

Forster was feeling ill, and feared that he might have tuberculosis. A letter—now lost—from Masood did arrive on January 2, Forster noting in his diary "Respondit," but Masood apparently had no intention of dealing directly with Forster's love and distress. Forster replied: "Dearest Boy, Your letter arrived. There is nothing to be said, because everything is understood. I agree. But oh you *devil*—! Why didn't you write at once? I was in an awful stew all Saturday & Sunday. You may say that this was not sensible of me, but when all that one is and can feel is concerned, how can one be sensible?"[23]

Emotions continued at a high pitch in early January, when Forster's grandmother died, causing his mother to go into a depression from which she never completely recovered, and making her more dependent than ever upon Morgan, her only child. Forster commented on the death: "Gran died the day before her birthday. A happy & dignified career. She knew how to live, and to the end took it out of those who did not, like Mother. . . . Here we are both without occupation for the coming year—I at the flood of fame, but with no further prospects. I will love, though."[24]

The close friendship with Masood, if not the relationship as Forster would have wished, survived both the passionate declaration and its tactful rejection. In 1912 the first visit to India took place. (The success of *Howards End* made it possible for Forster easily to pay for the trip.) He became more systematic in his reading about India, including a biography of Masood's grandfather, the founder of Aligarh, and was increasingly drawn to it as a subject. After Oxford, Masood returned to

India, married, and made his life there. But the correspondence between them, though sporadic, was for some years as intense as ever. In 1923 Forster wrote to him: "You are the only person to whom I can open my heart and feel occasionally that I am understood."[25] And in February 1924: "Yours is the only affection that remains with me as a solid unalterable truth."[26] After Masood's death in 1937 Forster acknowledged: "My own debt to him is incalculable. He woke me up out of my suburban and academic life, showed me new horizons and a new civilisation and helped me towards the understanding of a continent."[27] Perhaps his final feeling about the relationship is suggested at the end of *A Passage to India*—the novel dedicated to Masood—with its sentence "'No, not yet,' and the sky said, 'No, not there.'"

But this is to anticipate. In August 1910 Forster, on a walking tour on his own, wrote to Masood: "It isn't bad being alone in the country—the nearest approach we Anglo Saxons can make to your saints. There's such a thing as *healthy* mysticism, and our race is capable of developing it. . . . Now I have proofs to correct, and with luck I shall finish them next week."[28] He also wrote to a friend, Malcolm Darling: "I am bringing out a stodgy novel this autumn. . . . It's called Howards End, and dealeth dully with many interesting matters. I am correcting proofs now."[29]

One is struck with the speed of publishing at the time. He had finished the novel less than a month before, noting in his diary on July 28: "I have nearly done my novel, and mean to devote August to athletics and personal appearance."[30] It was published in October. He did have worries about the novel in September. When his mother read it she was deeply shocked, while Forster felt it was the least erotic novel he had written. He then also worried how his aunt and grandmother would take the book. "I do not know how I shall live through the next months." But by the end of the month he had regained faith in the enterprise. "The almost ceaseless worries of the last month have left me more interested in life!"[31]

In the novel, he was taking the "thingness" of the Victorian and Edwardian novel and, without scorning it, going behind it to the more transcendent and mystical aspects of life. As he had written in his diary the previous February: "Am grinding out my novel into a contrast between money & death—the latter is truly an ally of the personal against the mechanical."[32] In England, *Howards End* made him something of a celebrity, and it was ranked, alongside Arnold Bennett's novel *Clayhanger,* as one of the two most significant books of the season. Characteristically, Lady Ottoline, early in the new year, invited Forster to meet Bennett, but it is not clear whether this particular meeting took place. Forster replied to the invitation: "It is most kind of you to ask me to meet Arnold Bennett. I am sure I should like him, and no doubt he would not mind me."[33]

There is a certain irony that *Howards End* should share the honors of the season with *Clayhanger.* Bennett was rich and famous, and as a leading Edwardian novelist was customarily bracketed with H. G. Wells and John Galsworthy. In 1908 he had written his finest book, *The Old Wives' Tale; Clayhanger* probably is next in quality. He was incredibly prolific and more than willing to share his values. In 1910 he wrote a guide entitled *Literary Taste: How to Form It.* Bloomsbury had never had much regard for him. Clive Bell remembers that at a meeting of the Friday Club Ralph Hawtrey, the economist who had introduced Strachey into the Apostles, spoke favorably about Bennett: "'I mean since he took to writing good novels!' Lytton, from far back in the room and in his highest falsetto 'And when was that?'"[34]

Bennett wrote about *Howards End* in the *New Age* in a column about "Books of the Year" on January 12, 1911. Not surprisingly he doesn't mention his own book, and in effect he only discusses Forster's. In the brief piece, he alludes to *Dop Doctor* without giving its author and to Temple Thurston's *City of Beautiful Nonsense,* stating that they are selling extremely well, but that they can't count as books of the year because they are not part of the world of people "in the know," whom Bennett reckons to number 12,055! They are the élite and "without their aid, without their refined and judicial twittering, no book can hope to be book of the year. Now I am in a position to state that no novel for very many years has been so discussed by the élite as Mr. Forster's

'Howards End.'" He calls the book Forster's best to date, and "a very considerable literary achievement." He really does not make any criticisms of the novel, and he concludes that "if he continues to write one book a year regularly, to be discreet and mysterious, to refrain absolutely from certain themes, and to avoid a too marked tendency to humour, he will be the most fashionable novelist in England in ten years' time. His worldly prospects are very brilliant indeed. If, on the other hand, he writes solely to please himself, forgetting utterly the existence of the élite, he may produce some first-class literature."[35]

In 1924, in the high tide of modernism, Virginia Woolf would launch *Mr Bennett and Mrs Brown*, a sardonic attack on Bennett, Galsworthy, and Wells, the three most famous practitioners of Edwardian fiction. Significantly, Woolf's chief complaint against the three was that in their realistic, externalized descriptions of character they failed to penetrate to its essential reality. Forster she placed with the modernists; in fact he was less that than either Joyce or Lawrence. But in his attempt to "connect," to probe further inside his characters, to be more symbolic, perhaps to be more mystical, to achieve a greater sense of the essence of his characters, he was a newer sort of novelist. There is little question that Bennett, Galsworthy, and Wells were attached to the "thingness" of life. Forster had even published a short story, "The Machine Stops," in 1909 which parodied Wells's science fiction. The argument over the nature of literature was not new, as the correspondence between Wells and Henry James, a rupture between master and pupil, had painfully made clear. But its postwar direction is more pertinent in the contrasts between Wells, Bennett, and Galsworthy—triumphant middle-brow novelists—and the great outsiders, Lawrence and Joyce, and those who were much more securely within the middle class than they, Forster and Woolf herself.

Howards End marked Forster's transition from minor to major novelist. Could one call *Howards End* a Post-Impressionist novel? Possibly, yes—at least to the degree that it broke with conventional models then in favor, much in the way the Post-Impressionist pictures being shown in London in December 1910 would do. In contrast to Bloomsbury, Wells and Bennett were happy Philistines. Bennett wrote to his agent

J. B. Pinker: "*Clayhanger* will be a bit of allright." And three days later: "My first draft is always also the final writing. I would much sooner write a complete fresh novel than rewrite two chapters of an old one."[36]

Clayhanger was the other great critical success of the fall season, published on September 15, Bennett having written its considerable text from January to June in the same year. He kept track of the number of words he wrote, noting on the last day of 1910 that he had written 355,900. As well he measured his reviews by inches rather than their quality or whether they were favorable or not.[37] He was in many ways a fine writer, and there was a certain attractive defiant philistinism in his attitude toward his craft. But it was certainly a contrast to Forster.

Nevertheless, they were linked in readers' minds as authors of books of the time that were worthy of serious attention. For instance, Edward Marsh, Winston Churchill's secretary and a patron of the arts, wrote to a friend who was in South Africa: "There are some good new books—especially a gloriously long Arnold Bennett called *Clayhanger*—and a very interesting curious and amusing book by a little friend of mine, Forster, called *Howards End*."[38] *Clayhanger* too, in its story of Edwin Clayhanger, is a story of England as is *Howards End*, but with more emphasis on the Bast and Wilcox side. The anonymous reviewer of the book in the *Times Literary Supplement*, now known to be Percy Lubbock, commented on its "terrific zest for life" and went on to remark: "its poetry is the poetry of the sheer ordinariness of ordinary things and ordinary people. Its aim not to exalt or essentialize, or satirize, but to present life."[39] The contrast to what was the aim of *Howards End* is quite clear when one reads the remark made by James Douglas in the *Star:* "I think it is this physical verity which makes 'Clayhanger' so irresistibly human, so magnetic, so hypnotic. The organic detail is never tiresome."[40] Or as the *Manchester Guardian* remarked: "If his method is that of conscientious industry rather than inspiration he nevertheless achieves his end and creates the illusion and atmosphere of actuality."[41]

It is intriguing to note how books that have become classics were first received. In the case of *Howards End*, there were ardent reviews. The *Daily Telegraph* noted: "his stories are not about life. They are life." And

R. A. Scott-James wrote in the *Daily News:* "the novel rises like a piece of architecture full-grown before us. It is all bricks and timber, but it is mystery, idealism, a far-reaching symbol." There were demurrers: the *World* felt that *Howards End* was unfairly receiving more attention than *Clayhanger.* "There is no doubt that this novel has been one of the sensations of the autumn season, and in that respect, it has been made—not wisely—to overshadow Mr. Arnold Bennett's *Clayhanger,* which is a much greater book." Clive Bell wrote a rather even-handed anonymous review in the *Athenaeum:* "This novel, taken with its three predecessors, assures its author a place amongst the living writers who count. . . . The defects of this novel are that the protagonists are points of view rather than characters; that the two chief events—Margaret's marriage and Helen's seduction—are unconvincing; and that, in our judgment, the moral is wrong." In America the *New York Times* compared the book to Galsworthy, but felt that Galsworthy was better, while Elia W. Peattie of the *Chicago Tribune* insisted that the author must be a woman. "In feeling the book is feminine; but it is not to be gainsaid that a number of the strongest masculine writers of our times have been able to represent the feminine mind, with its irrational yet dramatic succession of moods, better than any woman can do it. It may be that E. M. Forster is one of these, but my impression is that the writer is a woman of the quality of mind comparable to that of the Findlater sisters or to May Sinclair."[42]

More complex than Forster's three previous novels, *Howards End* is a great Edwardian work that has won a place among the enduring novels of this century. It shares with the Edwardians their obsessive interest in money, but with a profound difference. The possession of money, we are shown, matters only to the degree that it may make possible the freedom to live a fulfilled life. Even then it does not follow as an immutable law: money is no more than a starting point—essentially, the without-which-nothing. The book is candid in recognizing the role of money and its importance in making England and those who lived there powerful. Forster's great theme was the need to connect—"only connect"—the prose and the passion, the world of the rich Wilcoxes and that of the sensitive Schlegels, money itself and what money could make possible. The materialism of the Wilcoxes is not sufficient as an end; it needs to be combined, to connect with the more spiritual interests of the Schlegel sisters and that of the first Mrs. Wilcox—a change in human character so that it will become capable of connection. There are both elements of hope and despair in the book; connection has mostly failed. But the illegitimate child of Helen Schlegel and Leonard Bast the lower-middle-class clerk will be the inheritor of the house, Howards End. The child is, perhaps, evidence of a more democratic and classless society that may be coming, something good amidst the defects that are part of the new age, the red rust of building that is creeping into the countryside from London.

Although there is little specific discussion of the politics of the period, the sense of turmoil and disorder, the goblins of Beethoven's Fifth Symphony, is present in the book, an unspoken reminder, perhaps, that Forster was doing his final work on the manuscript in 1910, that year of great political upheaval and of the growing militancy of the women's suffrage movement. (Although the suffrage question is not discussed, one feels that Helen would be a militant and Margaret a moderate—increasingly so—but both would have believed in votes for women.) But as Forster wrote to Edward Garnett about the novel: "It is devilish difficult to criticise society & also create human beings."[43]

Forster felt uneasy about his success, and had the common reaction of not agreeing with the praise, much as he enjoyed it, and taking the criticism too seriously. He wrote to Eddie Marsh about a captious review in the *Spectator:* "I haven't seen the Spectator, but it was to be expected. They would find the thing both irritating & easy to slate, and I shall agree with the strictures I fear, though I wish the paper to the devil."[44]

As his biographer, P. N. Furbank, has noted, Forster reacted to his success by returning to his evangelical roots in his attitude, writing in his diary on December 8:

Prayer. Not to imagine people are noticing me. . . . Let me not be distracted by the world. It is so difficult—I am not vain of my overpraised book, but I wish I was obscure again. Soon I shall be. . . . If I come an unholy smash let me never forget that one man and possibly two [H. O. Meredith?] have loved me. In old age I shall look back enviously to this year which gave me so much, but it is the material for happiness rather than happiness. I knew I shouldn't and I don't envy fame. Never forget nature and to look at her freshly.[45]

He wrote to his great friend Goldie Dickinson in November: "I go about saying I like the money, because one is simply bound to be pleased about something on such an occasion. But I don't even like that very much. . . . I am another Harmsworth darling. No, it *is* all insanity."[46] It was hard for a Cambridge Apostle such as Forster to handle worldly success, for Apostles tended to believe that that was really the world of illusion.

Success is rarely as satisfying as one might hope, and he felt it hard to return to creativity. *Howards End* argues the importance of money for providing an income to give one the freedom to do what one likes; yet in the end the freedom may be tainted. Forster recognized that the income from the novel would allow him to visit India, increasingly important to him in terms of his relation to Masood. As he wrote to Malcolm Darling in September: "My novel will be out in October, and you will receive a copy, if you will undertake not to dislike me for having written it. I am afraid it will give little pleasure to anyone. But the money, my boy! It helps me to get to India."[47]

One might have expected Forster to have a sense of purpose similar to Margaret Schlegel's: she came to know what she wanted. But in his own life, he seemed more unsure and tentative, and felt awkward about his great success. He did pursue, successfully, a campaign to have his short stories published, as happened the following year when *The Celestial Omnibus* appeared, with Fry's endpapers. In August 1910 he had written to Marsh: "I wish you would walk outside Sidgwick & Jackson's offices shouting nonchalantly 'Short stories are what *we* want.' They are considering mine, & even nibbling, but oh so feebly."[48] That month he had seen Fry, who had consented to do the work, and made a remark which suggested that he was thinking of taking bolder steps: "He said, among other good things, that talent has no chance today—only genius."[49]

In 1912 he began work on a novel, *Arctic Summer*, which he abandoned, and then during the next two years he worked on *Maurice*, his novel of an idealized, fulfilled, ultimately happy homosexual love, a "daydream book," so to speak, which could not be published. He may have actually started work on the book as early as 1910, perhaps in some sense a working out of his feelings about Masood.

Forster needed to come to terms with his success; he needed to come to terms not only with Masood's rejection of him as a lover but also with the continuation of their intense friendship. Less significant but vexing (and not without its comic aspect) was still another question that arose in 1910: whether or not he should be the godfather of the newly born son of his friend Malcolm Darling. Darling's elder brother had been an exact contemporary of Forster at King's. Malcolm, who entered the college two years later, became a great friend of Forster's. In 1904 he had joined the Indian Civil Service and had acted as a tutor to the Raja of Dewas State Senior, where Forster would visit in 1912, and would return to Dewas in 1921 to act as secretary to the eccentric Maharajah. Darling described Dewas as "the oddest corner of the world outside Alice in Wonderland. Dewas has 16,000 inhabitants, two Rajas, each with a salute of 15 guns, each with a Minister & a Palace."[50] Forster corresponded with Darling regularly, reporting on a variety of things, politics, publishing, the election over the House of Lords in January 1910, a walking tour with their Cambridge contemporary Hilton Young.

His ever-deepening love for Masood furthered and nurtured his interest in India; so too did his very different friendship with Darling, sustained by the flow of letters between them. There are suggestions in *Howards End* of moving away from Western rationality, which would become so much more decisive an element in *A Passage to India*. When Darling wrote to him of some incident involving an illogical yogi, Forster replied: "Wealth, success, friendship, love, are all one illusion, and reality, (whatever it may be) is obscured by them. But in practise one shrinks from this conclusion. The Western world, and in particular the Latin races, have too vivid a sense of surface-values. How wonderful—and how comforting—that the yogi should be illogical at the last moment too!"[51]

Darling wrote to Forster in May: "The English Mail is about the most romantic thing of this very romantic country. At Rajanpur it came to me on the camel's back; at Dewas a horseman would bring it to the door." He added as a postscript, pointing out that he was writing at nearly midnight from an encampment in a grove of apricot trees in the Himalayas: "Shall I tell you? Yes, I think I must, but you will be secret. We expect a third in July or early in August—most unwillingly at first, for it is pleasant to be two together, also Josie has suffered cruelly these last 6 months, almost unceasing sickness & other things. . . . Neither of us had really the least wish for a child. But it will at least be interesting. Write me another letter from Italy if this finds you there. I would barter the whole Himalayas for one little Umbrian hill."[52]

Forster didn't take his friend's doubts too seriously, replying: "You say that neither of you have been anxious for a child: when it comes surely you will feel differently, and realise it is the greatest of blessings. Children are so delightful—and something more besides."[53] The baby, John Jermyn, was born on July 14, and Forster wrote about him on August 12 very much in the spirit of *Howards End*. "I am pleased about the baby, of course, and more pleased than I can say that his coming has made other things better. He is the future, & our love for him is still hidden in it." In this letter, too, began the tiny rather Forsterian comedy of whether or not he would be a godfather to the boy. Forster at first refused. "I have only once said yes, and that was to parents whose atheism was even more pronounced than my own."[54]

Ten days later he wrote again, as the Darlings had written meanwhile assuming that he would be a godfather:

I do trust and think that you will both understood why I have refused. . . . I couldn't be of less use to him than my own official godparents have been to me, and perhaps it's the emptiness of my own experience in this direction that makes me behave like such a prig now. . . . The only present I ever feel inclined to give babies is to take away some of their toys. I do wish I could see him. . . . I am very fond of babies. Though I can't help laughing at them—they will more than pay me out for that in the future.[55]

It may have been that Forster's initial refusal had not reached the Darlings in time; a mutual friend who saw him thought he was the godfather. "Goodall thinks that I am already a god father willy nilly. . . . The fault of the bishop of Lahore, and his surpliced minions. Not my fault. I should have all the pleasure of authority with none of its responsibilities, if this report were true."[56] The issue continued on September 22, when Forster wrote: "Your letter about the godfather just received, & it is a comfort to know that you do not think I have been a pedantic ass."[57] Darling had suggested that Forster write a "catechism" for the child; Forster proposed that Darling and his wife write it themselves. But he became increasingly captivated by the idea, and finally did write something on November 20. On the 21st he appeared to consent to be a godfather, but on his own terms, and if the Darlings approved of what he written out: "I was not the least ashamed of my conduct in refusing & prevaricating at first, but felt that I had done quite the proper thing throughout; . . . For it is difficult to accept such a post quickly when one is definitely not a Christian."[58]

He changed his mind again, and decided not to act in the role. But he did pass on the "catechism" to Josie Darling, when she came to Britain in December because of the death of her father, Lord Low, a Scottish Law Lord, and also presumably to show the baby to her friends and relations. Before seeing the baby and her family, Forster, who had not met his good friend's wife before, wanted to see Josie on her own. There is a splendid series of notes from him—as if it were out of one of his own novels—arranging a meeting with her at the Tate Gallery to talk before going to tea at Malcolm Darling's mother's, where the baby would be shown.

So do let us meet at the Tate at 2:30, opposite Ulysses (Schlegel) defying Polyphemus (Wilcox) . . . I will bring the catechism with me—a meagre little thing which will not take two minutes. . . . If Ulysses [a painting by Turner] should not be at the Tate—I forget if he is still at N.G.—we meet in the room where the biggest Turners are. I shall not recognise you—it is not my habit to recognise people—and you will have to have a shot at me. I am now very stout.

He wrote again on February 20: "King Cophetua [Burne-Jones] 2.30, Wednesday, then. In case of disaster, parties shall not dash feverishly about, but shall repair for recriminations to the turnstile, and leave messages about each other with the man who guards it." On the 22nd he wrote to Malcolm: "I have at last seen J.J., and approve entirely. He is not a baby, but a very dear little boy."[59]

What of the catechism itself? Forster called it "Liking Being Alive" and entitled it as if it had been written by the Darlings, and then "Written out by E. M. Forster 20/11/10." It was in the form of a dialogue between the son and his mother, when the boy is eight or so—and he is asking her what a godfather might be, but he doesn't want the questioning to go on so long that it will delay his going riding. The boy says that he enjoys being alive, and the mother points out that his father does too, and when young "He liked to walk all night, sometimes with a friend, sometimes alone. As he grew older he began to care for other things. He read books." He became more and more aware of nature, and of the importance of friends. But his greatest discovery was love: "there came a thing that was more wonderful than all the other things put together, a thing that made his life—oh!—bigger than all the stars and the sun, brighter than any light you can think of, a thing so glorious so beautiful, so overwhelming that it was almost frightening to him."

The mother also talks about herself: "In some ways I have not been as happy as he has, because people think that girls ought not be as happy as boys, and instead of helping me to like life, they would give me orders about it, and this is never any help, never." For the parents "the wonderful thing was love, and out of our love you came. Because we cared about life, you are alive. You are the sign that we have loved, and all the beauty that we have seen." God is the name of all the good things that made the child. This is hard to understand, and godparents are to help: "They are to tell you about the things that they have liked in life. . . . They want you to be an inheritor of the Kingdom of Heaven. No one knows where the Kingdom of Heaven is—whether it is the place that the sun is flying to, or whether it is far behind that place or whether it is actually here on this beautiful earth."[60]

Anne-Marie Roman, in an interesting article on the catechism, puts more weight on a rather slight piece than it can comfortably manage, but her claim about its significance is intriguing. Its few pages do suggest the importance of nature, and of personal relations, for Forster, and also "the luminous revelation of love."[61] These, like many of the other elements that figure in the catechism, are already in place in *Howards End*—nature, connection, personal relations, the role of a baby. Even a more mystical approach to life has been adumbrated there, though it will become of far greater importance in *A Passage to India*. Perhaps in the catechism, Forster was half-consciously striving toward some sort of symbolic resolution to his personal dissatisfaction, as in his declaration a month later to Masood.

"Until 1910," Roman tells us, "the ultimate reconciliation of the seen and the unseen, the inner and the outer, appears only as an aim; but by way of writing out the catechism, Forster approached his ultimate goal: the formation of a link between art and life, the connection between the ideal and the real."[62] That, of course, had been an aim of *Howards End*, where Forster was arguing for a change in human character that would make possible a union between the ideal and the real. In a very simplified, even naive or childlike fashion, he was making the point again in his catechism for a godchild.

———

Finally, by contrast, Bloomsbury and the grown-ups. With the success of *Howards End*, Forster began to move into the wider world. As an Apostle he had always maintained very strong ties with Cambridge, but being slightly older than the generation of Bloomsbury Apostles, he had not yet established a bond with them in London. At this point the members of Bloomsbury, other than Fry and Forster, were more significant for what they promised to become than for what they had yet achieved. Roger Fry and Forster had done more than those younger friends who had "begun" Bloomsbury, which was still pretty much a private social group rather than a congregation of high intellects who would influence the values and artistic activities of Britain in the twentieth century.

Although Forster knew the Apostolic members of Bloomsbury, he had not actually seen much of them or of the other post-Cambridge Bloomsbury figures in London—he did not even meet Virginia Stephen until 1910. The crucial event that would lead to his becoming on friendly terms with the group took place in December, when he was asked to give a paper to the Friday Club. Yet he was quite diffident about becoming more active in the literary world. He had written in his diary on December 8: "Dont advance *one step more* with literary society than I have. Let the paper on the Feminine Note in Literature . . . be my last thing of this sort. Henceforward more work & meditation, more concentration on those whom I love."[63] Rather, giving the paper marked his further involvement in the literary world of his time, Bloomsbury in particular.

The suffrage movement was by then at its most intense; "Black Friday"—the demonstration that turned violent in front of the Houses of Parliament—had occurred on November 18; feminist questions were taking on a more immediate urgency. Forster gave a paper entitled "On the Feminine Note in Literature" on December 9 in which he argued in favor of a special feminine sensibility.[64] While he granted that differentiations between men and women were lessening, he rejected what he understood to be J. S. Mill's claim that there were no distinctions to be made between them. (Mill's *Subjection of Women* had been discussed at the previous meeting of the Friday Club.) Forster acknowledged that "A freer atmosphere is at hand, and the artificial products of the past—the Chatelaine, the Grande Dame, the Blue stocking—will be blown away and give place to the individual." But, despite Mill, he felt that "women . . . live nearer the truth of human nature. . . . The feminine note is—preoccupation with personal worthiness. The characters try not so much to be good as to be worthy of one of the other characters. . . . Men have an unembodied ideal. Women embody their ideal in some human being, be it a woman or a man. . . . Women have this strong practical vein, the desire to set up a sensible visible standard of righteousness."[65] Forster noted in his diary on December 11: "Miss Stephen said the paper was the best there had been, which pleases me."

Thus in 1910, through several comparatively private events of varying intensity—ranging from his impassioned relation to Masood to the social/literary pleasures of Bloomsbury and the Friday Club to the catechism for the Darling baby—and one great public event, the publication of *Howards End*, Forster had taken considerable steps forward. His character may not have changed, but his life had changed in public and private ways, and he had in *Howards End* made his private values shape the public world of his fiction.

6

Quakes in British Society

Nineteen-ten was a year of momentous events not only in the world of art but also in the world of politics, most markedly in the decline of the Liberal party in Britain. The party did survive the two elections of the year—in January and December—but it was not to win another, and the nascent Labour party, with which it cooperated, after the next election, in 1918, would replace it as the official party of Opposition. In 1924 Labour would be the governing party, albeit in a minority. The two General Elections in 1910 proved to be "terminal elections bringing to a close the electoral politics of pre-1914 Britain."[1]

The first of the two was over the question of the Budget, which had been approved by the House of Commons. Traditionally it was the prerogative of the House of Commons to deal with finance. But the Lords rejected the Budget at the end of November 1909, claiming that the taxes it proposed—necessary to pay for Liberal social legislation and also for increased armaments, most notably in the navy—exceeded the Commons' authority. A vast majority of the Lords, supporters of the Tory party, felt that the taxes on the wealthy and on land, in retrospect quite mild but significant as precedents, were the first steps toward a social policy of confiscation. The Lords maintained that they were the defenders of the true constitution of Britain. As such, they forced the Liberal party, in command since December 1905, to call a General Election to test the sentiment of the people. The previous General Election, resulting in an overwhelming victory for the Liberals, had been held in January 1906. In some sense it was a reasonable time to have another.

The interest was intense: many of the seats in particular constituencies had been uncontested in previous elections; now contested elections were the norm. The 1910 elections—the first over the Budget, the second over the power of the House of Lords—were probably the most important constitutional crises in British politics since 1832 and the hard-fought battle for the first Reform Act. To give the events, perhaps, an overly Whiggish interpretation, 1832 was significant for making British society more democratic. One might argue that British society is far from democratic even now. It could also be claimed that the decision taken in the second election in 1910—that the House of Lords be reformed so it could no longer permanently block any legislation—marked the introduction of a more "modern" form of democracy into the British state, its twentieth-century version. Some thought, particularly when taking into account reform of the Lords, labor issues, the question of Ireland, and the women's vote, that British society was on the verge of revolution. The outbreak of the first World War in 1914 ended any such possibility.

Perhaps it was from 1832 to 1914 that politics held its most compelling interest for the British public. All through the nineteenth century it had been a national pastime and preoccupation, heavily covered in newspapers, and much debated. At the latter part of the century it was even better covered, for newspapers had far advanced technically and grown considerably in circulation. In 1910 other sources of entertainment, except for the music hall, were less pervasive than they would presently become—the cinema was available, but had far to go, radio though it existed was hardly a popular force, and television was in the future. In theory there was universal male suffrage but it would not truly come into being until 1918. Between the theoretical achievement of universal male suffrage in the Third Reform Act of 1884 and the Representation of the People Act of 1918 that also gave votes to women of thirty and older, many men were technically disenfranchised through registration and residence requirements. But being disenfranchised did not necessarily mean that one was politically inactive or without political effect, as the agitation for women's suffrage richly demonstrated.

The "swing of the pendulum" which was such a factor in the classic Victorian political years from 1868 to 1886, when Irish and other issues changed the landscape, would lead one to expect that the Tories would have recovered quite a bit in the election in January 1910. There was a very high turnout of the voters: 6.6 million voted, 87 percent of those entitled to do so. Liberals maintained their majority, but just, with 274 MPs on the basis of 44 percent of the vote. The Conservatives had 272 MPs, with 47 percent of the vote. There were 40 Labour MPs, based on 7 percent of the vote, and 72 Irish Nationalist MPs. The Tories had gained 105 seats; the Liberal majority, counting the uncertain support of the Irish and Labour, was down from 334 to 124 seats.[2] It was a different political world. In order to assure their continuing in power, the Liberals would have to do more, not less, for the interests of Labour and the Irish.

Having won the election, the Liberals had received a mandate from the "people" for the Budget. The next issue was the question of the power of the House of Lords. In the Speech from the Throne on February 21, Edward VII stated that steps would be taken to strengthen the authority of the House of Commons. But the overly loyal prime minister, Herbert Asquith, had failed to ask for guarantees for the creation of peers, setting off a revolt of the Irish members who threatened that they would not vote for the Budget unless he did so. The Liberals were not in a position to move forward on Home Rule for Ireland, but Asquith did more or less promise to do something in that regard at the end of the session. The Budget was finally passed by the Lords at the end of April. The crucial issue was whether the Lords would agree, by vote, to a curtailment of their power, or would be willing to have their chamber diluted by the creation of enough new peers by the king, on the advice of his prime minister, to outvote the Tory Lords. But whatever commitments the king might have made to Asquith were ended by his death in May and the coming to the throne of his son, George V.

Starting in June and ending in November, there were twenty conferences participated in by the leaders of the parties in an attempt to resolve the constitutional issue of the role of the House of Lords. All were ultimately unsuccessful. There was also the interesting constitutional issue of whether the leader of the Tory Opposition, Arthur Balfour, could be asked to form a government, as he was willing to do, even though he led the minority party. With supreme tact, Sir Arthur Bigge, the king's secretary, decided that it would not be proper for him to inform the new king of this willingness. Balfour's attempt to form a government might have precipitated even more of a constitutional crisis. There was a sense of living in parlous times. That these crises were diminished in retrospect by the advent of the First World War does not mean that they were not regarded as being extremely momentous when they occurred. Bloomsbury might not be deeply interested or involved in the political details but it was part of the metropolitan world that the professional middle classes shared with the politicians of the day. Keynes knew this world, Francis Birrell's father was in the Cabinet, Asquith might well appear at Lady Ottoline's evenings.

Bloomsbury took limited notice of the death of the king on May 6. Lytton was in Cambridge at the time, and found the atmosphere of the town too oppressive; it was at occasions like these that the ancient universities were determined to demonstrate their loyalty to established institutions. Keynes, however, was bored with it all. "I attended two mock funerals here, clothed in full sacredots, and have never been so much bored in my life."[3] Duncan, on the other hand, looked forward to watching the funeral in London. "I think it ought to be amusing."[4] Nevertheless, the event demonstrated what it meant that Britain was a monarchy. For a period much of its public life was quite profoundly affected by the death of the king. The *Times,* in its review of the year, claimed in its loyalist prose that "everywhere the sense of loss was keen and personal. . . . Never before had so many Kings met together in London."[5]

───────────

It was during this year that the Bloomsbury figures became friends of Lady Ottoline's. Although they had not taken much notice of her husband's defeat in his Oxfordshire constituency in January, some of them were quite concerned with the question of whether he would come back into the House from his new Lancashire constituency. But Bloomsbury's most direct connection with both elections was through a friend, Hilton Young, who was running, without too much hope of success, against Austen Chamberlain in the constituency of East Worcester outside the Chamberlain's family fiefdom in Birmingham.

Hilton Young was the son of a mountaineering friend of Leslie Stephen's, Sir George Young; he had grown up with the Stephen children, was a Trinity contemporary of the Bloomsbury men, and was one of the possible fiancés of Virginia. He was liked, although found to be rather pompous. In 1910 he was an assistant editor of the *Economist* and was anxious to enter Parliament; he did so in 1915 while serving in the war.

In both of his campaigns his friends came to help. Keynes, who journeyed to Birmingham to speak, wrote to Strachey: "Life without a howling audience to address every evening will seem very dull."[6] He went into a little more detail to his family: "The rural districts are solid liberal, but are quite swamped unfortunately by the outlying parts of Birmingham. I'm going to enjoy myself very much, I think." And a few days later: "We had a splendid meeting last night, packed and enthusiastic, at least 1200 present, in *Birmingham* itself. But I fear that when on Saturday next the Birmingham divisions have polled the Tories will put forth their full strength and flood E. Worcester."[7]

Forster felt that the world had changed already, and that the election brought out the worst in everyone. His particular concern was Young. He was a good friend, and in October 1909 the two men had taken a walking tour which sounds as though it were a successful version of Leonard Bast's walk in *Howards End*. In the tradition of Leslie Stephen, these Cambridge men were great ones for walks. Forster wrote about this particular one to Malcolm Darling: "After a few miles we took to the grass and with compass & bicycle lamp he [Young] steered us through a black night and torrential rains, and was only half a mile out at dawn. We broke into Stone Henge at midnight, and ate on the altar stone, which may have been sacrilege but was more probably the other thing. . . . It was about 30 miles; at 9.0 we reached the so called cottage—thatched it is true, but replete with hot baths and the novels of Arnold Bennett."[8]

Forster later wrote to Darling in India a general rather snobbish comment about the election:

> The German scare and snobbery seem doing their worst, and the appeals this election are made to the lower instincts, than heretofore. Dishonest, illiberal, the spirit of petty tradesman, who doesn't mind if he's found out to morrow, so long as he cheats you today—that's the spirit of both sides as it appears to us: and I have continually to remind myself that there must be honest effort & conviction somewhere, hidden behind the froth of either party.

In his next letter he reported that Dickinson "has been electioneering, and I ought to have done the same, but do dread it, and am so ignorant and incompetent. Hilton Young stood against Austen Chamberlain. He was defeated heavily."[9]

Strachey was pessimistic about the results in that election, writing to Keynes: "I suppose there's no chance of dear Austen being booted out." He wrote that his brother James and Gerald Shove had gone to the Palace Music Hall to hear results: "The whole audience was violently Tory." The two had spent part of the day soliciting signatures on behalf of women's suffrage, and Strachey reported the following conversation: "'I don't approve of it', said a rich & respectable voter. 'Why'? said James. 'Because it's unnatural', was the reply. 'Do you think everything that's unnatural bad?' James asked. 'Well', answered the voter, 'in love affairs I do', and left James pulverized amid a crowd of highly amused & exquisite boys, who'd gathered around during the conversation."[10]

Some of the Cambridge young men rallied again in the next General Election the following November and December, as Sydney Waterlow recorded in his diary from Young's constituency: "George Trevy [Trevelyan] came & made a speech. . . . Altogether there were days of great enjoyment & excitement, talking to all kinds of people in the Club, in shops & mean houses, & in the street."[11] Keynes was following the results in Cambridge, where he remarked to Duncan Grant that the General Election "occupies our tongues appallingly and we go to the Union every night to cheer the results,—where it appears that all Tories have bass voices and all Liberals tenor."[12]

Even after the new king had pledged to create peers, the Lords were unwilling to vote until another election had taken place. Despite the failure of the interparty conferences, Arthur Balfour, the leader of the Tory party, was still hopeful that somehow—it was unclear how—the standoff between the two Houses of Parliament could be solved without an election The Liberals felt that there was a need for a breakthrough to a new sort of politics freer of the role of tradition. With the failure of the conferences, the Liberals concluded that politics had reverted, as their leader Asquith stated in Parliament, to

> a state of war. . . . We believe that a General Election which can be brought to a close well before Christmas will cause the least distur- bance to business interests and the general convenience of the nation; and we are satisfied after two judgments, pronounced in the same sense, by two successive Houses of Commons, the time has come for this controversy which obstructs the whole path of progressive legisla- tion to be sent for a decisive arbitrament to the national tribunal.

He also stated, as a clear indication of the wooing of the Labour party and of breaking with the old politics, that in the next session a bill would be introduced for the payment of the members of Parliament, an im- portant change in the relation of politics and class. The dissolution was announced for November 28.[13] The political and the artistic consensus were challenged in the same month. The Tory party, like old-style painters and traditional art dealers, was increasingly becoming the party of the business interests, as was fully indicated in 1911 when the businessman Andrew Bonar Law replaced, after a raucous campaign of B.M.G.—"Balfour Must Go"—the patrician Balfour as leader of the Tories in the House of Commons, in effect head of the party.

The *Times*, so often the voice of establishment values, seemed to be obsessed with the question of commerce, and considered the actions of the Liberals as subversive of long-held values as the Post-Impressionist painters who were also being displayed during the Christmas season. It commented editorially on the calling of the election:

> That it would be unmitigated nuisance to the whole community, and a positive disaster to large trade interests which have their best market in the weeks before Christmas, no one can seriously deny. It has been usual to consider public interest in these matters and to avoid December on that account; but the coming election has nothing to do with public interest. . . . Readers will scan MR. ASQUITH'S speech in vain for any valid justification of the course the Government had decided to take.[14]

It was unclear why it would not be possible to shop and participate in the election at the same time, particularly as women did not have the vote.

Virginia Woolf would appear to have had a somewhat parallel attitude toward the election, as least while speaking in the character of Helen Ambrose in *The Voyage Out*. (To a degree, Helen was based on Vanessa Bell, who was alleged to have sat next to Asquith at a dinner party and turned to him and asked him what he did.) In a letter home, to Bernard, not otherwise identified, from the South American location where the novel takes place, Helen writes:

> It seems incredible . . . that people should care whether Asquith is in or Austen Chamberlain out, and while you scream yourself hoarse about politics you let the only people who are trying for something good starve or simply laugh at them. When have you ever encouraged

a living artist? Or bought his best work? Why are you all so ugly and so servile? Here the servants are human beings. They talk to one as if they were equals. As far as I can tell there are no aristocrats.[15]

Woolf's disdain, but also her view of politics, can be seen in the character of Richard Dalloway in *The Voyage Out*. Perhaps by the 1920s, when it appeared that Labour had a chance, Woolf felt that politics had become more attractive. Dalloway is a villain in the earlier novel, and demonstrates the pomposity and received thinking of politicians of the time. The Dalloways impose themselves into the party of friends and acquaintances on the ship, with the easy arrogance of the English upper classes: "'Mr. Richard Dalloway,' continued Vinrace, 'seems to be a gentleman who thinks that because he was once a member of Parliament, and his wife's the daughter of a peer, they can have what they like for the asking.'"

The author would appear to have doubts about both Liberal and Tory parties: "I call myself a Conservative for convenience sake,' said Richard, smiling. 'But there is more in common between the two parties than people generally allow.'" Needless to say, he is opposed to votes for women. "'Nobody can condemn the utter folly and futility of such behaviour more than I do; and as for the whole agitation, well! may I be in my grave before a woman has the right to vote in England! That's all I say.'" He later remarks to Rachel: "'No woman has what I may call the political instinct. You have very great virtues; I am the first, I hope, to admit that; but I have never met a woman who even saw what is meant by statesmanship. I am going to make you still more angry. I hope that I shall never meet such a woman.'" The climax of their relationship is when "Richard took her in his arms and kissed her. Holding her tight, he kissed her passionately, so that she felt the hardness of his body and the roughness of his cheek printed upon her. . . . 'You tempt me,' he said."[16]

Woolf herself was only active in a comparatively minor way in the suffrage movement, but she did see quite a bit of those who were much more involved than she. In 1889 her mother had signed the anti-suffrage petition organized by Mrs Humphry Ward, but presumably her daughter did not take that position very seriously. In 1909 Duncan Grant had designed a poster for the Artists' Suffrage League, sharing the first prize of five pounds. He probably knew about the contest through his cousins the Strachey sisters: Pernel; Philippa, who was secretary of the London Society for Women's Suffrage; and Marjorie, also active in the cause as was Ray Costelloe. The secretary of the Artists' League had suggested that the scene should be "A man in a *sailing* boat, (the sail represents the Vote). A woman with only *oars*—out in the sea *of Labour.*" The rather vivid result was called "Handicapped." The suffrage publication *Common Cause* liked the poster, commenting on the "stalwart young woman of the Grace Darling type." She is trying to reach Westminster "while the nonchalant young man in flannels glides gaily by, with the wind inflating his sail—the vote."[17] During the election in January Grant went to a polling station in Hampstead in order to collect signatures on behalf of women's suffrage.[18]

Virginia saw something of Ray Costelloe at this time. She went to visit her and the other Pearsall Smith ladies outside Oxford, apparently causing some consternation as a formidable intellect. Mary Berenson, Ray's mother, wrote that she was "paralyzed at the prospect and have tried to plan out every half hour." The next year Ray would visit Virginia at Firle and they would discuss Ray's growing attraction to Oliver Strachey, particularly as James and Lytton displayed no interest in her, although Keynes had.[19]

In terms of suffrage activity, 1910 climaxed in November, at the same time as the opening of the Post-Impressionist Exhibition. Starting in the summer of 1909, violence was part of the suffrage movement, particularly associated with the more militant organization, the Women's Social and Political Union, led by the Pankhursts. The emotional and physical levels were rising, as in the same period the hunger strike became a response to being arrested for suffrage activities. For most of 1910, though, there was a truce and little violent activity.

There was, however, the notable exception of a week in November 1910. The suffragists, the moderates, and the suffragettes, the more

Handicapped by Duncan Grant.

militant, felt, perhaps wrongly, that they had been a major factor in the lessening of the Liberal majority, having urged sympathetic male voters not to support those Liberals who did not, in their turn, support votes for women. There was some possibility that the Liberal party might move in the direction of granting the suffrage through a private member's bill. During the summer the more moderate suffrage group, the National Union of Women's Suffrage Societies (NUWSS), headed by Millicent Garrett Fawcett, the widow of Henry Fawcett, a Liberal intellectual and politician (whose biography Leslie Stephen had written in 1885), participated in a considerable campaign for the Conciliation Bill, arranging a demonstration of 10,000 in Trafalgar Square on July 9 in its support. There was some debate in Parliament when, to the distress of its supporters, Churchill and Lloyd George expressed concern about the "antidemocratic" aspects of the bill, namely that as it would enfranchise only better-off women, it was likely to help the Tories. The constitutional crisis over the House of Lords was used as a reason to forget the bill for the moment. The NUWSS continued to agitate when Parliament reconvened on November 15, leading further demonstrations, but with dissolution imminent there was little hope. In the view of the NUWSS, a militant response by the Women's Social and Political Union would further diminish the chance that the bill might pass.[20]

A women's suffrage bill, even if a private one, would still require government support in the fall in order to move through the House of Commons. This Asquith was unwilling to give. The proposed bill was deliberately made fairly conservative to attract Tory support, granting the vote only to women who had some limited property qualification. (Of course this was the very aspect that concerned those on the left: that such a bill would increase Tory strength.) On November 18 in Parliament Asquith made no mention of allowing the bill to go forward at that time. Keir Hardie, the Labour leader, spoke on behalf of the women:

For the past six or seven months, there has been a cessation of what are called active hostilities on the part of the militant section of the Women's Movement, but if this question, in which they are so deeply interested, is to be passed over without even a word of recognition from any Member of the Government, then no one need be surprised if those hostilities are resumed in an even more militant form than has been the case in days gone by.[21]

The Women's Social and Political Union was meeting at the same moment at Caxton Hall, and on hearing the news, more than three hundred women marched on Parliament (115 of them were ultimately arrested) and were treated with more brutality than before. The day became known as Black Friday in the movement. The attack by the police was frequently sexual, involving, among other indignities, the manhandling of breasts. The riot went on for six hours as, unlike the case in some other demonstrations, no arrests were made at first which would have limited the violence. There was a sense of a contrast of the two worlds, that of allegedly reasoned discourse within the House of Commons and violence outside of it, suggesting vividly the force that lay at the heart of the state, that made it possible. One member of Parliament, Thomas Kettle, a young Irish Nationalist MP, declared: "I do not think that many Members are aware that while this great question of constitutional freedom has been discussed inside this House there has been re-enacted in Parliament Square and in the adjoining streets scenes such as those which have disgraced British statesmanship for more than a year past."[22]

Perhaps it was at that demonstration that the character of the fight changed and it became more explicitly sexual. This was further demonstrated on November 22 in reaction to Asquith's vague promise of allowing the bill to be discussed in the next Parliament, not necessarily the next *session*, and in permitting so many amendments that the bill was very likely to be defeated. For another year, the WSPU abandoned militancy. Whatever course the suffrage movement took, it was not achieving its objectives. The situation would hardly increase Virginia's belief in the general reasonableness of males.

Violence was certainly in the air and on the walls of the Grafton Gallery. As reported in the *Times* of November 29, Hugh Arthur

Franklin, the nephew of the Postmaster-General in the Cabinet, Herbert Samuel, had attempted to strike Winston Churchill with a bullwhip, saying: "Winston Churchill, you cur, take that for your treatment of the suffragettes." Churchill was now Home Secretary and thus ultimately responsible for the police and the extreme way they had acted in their handling of the women outside of Parliament. Many thought it was his fault that the police had been so brutal. It may have been more the case that a police group new to the work was ill-advisably used, one accustomed to working in the East End where violence did not produce articulate complaints, as it had among the militant women, many of them middle class. When Franklin was brought to trial on December 6, Churchill was there to plead for leniency, making the point that he did not consider the assault as personal as it appeared, but rather believed it was intended to bring money to the movement through publicity.

Franklin claimed he had been deeply outraged by the behavior of the police at the November 18 demonstration. He had been arrested there for reprimanding a policeman for the way he was treating a woman. (The class implications of the whole matter are quite intriguing.) The magistrate, Sir A. de Rutzen, thought the attack had been "in cold blood." He sentenced Franklin to six weeks in prison as an ordinary prisoner (not as a first division, who were better treated, a category that women suffrage prisoners had secured), stating that his severity was curtailed by Churchill's plea but that he, the magistrate, was not influenced by either the politics of the situation or the fact that the man attacked was the Home Secretary.[23]

Churchill was to some extent pursued over the issue. Thousands came to hear the politicians as they stumped the country for votes. On November 30, Churchill had spoken at Sheffield before 6,000. Only three ladies were allowed to attend, his wife, his mother, and another relative. In the speech he made mock of the House of Lords, stating that "only a year ago the patriotic, fearless, impartial backwoodsmen were summoned from their sylvan retreats at the imperious call of the Tory whips to stand between the nation and the socialist scheme that would ruin our trade and go far to destroy the fabric of British society."

At the pause caused by laughter, a man called out, "You are wrong in not giving women votes." That man was ejected, and a minute later there was another similar charge, and when the second heckler was being removed a fight broke out between his friends and the stewards. Churchill took no notice but pursued his attack on Tariff Reform—which had been the issue, after all, over which he had left the Tory party.[24] Votes for women had become a question that cut across party lines and further destabilized the political structure of the day.

These incidents were signs of some disintegration of British society in the years before the first World War, though compared to the modern Western world of a few years later, it was a period of comparative security. Certain other violent events of the year 1910 seemed to suggest the growth of instability or, at the least, captured the imagination of the time. Such was the trial of Crippen for the murder and mutilation of his wife, and his execution at the end of November. In the *Times* review of the year, Crippen and the murder of three policemen at Houndsditch in December, possibly by foreign anarchists, were the two crimes marked for notice, the latter providing more fuel for the further tightening of Britain's immigration laws. The *Times* commented that the Houndsditch murders "argued a disregard of human life and resolve to go to all lengths in crime which is happily not English. . . . The crime has helped to convince even sentimentalists that something must be done to prevent the importation of foreign desperadoes from Eastern Europe."

One can transpose this attitude to that taken toward foreign painting. In the same review of the year, the *Times* remarked: "A much-discussed show of recent French work, now being held at the Grafton Gallery, has not convinced the majority of English art-lovers that Post-Impressionism is progress in art." The newspaper did recognize that there were limits to connecting politics and art: "Politics and the state of trade cannot be held entirely responsible for the singular dullness and ill-success of the drama."[25] That seems a little hard on the year that saw the opening of Galsworthy's *Justice,* Shaw's *Misalliance,* and Granville Barker's *Madras House.*

Were these events sufficient to support the contention Virginia Woolf put forward in a rather hyperbolic way fourteen years later? Then she wrote: "All human relations have shifted—those between masters and servants, husbands and wives, parents and children. And when human relations change there is at the same time a change in religion, conduct, politics, and literature. Let us agree to place one of these changes about the year 1910."[26]

Some of the issues she listed were very much part of the year. The relation of husband and wife was the subject of a Royal Commission on Divorce that had yet to conclude its deliberations. For "master and servants," she probably was thinking in terms of domestic service, but such language was the traditional if by now rather old-fashioned way of referring to questions of labor relations. In the latter part of 1910 strike activity became more prevalent, with union members less subservient to leadership than had been true formerly. The Osborne judicial decision of 1908, which the Liberals had not yet pledged to repeal by legislation, meant that union members need not support the Labour party unless they individually decided to do so—they had to opt in, rather than opt out. It suggested that workers would have to reconsider the idea that the government might assist them, and return to the more direct action of strikes. As with so many other events of the year, it had an unsettling effect. Unions were increasing the intensity of their agitation against the Osborne judgment; they wanted to be more politically active at the same time that there was a rise of industrial action. Both sides were becoming shorter tempered, one indication being the employers' use of the technique of the lock-out against the workers. The idea of a class war became more prevalent even though British workers observed that a railway strike in France had been crushed by a militarization of the workforce, a response that could not happen for legal reasons in Britain.

There was the possibility, however, in Britain of the employment of troops and non-local police to contain the workers. The divisions of society, with their implications of threat and change, were most evident in 1910 in the violent incidents which took place during a Welsh miners' strike, especially in the village of Tonypandy. The Liberals, and

Churchill in particular, as the responsible cabinet minister, were not allowed to forget them. Thirty thousand miners struck in the Rhondda and Aberdare valleys in South Wales. Churchill sent troops and London constables to maintain order after the village of Tonypandy had been in a state of riot for three days, starting on November 7 when the main street was wrecked. There was a "festival of disorder."[27]

The violence which some saw in the new paintings at the Grafton Gallery was also on the streets of London on Black Friday, and in a coal mining village in Wales. Keir Hardie, the Labour leader in Parliament, pressed the government both on the issue of the use of troops against the workers and on its negative attitude toward votes for women. Disorder was not expected in the Britain of the twentieth century, nor that passenger trains would be stoned in Wales, presumably by disgruntled miners, and as the correspondent of the *Times* wrote on November 23: "Tonypandy presents a very strange appearance for a British town. The main street shows ample evidence of the disgraceful rioting of the last fortnight. In nearly every case the shop windows have been boarded up."

As with the suffragettes, there were charges of police brutality against the workers. The class war was in evidence, but more on the part of the propertied interests who regarded the police and their back-up, the troops, as their agents against what they feared was revolution. Even in the trade unions, the forces of order were being ostensibly undermined; the Miners' Federations and the miners' agents disapproved of the strike. Churchill (who would be more virulently anti-labor at the time of the General Strike in 1926) had Tonypandy thrown in his face for the rest of his career. In fact he, and General Nevil Macready, the troop commander sent to Wales, had exercised restraint. With characteristic condescension, the *Times* pointed out that despite the violence in Wales no lives had been lost, as, it felt, would undoubtedly have been the case on the Continent or in the United States.[28]

Strike action increased during the remaining years before the First World War. In the Tonypandy strike, Macready had to cope with the beliefs of the British upper bourgeoisie that the police and troops were there to reinforce its values. Macready was aware "that the situation was dangerous, and that the strikers were in a violent mood, but he saw the cause of the crisis not in revolutionary conspiracy but in the overweening intransigence of the management. The automatic enlistment of the forces of the state to support the imposition of wage cuts was in his view subversive of consensus and legitimacy." At the same time, over a glass of ginger beer, he warned the strikers' leaders that he would react very strongly to any shooting or bottle throwing.[29] The troops remained there until October 1911, when the strike ended with the workers' defeat.

More peaceful, and a cultural event of some significance, was the publication in December 1910 of the famous eleventh edition of the *Encyclopedia Britannica,* which subsequently has been taken to represent a *summa* of knowledge before the First World War, when Britain ruled the waves and all seemed to be right with the world. As one of the *Encyclopedia*'s historians has remarked, the great age of the encyclopedias began with Diderot in 1751 and ended with the eleventh edition: "One rang in the age of reason, the other rang it out. . . . Its [the eleventh edition's] writers shared a common rationality, and even a common idea of human destiny. The world was a rational and ultimately a harmonious place."[30]

And in many ways it seemed to be, particularly on the cultural side, with Edmund Gosse as the *Britannica*'s chief adviser in that area. He represented the older established literature, despite having written a sensitive book about his conflicts with his father, *Father and Son,* published as recently as 1907, that reflected with justice to both the battle of generations. Gosse hoped to reinforce settled literary values through the creation of an academy. As such, he was a prime figure in the world Virginia Woolf was to attack in favor of a view of literature and art that was fresher, unsettling, and looked far more deeply into "life." There was no entry for Freud in the eleventh edition; Marx is there, credited as an economist but not as a political analyst or prophet. The *Encyclopedia* was premised on a rational world, not dissimilar from the world of fact and appearance recorded by the Edwardian novelists.

The *Britannica* had been established in 1768, but had in recent years fallen on hard times. The eleventh edition is now perceived as a deeply British institution, particularly as in 1920, while maintaining its name, the *Britannica* migrated to the United States. But in fact its revival—in this sense serving as a herald of the shift in power relationships that would take place after the First World War—owed a great deal, even before the war, to the enterprise of a go-getting American entrepreneur, Horace Everett Hooper. He had joined the *Times* to help in its advertising and to bring it into a competitive position with the more aggressive press of the day. The culmination of this tendency was when, partially thanks to Hooper, the *Times* was acquired by the great British newspaper magnate Lord Northcliffe in 1908. The tenth edition of the *Encyclopedia,* a reissue of the ninth edition with eleven new supplementary volumes, appeared in 1902. Through aggressive marketing techniques, Hooper made it a great success not only in Britain but in the United States.

The eleventh edition of twenty-nine volumes was to claim to be entirely new, with 40 million words—not actually that much more than previous editions—40,000 articles (far more shorter articles than the previous edition that had contained only 17,000), and 1,500 authors, many of them serious journalists rather than academics. Some articles were revisions, and there were some accusations that the edition was already out of date. The volumes were dedicated to George V and William Howard Taft, the president of the United States. It was all you needed to know if you were lucky enough to be a member of the English-speaking world. Indeed, it sold even better in the United States than in Britain. It was the apogee of "power, knowledge and self-confidence."[31] The underlying assumption and justification was that progress was a matter of the acquisition of new facts. The *Encyclopedia* was the triumph of positivism.[32]

The *Times* was full of advertising for the forthcoming edition, now sponsored by the Cambridge University Press, as well as printing innumerable news stories about the gatherings being held in honor of the contributors to the edition, most prominently a dinner at Claridge's, presided over by the chancellor of Cambridge University, the scientist Lord Rayleigh. Like the Edwardian novelists, but unlike the modernists, the eleventh edition was designed to reach out to the "ordinary" reader, not to the highbrow or academic, although over the years it has acquired a somewhat more refined patina.[33]

Of course the most important news stories in the weeks before the end of the year concerned the General Election. The second election campaign in late November and early December 1910 was briefer than the first and fewer seats were contested, but it was still intensely fought. Again, it was a victory for the Liberals but they could hardly have known that it was to be their last ever. It was taken for granted that they would continue as one of the two great political parties in the nation.

Lloyd George used all the power of his considerable rhetoric to attack the peers and their presumption of power to oppose what he saw as the wishes of the people. The king had had no choice but to provide Asquith with guarantees that, if necessary, he would create enough peers who would vote to deprive the House of Lords of its veto privilege. Although the importance of the House of Lords had declined over the previous centuries, such an action would prove a definite punctuation point, an indication that British political society had changed in a fundamental way: that the declining economic power of the aristocracy was now combined with a definite loss of political power. The Tory alternative, which Balfour, the leader of the party, was unenthusiastic about, was to find the necessary funds for military and social programs through tariff reform. Quite a few members of the political public were not ready to discard that central principle—free trade—of the nineteenth-century political world. Even so, the two elections marked a decline in political consensus, the lessening of the shared assumptions of the previous century. The groundwork was being laid for at least some consideration of socialism as an alternative, a form of political modernism.

The political system had been destabilized in a modernist way; those on the right, to a degree, had been alienated from the system, as they had first lost on the Budget, which they regarded as confiscatory, and now they had lost on the question of the House of Lords. The Liberal party had won, but it was hardly the victory of 1906, and its great supporters, many members of the middle class, were deeply disturbed by the abandonment of its old principles of Peace, Retrenchment, and Reform (and limited government action) and by its spending money raised by taxation on military preparedness and on new social programs. Lloyd George's rhetoric scared quite a few who felt they had a stake in their society. For instance, Stella Benson, the future novelist, then only eighteen, noted in her diary: "And then I don't know what will become of us. They say it may end in Revolution as Lloyd George wants it to."[34]

For various reasons, much debated by historians, the Liberal party did not ultimately succeed in persuading working-class voters to support it rather than the Labour or Tory parties. Asquith attempted such an appeal in his speech in Parliament about the dissolution, saying that in the future the Liberal party would remove the disqualification that meant that paupers could not receive old age pensions, and would facilitate working-class politics by introducing payment for Members of Parliament—a way of recognizing, in part, the Liberals' need for the support of Labour MPs.

Asquith concluded his remarks graciously, far different from the "new style" of political rhetoric that would enter the chamber the next year with the debate over the future of the House of Lords. Asquith had a sense of what might happen: he mentioned that the failure of the constitutional conferences meant the parties had reverted to a "state of war." Yet he wished to maintain civility—that was his strength and his weakness. "Outside these walls before we are many days or perhaps many hours older we shall, I imagine, be all brandishing our dialectical swords, and possibly some of us slinging the stones of invective. . . . I do not desire to-day to anticipate, if I can avoid it, the approaching tumult of the electoral arena." To a question about the king and the Lords from Captain Wedgwood, of the radical pottery family, Asquith answered in the then-current language of deference: "The King stands aloof from all our political and electoral conflicts, and it is the duty of all his subjects and of his Ministers to maintain and secure his absolute detachment from the area of party politics."[35] But Asquith did not allow for the violence that was going on outside the chamber as he spoke. With the elections of 1910 there was a new sort of class politics. If the war had not intervened there would have been another election in, presumably, 1915. Technically, the Liberal party remained in power until 1918, but by the end of the war, largely because of the activities of Lloyd George, the party was in shreds.

The new sort of politics that had come into being was very different from the premises that had governed the nineteenth century. The cultural changes foreshadowed in 1910, in which Bloomsbury would play an important part, were also, like the new politics, significant aspects of the undoing of the Victorian world view.

The polling in the second election continued from December 5 to December 16. Such a long period made it seem even more exciting, even more of a contest, as the position of the parties might change each day. It was the great sport of the time. Harrods had installed a tape machine connected with the news agencies, and ran an advertisement: "See the Election Results while doing your Xmas shopping at Harrods." It also offered to send free "a handy little Pocket Election Chart for recording the exact position of the parties day by day."[36] On December 8 there were 184 Liberals and their allies and 169 Conservatives, and the next day it was 225 Liberals and allies and 193 Conservatives.[37]

The final results, however, were hardly different from the positions before the election. At the end of the polling there were 272 Liberal MPs and 272 Unionist MPs, but the Liberals were, officially, supported by 42 Labour MPs, 75 Irish Nationalists, and 7 Independent Nationalists. The *Times* was rather cranky in its editorial: "The net result of all this costly and troublesome search for more emphasis is that in the new Parliament, as in the old, the two great parties are exactly equal."[38] Nevertheless, the understanding, at the very least, was that the House of Lords would have its powers sharply curtailed; even that took some time to accomplish, but without the threatened creation of new peers. In December 1910, after the election, one would not have necessarily said, to use Virginia Woolf's phrase, that "a hen had laid an egg," but the character of British politics had changed all the same.

7

On the Way to Post-Impressionism

Roger Fry had over the past few years become increasingly interested in modern French art, in particular the work of Cézanne. Even during 1910 he was still in a somewhat transitional phase, as we have seen, having lost his job at the Metropolitan and not having succeeded in becoming Slade Professor at Oxford. At comparatively short notice, the Grafton Gallery, which had a large exhibition space, informed him that it did not have anything scheduled for the end of the year—a slow time in any case—and proposed that he assemble an exhibition of some kind. It would be a sort of "filler" that was unlikely to make any money. Fry seized the unexpected opportunity and, amazingly quickly, assembled an extraordinary exhibition. He didn't do it alone; the "scouts" that assisted him were Lady Ottoline, Clive Bell, and Desmond MacCarthy, who was offered the secretaryship of the exhibition.

Desmond MacCarthy has not formed part of this story up to now, although he and his wife Molly had been for some time great friends of the Bloomsbury figures, and are generally reckoned as part of "Old Bloomsbury." Coming closer to the circle in 1910, MacCarthy was a significant factor in the increase in emphasis upon aesthetics. Born in

1877, he was of the older generation of Apostles. Through the Society, while an undergraduate, he had become quite friendly with Fry.

In London MacCarthy first made his mark as a drama critic, particularly as an appreciator of Shaw and Ibsen. He published his first book in 1907, a discussion of Shaw's and other plays performed at the innovative Court Theatre. Although he had a full and influential career as a literary critic, he never had the more substantial achievements that his friends expected. A famous conversationalist and a great charmer, throughout his life he held out the promise of being a wonderful novelist, but if so, he talked his novel out and never committed it or any other considerable sustained work to paper, although his essays were eventually gathered together in six volumes.

Perhaps typically, his unfinished memoir of Bloomsbury, written in 1933, is only a few pages in its published form, although the manuscript, presumably a talk to the Memoir Club, is quite a bit longer. As published, all he records is his meeting with Clive Bell in a first-class compartment of the Cambridge-London train in 1901. (How important that train appears to be in the history of Bloomsbury!) Through Bell, MacCarthy came to know the young Cambridge men who would form much of Bloomsbury (and whom he published when he was editor of the *New Quarterly*). He was perceptive about the young Bell, still an undergraduate: "He seemed to live, half with the rich sporting-set, and half with the intellectuals."[1] He married Molly Warre-Cornish in 1906 and she too became a close friend of Bloomsbury; she coined the term "Bloomsberries" for the group in 1910. Although Virginia had been at her wedding, it was not until that year that they really became friendlier, Molly spending time with Virginia at Studland in September while Desmond was abroad selecting pictures.

MacCarthy was always deeply involved in the life of a man of letters, and his publication in 1910 indicated a tie to nineteenth-century liberalism. He had at long last finished the editing, with Lady Agatha Russell, the daughter of the subject, of *Lady John Russell: A Memoir with a Selection from Her Diaries and Correspondence,* which he found a rather boring project. He had been led into it three years before, on the request of the family, through his friendship with Lady John's grandson Bertrand, whom she had raised after the early death of his parents. Desmond and Molly—although she had come back earlier—had spent the first part of 1910 in the Union of South Africa, taken there on an all-expenses-paid tour by his patron, George Arthur Paley.

Desmond was rather at a loose end, looking around for journalistic activity. Molly was after him about money matters and felt that he wasn't working hard enough. So Fry's involving him in the adventure of the exhibition came at a good time. He agreed to be its secretary—the general assistant who would help in getting the show together and then would actually be there while it was at the gallery. In return he would receive £100 and half of the profits, of which it was assumed there would be none. In fact his ultimate share was £460, quite a considerable sum. The expenses were low, £150 for transportation of the pictures, and £100 for advertising.[2]

It is quite astounding how comparatively rapidly this large, and epochal, exhibition was put on. (Nowadays exhibitions—admittedly more the case with museums than commercial galleries—are planned years in advance.) Apparently Fry had started thinking about such an exhibition the previous May, although originally he had thought of having it of Russian pictures. Rather casually he had written to his mother: "I am hoping to have a picture show in the autumn and I may arrange for a course of lectures in London. These may keep one going till the end of the year."[3]

MacCarthy came down with influenza at the end of the summer, but Fry bolstered him up with a promise of a bottle of champagne and they were on their way to select the pictures. MacCarthy rather diffidently recalls that Fry valued him more for his company and his perceptive remarks about pictures than for his efficiency. Presumably he was a delightful companion, even if ill. Fry also used the lure of some days of bicycling in France as a reward. MacCarthy wrote an account of the beginning of the trip in a letter on September 8:

> I am now exceedingly keen on the Exhibition. He [the unnamed director of the gallery] agreed it was quite clear I must go to Paris and

then on to Munich without delay, there being nothing to do in London, until the pictures were chosen. I saw Fry at 6 o'clock . . . and to my dismay, he said that *if* my health would stand it, I ought to come with him that night, as all had been arranged—dealers told we were coming, Paris agent for the exhibition waiting with lists of pictures—etc. in short everybody had got together and as he (Fry) would only have one day in Paris, it was practically my only chance of getting much done in a short time to go at once. Well, of course I said I would come. I rushed to flat to pack and dine at Vic[toria] Station. Off we went, R.F. bought a bottle of champagne (in case I should fail by the way) and I laid down a small medicine store.[4]

Fry was in France from September 3 to September 15.[5]

MacCarthy, because of his illness and the vibrations of the ship, couldn't sleep, even after they had drunk the champagne on deck (thirty-five years later he remembered drinking the champagne before even setting out) on the way to Paris. (Of course there may have been several bottles! Frances Spalding in her biography of Fry has the trip start in the morning with a bottle of champagne.)[6] MacCarthy did have a three-hour nap at a hotel, a delicious lunch, and then he and Fry went around to see dealers, accompanied by Robert Dell, the Paris correspondent for the *Burlington*. Dell had organized the important and large exhibition in Brighton the previous June that Fry had reviewed, and must have been a major reason that Fry and MacCarthy could operate so quickly. In the one afternoon they selected fifty pictures, somewhat less than a third of the exhibition. "Dell . . . took us round to the dealers and I enjoyed choosing the pictures (which will by the bye give you the most tremendous shocks.) . . . At these interviews with dealers I used to pose as M. le Publique, and on one point my verdict was final: Was there, or was there not, anything in some nude which might create an outcry in London?"[7] Presumably the theory was to produce only one sort of shock and not compound the situation through more traditional ways of offending conventional morality.

It was not a matter of going to obscure places to find the pictures; indeed most of the painters selected were already major figures in Paris, demonstrating the differences between French and English attitudes toward the modern. On this visit and a second one, Fry and MacCarthy, and later with advice from Bell and Lady Ottoline, acquired paintings from well-established dealers: Cézannes, Gauguins, and Vlamincks from Vollard; Cézannes and Rouaults from Druet; Vlamincks and Derains from Kahnweiler; Manets, Van Goghs, Signacs, and Seurats from Bernheim-Jeune. There were also a few pictures from individuals: Picasso's *Nude Girl with a Basket of Flowers* from Leo Stein (the other Picasso in the exhibition, a portrait of the art dealer Sagot, probably came from Sagot himself) and a Matisse from Fry's old friend and mentor Bernard Berenson. Fry later regretted not having more Seurats. In the Retrospect in 1920 of his *Vision and Design,* he wrote: "my most serious lapse was the failure to discover the genius of Seurat, whose supreme merits as a designer [significant word] I had every reason to acclaim."[8] Cézanne, Van Gogh, and Gauguin were the dominant painters in the selection.

Writing about the experience in 1945, MacCarthy makes it a slightly more leisurely affair, saying that he and Fry spent "day after day looking at pictures."[9] Even at this point it did not appear absolutely certain that the exhibition would take place. Fry wrote to his mother on September 16: "I went to Paris to help arrange about an exhibition of modern French pictures in London wh. I hope will come off."[10]

On September 8 they bicycled to Meaux and then arrived at Reims on September 10; Lowes Dickinson was supposed to be a member of the party, but he had to cancel and Desmond used his bicycle. From Reims he wrote to Molly:

> I think I told you in my last letter that the pictures will raise a howl of fury & derision. If people can be persuaded, however, to give them a chance—that is to say not to condemn them on their first impression—they will see something in them. There is a postman [by Van Gogh] which I expect will send people to the turnstile clamouring for their money back. He is so wonderfully hideous, alive, and as disconcerting as a face put suddenly three inches from one's own.[11]

MacCarthy went to Munich the next day to look for more pictures. Although half-German, he felt more friendly to the French. As he wrote from Munich to G. E. Moore: "Fry and I had an amusing day or two in Paris, looking at pictures. I like the French so much better than the Germans now. . . . I wonder what you will think of the pictures."[12]

It is somewhat unclear what happened in Munich as there were no German pictures in the exhibition. His connection in Munich was with Dr. R. Meyer Reifstahl, an expert on Van Gogh, who was about to publish articles on the painter in the November and December issues of the *Burlington*. MacCarthy didn't enjoy himself, and took against the "unpleasant German language, in which it seems impossible to say anything about a work of art without seeming to analyze it as though it were a prescription composed of doses of this & infusions of that."[13] He also went to Amsterdam, where he acquired Van Goghs from the artist's sister-in-law, Mme. Gosschalk-Bonger, notably the *View of Arles, Iris, Cypresses, The Postman, Sunflowers, Orchard under Rain,* and *Cornfield with Crows. Factories* came from Bernheim-Jeune and *Dr. Gachet* from Druet.[14] "When we came to price them she was asking a hundred and twenty pounds or less for some admirable examples of his art."[15] (Ian Dunlop believes that these prices cannot be accurate as "Van Gogh's prices were rising and by 1913 a still-life had been sold at auction for £1,450.")[16] He then returned to Paris and settled how much the Grafton would receive from sales. He had not received instructions and said 20 percent, only to discover upon his return to London that the Grafton had been accustomed to receiving only 11 percent. The Paris galleries had not objected, so MacCarthy felt quite pleased with his business skills.[17]

Even at the end of September, Fry appeared to be rather diffident about the exhibition, or perhaps in writing about it to his mother he felt that she might be a little shocked and he wanted to distance himself from what was happening. On September 23 he wrote to her: "I've perhaps foolishly been the instigator of an exhibition of Modern French Art at the Grafton Gallery this winter and tho' I'm not responsible and have no post in regard to it I'm bound to do a good deal of advising & supervising and I must go to Paris again."[18]

This was the second trip, in October, to Paris to select further pictures. The party consisted of Fry, MacCarthy, Lady Ottoline, and Clive Bell. Lady Ottoline had become more familiar with recent developments in art through her role as a founder of the Contemporary Art Society and her love affairs with Augustus John and later Henry Lamb. Her relationship with Fry himself was becoming increasingly intense, although they would be actual lovers only very briefly in the spring of 1911 just before Fry went off with the Bells to Turkey. In the fall of 1909 Lady Ottoline had visited Paris with Dorelia John, Augustus John's wife, seeing Gertrude and Leo Stein, the art dealer Ambrose Vollard, with his Manets, Gauguins, Picassos and Cézannes, as well as the Manets and Cézannes belonging to Auguste Pellerin in Neuilly.

Lady Ottoline, like Horace Cole in his decidedly different way, served as a bridge between Augustus John's circle and Bloomsbury. It was a moment when John was very much part of the avant-garde; in fact his exhibition at the Chenil Gallery at the same time as the Post-Impressionists garnered a somewhat similar negative reaction. John himself was indecisive about the Post-Impressionists, at first finding the exhibition rather "bloody" but then becoming fonder of it. He would shortly thereafter turn away from modernism, but at this point he was part of Lady Ottoline Morrell's world, and joined her in her support of the new. During the summer of 1910 she visited him in Provence, and they went together to Cézanne's house, where there were still some of his paintings.[19] She traveled on to Venice, where Fry wrote to her and asked her to meet him in Paris to help him to continue to pick pictures.

It was at this point that their friendship was at its closest, before it was ruptured either by her belief that Fry had boasted of their brief affair or because he accused her of saying he was in love with her. He was a frequent visitor to Peppard Cottage at this time. There was a limit to Lady Ottoline's bohemianism; she was a grand lady who enjoyed being part of various worlds, and had affairs in a rather aristocratic manner, which was perhaps one reason she and Bertrand Russell were well matched when their grand passion started the next year.

In September Fry wrote to her that he was going to France and wondered if they could meet on her way back from Venice. The letter has the air of being written by a lover, or at least a wooer:

> How I wish I were with you in Venice of all places in the world. Such things seem to belong to an impossible dreamland now. Why can't I chuck everything & just come. But it's not possible. . . . The last thing has been the arranging for this modern French Exhibition at the Grafton which is a good work but has meant a lot of worry, and will mean a lot of abuse when it comes off. . . . I never got my tour with Goldie Dickinson. He failed me so I pottered round Paris Rheims, and the Oise for five rather grey cold days & got back. Still I saw some splendid things & some very sad ones for the French are ruining all their cathedrals as hard as they can with senseless restorations. I must make some protest. It's so gratuitous & so infernal. Now about plans. I must have one really delightful thing this horrid year & have decided that it is to be meeting you in Paris & going to the Autumn Salon & looking at some of the Cézannes Van Goghs etc. wh. are to come over to England. So please tell me at once when you will be there. My best time would be round about Oct. 5–15. . . . Now do help to bring this about. It would make all the difference to me if we can arrange it.[20]

They did meet in Paris, although it is not clear what the schedule was, and to what degree Lady Ottoline actually chose pictures to be in the show. Through the Contemporary Art Society and privately, they had spent much time together discussing pictures. Fry wrote to Dickinson on October 15: "She is quite splendid. . . . I am preparing for a huge campaign of outraged British Philistinism."[21]

Vanessa, in England with the children, was apparently somewhat jealous of her husband and friends having a good time in Paris. She wrote to Clive on October 9: "Oh dear. I own I should rather like to be in that exciting atmosphere where people really seem to realise the existence of art." And then the next day:

> I wonder whether you'll come across a new genius in Paris & even perhaps invest in one of his works. I give you leave to do so if you feel

inclined. Who is the newest sensation? I am longing to hear from you about it all but I suppose you wont have much time for letter writing. . . . I think Ottoline must be rather incongruous in Paris. She seems to me too essentially a part of Bloomsbury culture to mix well with Paris. What do the French think of her?[22]

This was just a few weeks before the exhibition was to open.

There was a growing sense that something dramatic was about to happen, and that English art, and perhaps writing as well, might be put on a different path. Two of the pioneers in England up to this time, and good friends, comrades in the good fight, had been Fry and William Rothenstein. Born in 1872, Rothenstein became a dominating figure in the New English Art Club. He had studied in Paris, where he was influenced by Whistler, Degas, and Pissarro. Up until 1910 he had been a leader of the advanced in English art, but one must keep in mind the subdued nature of that activity in England. As Ian Dunlop has commented:

> There is no equivalent to the Latin Quarter in London: Whistler's Chelsea was never an artistic *quartier* in the Parisian sense. . . . Instead of wild gatherings, like the celebrated banquet for Rousseau given by Picasso and others at the *Bateau Lavoir,* there were the endless dinner parties arranged by Rothenstein and his friends at the Chelsea Arts Club—usually ending with speeches. The lack of an *avant-garde* tradition explains the almost incredulous surprise that greeted some of the paintings in the Post-Impressionist exhibition.[23]

Fry thought Rothenstein would agree with him that French painting was not sufficiently influential in England. He had bought one of Rothenstein's paintings for the Metropolitan Museum, and had supported an exhibition of Rothenstein's work early in 1910. The attention the exhibition had received at first was negative, and Fry did his best to reverse the situation. "I set to work at once & wrote an article for the Nation wh. I hope they will put in. It's terrible now that no critics have any independence of mind. I hope it may start things, meanwhile I've talked all I can."[24] And indeed Fry's praising piece on Rothenstein appeared in the June 11 issue of the *Nation.* (One should note how prodigious Fry's energy was. He wrote twenty-eight pieces for periodicals during 1910.)[25] And in June, despite their growing disagreements, Fry wrote in the *Nation* in praise of Rothenstein's Indian paintings exhibited at the Chenil Galleries.

Fry was becoming increasingly impatient with what he regarded as the "milk-and-water" Impressionism of the New English Art Club, the thinking of those whom he referred to when impatient as the "Custard-Islanders." Yet he still felt close to Rothenstein, writing to him and his wife in friendly terms, confiding his worries about his wife, money, and his chances of becoming Slade Professor. He was also busy in midsummer (how did he find the time?) painting a ceiling decoration for Sir Andrew Noble, a physicist and armament manufacturer, for his house in Scotland. In October of the year, with everything else, he was working, not particularly successfully, on restoring the Mantegnas at Hampton Court. He worked on the ceiling in a barn he rented near his house in Guildford. For it, he painted Apollo driving two horses across the sky, and exhibited it in November at the New English Art Club, despite his doubts about the club, where in its comparative conventionality it made an odd contrast to the Post-Impressionists he had arranged to be on show at the same time.

Fry did have doubts about the ceiling, which he expressed to D. S. MacColl. In August he was feeling better about it, although he wanted Rothenstein's advice. As he wrote to Mrs. Rothenstein:

> I'm doing a great ceiling decoration for Sir Andrew Noble. It's nearly done but I wld. give a good deal to have Will's criticism at this stage. I think its come rather well. I hope . . . that Will is happy in his work. I still think that people must come round to understanding it before very long, but it is a terrible fight. Only all creators who have really created anything have the same kind of fight. I am sure people really want always the old truths which have had time to become lies. If anyone can dress them up so as to look new he can command the world.[26]

It should be noted that Fry's own painting, stronger than its general reputation would have it, nevertheless seemed less influenced by the Post-Impressionists than other British painters were, most notably Vanessa Bell and Duncan Grant. In an undated note to Rothenstein he wrote: "I have a big idea, if I fail to get the Slade, which might I think do a great deal of good. I want to talk it over with you."[27] Was this the Post-Impressionist exhibition over which their friendship would founder?

At least looking back in 1920, in the Retrospect to *Vision and Design*, Fry saw his development as all of a piece, moving on from his interest in the Renaissance and Impressionism to something new and to something better, a return perhaps to the geometric parts of the Renaissance that he associated with Piero della Francesca.

> After a brief period during which I was interested in the new possibilities opened up by the more scientific evaluation of colour which the Impressionists practised, I came to feel more and more the absence in their work of structural design. It was an innate desire for this aspect of art which drove me to the study of the Old Masters and, in particular, those of the Italian Renaissance, in the hope of discovering from them the secret of that architectonic idea which I missed so badly in the work of my contemporaries. . . . I became increasingly interested in the art of Cézanne and those like Gauguin and van Goch [*sic*] who at that time represented the first effects of his profound influence on modern art, and I gradually recognised that what I had hoped for as a possible event of some future century had already occurred, that art had begun to recover once more the language of design and to explore its so long neglected possibilities.[28]

It was over these ideas that Fry and Rothenstein began to part ways, that a fissure developed between Edwardian progressivism and the development of modernism. Perhaps Rothenstein became a little too enamored of respectability. He was increasingly part of the art establishment, particularly involved with art education. When looking back in his memoirs he gives the impression that he was fighting with Fry for the leadership of the young, and that he felt Fry had won. He depicts himself as having stood aside from competing for the Slade professorship out of friendship for Fry. He seemed to feel that it was almost coincidental that Fry became so prominent, that he became the leader of the younger artists. Rothenstein commented rather sourly that Fry, having failed to secure the Slade professorship,

> was soon to find an outlet for his restless and varied energies else-where. . . . As Fry had from the first been my warmest supporter, he expected that I would now support him; but since I held aloof, the good Roger, who can always convince himself as magically as he convinces others, discovered that my work was no longer of any importance. Fry's first idea was to show a group of Russian paintings; finally he got together an exhibition of what was then, or just after-wards, called French Post-Impressionist paintings, which provided a greater sensation than any collection of Russian paintings would have done. Fry thenceforth became the central figure round whom the more advanced young English painters grouped themselves.[29]

But at the time, when they were still friends, he was much more positive. In his letter of commiseration about Image becoming the Slade professor instead of Fry, Rothenstein wrote: "I feel there never was a time when so much could be done as now, & I know you are the person to make people aware of essential things; indeed I am personally certain there is no one else."[30] Yet, even then, he had doubts about the exhibi-tion, writing to his wife on January 4, 1911, that because of his trip to India he was "glad to miss the senseless chatter over the French show; if I could only never hear any of that salon nonsense how much pleas-anter my life would be. Fry is really in a sort of pit, I fear, with Bedford Square [Lady Ottoline] at his coattails."[31]

Fry, despite being something of a rebel and a Quaker, was still more of an insider than Rothenstein, a Jew from Bradford. One mustn't forget the class aspects of what was going on in 1910. The Bloomsbury figures were in the upper reaches of the middle classes, they either had small private incomes or acted as if they did. They resided upon the golden islands depicted in *Howards End* or to use the image that Virginia Woolf employed in a later famous essay, they viewed the world from a tower, still standing upright, built of money and assurance, in the years before the First World War, after which it started to lean.

I believe this is a crucial factor in trying to understand how changes take place in England in any area, be it political or cultural. Those who are in a position of authority, conferred upon them generally by their class position, are far better placed to effect change, if such be their intention. Reform from within has almost always been the English way. Bloomsbury's ideas in art, starting in this year; in biography, most notably marked in 1918 with Lytton Strachey's *Eminent Victorians;* in literature, despite her earlier important novels, with Virginia Woolf's taking off in a more dramatic direction with *Jacob's Room* in 1922: these were important steps in the development of modernism. But one should not forget that they were English "rebellions," ultimately more easily accepted because they came from members of the upper middle class. And these "rebellions" were muted by the class position of their perpetrators.

It is this mixture of respectability and rebellion that can make such figures so fascinating, but also at times so irritating. They had a sense of security but they rather enjoyed mocking the world that had given it to them. At the same time that sense of security made it possible for them to charge off in new directions, to tamper with the conventions that were part of their world. Bloomsbury wished to take a "voyage out" to try to discover the reality that lay beneath the appearances that they found about them. For Fry, Cézanne increasingly became the prophet of that reality. From his position as editor of the *Burlington* and elsewhere, he championed Cézanne.

For most of the year, however, Rothenstein and Fry were on good terms. In January Fry sent a very cordial letter to Rothenstein including an invitation to come and see his new house, about which he said: "I think you will like it as an attempt to make a house very economical and yet expressive of the needs of our sort of life." He also sent a copy of the January issue of the *Burlington*, as he thought the article in it on Cézanne by Maurice Denis would interest Rothenstein. He wanted increasingly to make the journal a force for those who were

keen about the future of modern art, from artists and craftsmen so that gradually the *Burlington* may become a real power in that direction.

Do do what you can. Also of course I shall want an article from you on some subject—perhaps a quasi-philosophical one would be the most interesting. Have you anything in mind? Well, when we meet we shall strike out some idea, I hope.

I feel a new hope altogether about art, and all those who care and who are not fossilized must get together and produce something.[32]

In his chatty letter to Mrs Rothenstein in August Fry shared, in a rather insouciant way, his concern about money: "I sometimes worry about money & you know what that is but I don't believe its even worth while to bother about that."[33] In October Rothenstein went to India and did not return until January 1911. It was almost as if he returned to a different world, and he and Fry would have an increasingly acrimonious correspondence. The relationship between them represented, I believe, the differences in England between the previously advanced but still traditional forms of artistic developments, and those artists and critics who were heralds of a new artistic movement, which we now know as modernism, those who believed they could truly understand Mrs Brown.

8

The Exhibition

We now come to the exhibition itself, that extraordinary compilation of modern French pictures, quite a few of which are now canonical works of the modern movement. The first step was to gather together an honorary sponsoring committee. A series of letters were written to the "great and the good" pointing out that they needn't necessarily endorse the works of art. Rather they would be merely supporting, Fry assured them, the right of the pictures to be seen.

The sponsoring committee consisted of twenty-two eminent figures such as Lord Ribblesdale—he of that ultimate portrait of Edwardian luxury painted by Sargent in 1902. Master of the Buckhounds, Lord-in-Waiting, Liberal Whip in the House of Lords, Ribblesdale, by serving as a sponsor, inadvertently was helping to challenge the values of his Edwardian world.[1] There were other politicians on the committee: the Earl of Plymouth, who was commissioner of works in Balfour's Tory government from 1902 to 1905, and Lewis Harcourt, who had the same position in Asquith's Liberal government. (As such they were in charge of government buildings and presumably their contents, including works of art, so they were in some sense singularly appropriate as committee members, even if they were unlikely to approve of Post-Impressionist works of art going into government buildings.) Plymouth, Ribblesdale, and Harcourt were all already part of the art world, for they were also involved in the Contemporary Art Society as trustees, along with, improbably, Lord Northcliffe.

Other sponsors included the director of the National Gallery, Sir Charles Holroyd, who once he saw the paintings asked that his name be removed.[2] The Duchess of Rutland, a sculptor herself, who with her daughters was happy to attend *Salome,* was at one point on the committee, but she too asked for her name to be taken off. She wrote to MacCarthy: "I am so *horrified* at having my name associated with such an *awful* exhibition of horrors. I am very very much upset by it. . . . I suppose it is not possible to erase it somehow, on the unsold copies [of the catalogue] you now have? I am very sorry to be so strong in my horror—but I can hardly tell you how sorry I am, I should have had my named used in such a hurry—without a chance of knowing *what* I was patronizing." Her name was duly removed.[3]

Other members of the committee were the financier and diplomat and supporter of art galleries Sir Edgar Vincent, later Lord D'Abernon; Lionel Cust, famous man about town, but also Fry's co-editor of the *Burlington,* and surveyor of the king's pictures; and Lord Henry Bentinck, Lady Ottoline's brother and involved with the Contemporary Art Society. Fry also asked Charles Holmes, whose term as Slade Professor at Oxford was just ending (creating the opening for which Fry had competed and lost), and who was director at the time of the National Portrait Gallery, where he had replaced Lionel Cust.

Holmes did write a short guide to the exhibition, *Notes on the Post-Impressionist Painters,* which was mildly favorable and was on sale at the gallery. It did certainly capture the establishment tone. Holmes attempted to steer a middle course, granting that the exhibition was "stimulating. . . . And in the arts, I am inclined to think that a stimulus of any kind is healthy."[4] He half praised Cézanne as a genuine artist of a modest rank, though clumsy. Despite his lukewarm position, Holmes was attacked as a defender of the exhibition. He wrote years later:

The violence of the controversy roused by the show, the criticism of officials, like . . . myself, for backing what was deemed aesthetic Bolshevism, and the earnest wish of my friend Lee-Warner [the publisher] that I would write something for him, drove me to put together, very hastily, my first thoughts about the Movement. "Notes on the Post-Impressionist Painters," an attempt in my usual rather cautious way, to survey the exhibition without bias, seemed to please nobody.[5]

As Clive Bell remarked in a brief review of the *Notes:* "It is greatly to the credit of Prof. Holmes that, in spite of an official position, he has not hesitated to express his favourable opinion of the 'revolutionaries.' These notes are the weighty judgments of a powerful, cultivated, but somewhat uninspired mind. . . . Prof. Holmes has hardly realized the full significance of this revolution."[6]

The pamphlet was quite unbearably patronizing in an understated way, as it appeared to judge the pictures on the basis of how well they would work out in a scheme of interior decoration. Holmes concluded that the Post-Impressionists were moving "towards a larger and more decorative style of pictorial expression—in itself of very modest value, owing to its obvious limitations, but with potentialities of future personal refinement which are almost unbounded."[7] As Fry commented in the *Nation:* "All through Mr. Holmes's criticism runs the question whether a picture is 'serviceable' or not, a question which suggests an odd idea of the artist's function, as purveyor to the conveniences of the middle classes. It was certainly not so that these artists worked, nor so, I believe, that any noble or lasting creations were made."[8] Holmes was committed to a middle position, and in his reminiscences, published in 1936 two years after Fry's death, he spoke up on behalf of responsibility and respectability: "For me, Fry's rapid improvisations of perception and theory came too near to opportunism;—brilliant, suggestive and stimulating, no doubt, but compelled, by the need for momentary predominance, to obscure or denounce all other beacon lights, even those which time has shown to be trustworthy."[9]

An interesting anonymous review of Holmes's short book in the *Times Literary Supplement* at the end of December criticized Holmes for not being sufficiently positive and revealed a strikingly level-headed view of the Post-Impressionists, very sympathetic to Fry's ideas: "He [Holmes] is, we think, unjust to Cézanne, praising his sincerity, but blaming him for his 'consistently personal clumsiness of touch.' Cézanne often is clumsy, as Wordsworth is clumsy. . . . [His paintings] have a kind of unwilling beauty which is more convincing than the too eager beauties of other painters."[10]

The aspect of musical chairs on the committee—the trading of posts its members represented—makes vivid the tightness of the English official world. Fry used this world but also was interested in breaking it up. Change in England is often caught in this dilemma, and is likely to remain within accepted dimensions. The continual question in England is who has won, the forces of change or those of continuity? The answer is generally both or neither. Holmes had also been an editor of the *Burlington Magazine* from its founding in 1903 to 1909, and Fry had replaced him in that post. The executive committee of the exhibition consisted of Fry, Cust and Holmes, Lady Ottoline and Lord Henry Bentinck, as well as Meyer-Riefstahl from Munich and Dell from Paris, presumably in recognition of their work in helping to bring the show together at remarkably short notice.

Such a group as the honorary committee makes a splendid example of how names are gathered for such events, uninvolved though some of them may have been. It also included the directors of the Glasgow and Scottish Art Galleries, the keeper of the Louvre, some of the French dealers who had supplied the bulk of the pictures, as well as Clive Bell, Count Harry Kessler, and the famous French dandy and model for Proust, Comte Robert de Montesquiou-Fezensac. This committee was exonerated from support of the specific paintings: "They are not responsible for the choice of the pictures, [but] by lending their names [they] have been kind enough to give this project their general support."[11]

In the need for the new to authenticate itself, the risk was of being absorbed into establishment values. Fry was aware that these figures might well regret lending their names, as had happened with Sir Charles Holroyd and the Duchess of Rutland. He wrote to Holmes when asking him to be on the committee: "It's purely formal, just to a blessing not to the pictures themselves but to the idea that people may be allowed to look at them."[12] Fry may have felt more comfortable having on the executive committee figures associated with the avant-garde who were safely abroad, such as Meyer-Riefstahl and Dell.

MacCarthy decided it would be a nice touch to invite the French ambassador to open the exhibition, a gesture that might have given the public some pause. On September 26 he wrote to Eddie Marsh asking him to be in touch with the private secretary at the Foreign Office to find out the best way to go about asking the ambassador. (Presumably he did not concern himself with the possibility that the Foreign Office might know that the perpetrators of the *Dreadnought* hoax were friends of the organizers, but even so it probably wouldn't have made any difference.) Nothing apparently came of this. He also asked Marsh to alert his grand friends to the exhibition; MacCarthy clearly wanted to stir things up.

> The cat has been out of the bag frisking about and it is no use now trying to thrust it in again. In fact, the more it jumps the better. The exhibition will be confined to the post impressionists [suggesting that the name had been decided upon comparatively early]—no neo-impressionists—Gauguin, Van Gogh, Cézanne, Matisse etc. I expect howls of derision and fury. "Synthesists" I found they were called in Germany where they are all dead, dessicated & dissected, but synthesists won't do. It sounds so much like the hiss of any angry gander to be a happy appellation.[13]

MacCarthy so liked this phrase about the gander that he incorporated it into his introduction to the exhibition.

Fry was becoming more and more enthusiastic about the pictures that had been gathered, perhaps rather arbitrarily, in the brief visits to Paris. Virginia Woolf has written a description of him contemplating and explaining them which seems rather contrary to her sense of a great break happening in December 1910:

> There they stood upon chairs—the pictures that were to be shown at the Grafton Gallery—bold, bright, impudent almost, in contrast with

the Watts portrait of a beautiful Victorian lady that hung on the wall behind them. And there was Roger Fry, gazing at them, plunging his eyes into them as if he were a humming-bird hawkmoth hanging over a flower, quivering yet still. And then drawing a deep breath of satisfaction, he would turn to whoever it might be, eager for sympathy. Were you puzzled? But why? And he would explain that it was quite easy to make the transition from Watts to Picasso; there was no break, only a continuation. They were only pushing things a little further. He demonstrated; he persuaded; he argued. The argument rose and soared. It vanished into the clouds. Then back it swooped to the picture.[14]

What to call the exhibition? According to MacCarthy, Fry was being pressed by a journalist who was helping with publicity for a title. Fry suggested "expressionism" among other possibilities, but the journalist wasn't satisfied. Finally Fry said, "Oh, let's just call them post-impressionists; at any rate, they came after the impressionists."[15] As J. B. Bullen points out, Frank Rutter had used the term about the painter Othon Friesz in an issue of *Art News* on October 15, and in the same issue there was an advertisement for "The Post-Impressionists" of France. But here, with the conjunction of a sizable number of paintings by Cézanne, Van Gogh, and Gauguin, the term entered the language.

The poster too featured these painters: the only names given were Manet, Cezanne (without its accent), Gauguin, Van Gogh, and Matisse. The illustration was a rather hieratic Gauguin, *Poèmes Barbares,* a bust of a Tahitian woman, with a small dark figure, perhaps an idol. It emphasized the connection with the primitive which was already becoming such an important factor in the development of modern art—most overwhelmingly in Picasso's *Demoiselles d'Avignon* of 1907—and such a contrast to the overly "civilized" quality of paintings that were shown at the Royal Academy annual exhibition, particularly as the contemporary English portrait style favored a pseudo-eighteenth-century look.

The catalogue had to be hastily assembled, and it is an unreliable guide to what was there. Although the exact number and contents of the show will never be known, it was unquestionably a large exhibition created very quickly. Perhaps the enterprise reflected that particular combination that seems more common in England than elsewhere: an extraordinary range of knowledge combined with a certain amateur spirit—perhaps it is just a trifle vulgar to be *too* well organized. With Fry's myriad other activities, his personal problems, and the great speed with which the exhibition was assembled, the comparative casualness of this event is not surprising. Not everything on display was listed in the catalogue; quite a few of the titles given are too generic to make it possible to decide the exact work of art, as there were several paintings of the same title by the same artist, and some of the titles have been modified since 1910. As Benedict Nicolson has remarked, even in its limited way the catalogue was quite inaccurate, going so far possibly as to identify one Gauguin as a Van Gogh.

MacCarthy was aware of the casualness of it all. As he wrote:

The hurried agonies of that picture-hanging are still vivid to me. Roger was entirely absorbed in deciding which picture would look best next another, while it lay with me to number them. As he was continually shifting them about when I was elsewhere, I was terrified that the numbers and titles wouldn't always correspond, with the effect of increasing the mockery, which I now felt certain the exhibition would excite. It was four a.m. before I got to bed the night before Press day, and then I couldn't sleep for worrying. When the newspaper was brought to me with coffee in bed, although it happened to contain a long and laudatory review of a book I had just published [about Lady Russell], I couldn't even read that. The prospect of public ridicule owing to having, say, catalogued a nude girl as "Station-master at Arles," made my walk to the gallery more like a walk to the gallows.[16]

The catalogue listed 159 paintings, 52 drawings, 13 sculptures, and 9 items of faience pottery. Despite his prominence in the title of the exhibition, there were only eight works by Manet, all jointly owned by the Paris dealer Bernheim-Jeune and the Berlin dealer Paul Cassirer. Manet was the senior artist who would, in effect, the organizers hoped, bestow his blessing upon the others. He was the only Impressionist in the exhibition, but his works shown included what has become one of his most famous paintings, his last major work, *A Bar at the Folies-Bergère*, of 1881–1882. It had actually been displayed before in London, in 1905, in the exhibition at the Grafton organized by the Paris dealer Durand-Ruel. It would go through a series of owners and galleries before being bought by Samuel Courtauld in 1926 and presented by him to the Courtauld Institute of Art in 1934.[17] If it had not been for Courtauld's acquisition of the Manet and other Post-Impressionists, English public collections would have had to wait much longer to have representative pictures to display. Despite the fairly rapid critical turnaround, the public, and those who purchased on its behalf, were slow to catch up with the canons of modernism.

The three painters who dominated the exhibition, however, were Cézanne, Van Gogh, and Gauguin, the greatest of the Post-Impressionists, and theirs were the works that caused the most upset. Twelve of the Van Goghs were from his sister-in-law, the others from Paris dealers, as were most of the paintings in the exhibition. The only considerable exception was the drawings. Matisse had lent four of the twelve of his that were displayed, and Mrs. Emily Chadbourne, a wealthy American collector who had a house on Park Lane in London, had lent three Matisses, as well as eight of the ten Gauguin drawings.

As Stella Tillyard has recently shown, there were more favorable reactions to the exhibition than tradition allows, and some of the Post-Impressionist painters were more rapidly accepted in England, at least among the cognoscenti, than might have been anticipated. But as we shall explore, in the short term there was violent reaction. And more important, in my view, as an indication that the exhibition was a watershed, was that critics who until then had been supporters of the new, such as Robert Ross, D. S. MacColl, and Charles Ricketts, turned on this art, even though on the continent there was a far greater acceptance of it. In Paris the "art-quake" of 1910 was concerned with Cubism, which made a much more severe break with "reality."

In the exhibition there were twenty Cézannes, mostly from his earlier periods, and somewhat less exemplary of the doctrine of significant form in his work, as advanced by Clive Bell in his *Art* in 1914. The Cézannes included *Les Maisons Jaunes,* purchased from the exhibition itself by the Helsinki Museum, probably through the art historian Tancred Borenius, a friend of Fry's and an adviser to the museum. (The short pieces about the exhibition written years later by MacCarthy and Bell have to be used with some caution. Bell remembers, presumably accurately, that he wished to buy the Cézanne that the Finns acquired—but as a *Montagne St. Victoire* for which he could not afford the £400 asked.)[18] There was also an 1877 portrait of Mme. Cézanne, now in the Museum of Fine Arts in Boston, and his *La Vielle au Chapelet* of 1895–1896, now in the National Gallery in London. The Museo de Arte in São Paulo, Brazil, eventually acquired several of the paintings on display: Cézanne's *Le grand pin* of 1892–1896 and Gauguin's *Joseph and Potiphar's Wife* as well as two of the Manets.

In the catalogue there were 36 Gauguin paintings and ten drawings. One of the Gauguins that became best known was his *L'Esprit veille* of 1892, as it was listed in the catalogue, now called *Manao Tupapau, The Spirit of the Dead Keeps Watch;* it is in the Albright Knox Art Gallery in Buffalo, New York. Another powerful Gauguin, *Parau na te varua ino,* was exhibited then as *L'Esprit du Mal.* It is in the National Gallery in Washington. The picture depicts a nude woman holding a cloth over her genitals in what might be seen as a gesture of modesty but might well have been so disconcerting to the 1910 public as to call attention to them. Behind her is a seated male figure who may be Satan.

There were twenty-two Van Goghs, including the overwhelming *Crows in the Wheatfield,* painted in 1890 just before his death and now in the Van Gogh Museum in Amsterdam, and one in the *Sunflower* series now in the National Gallery. There was also his *Dr Gachet* and *Le Postier,* one of six he did, this one in the Barnes Foundation. There was one of the five portraits of the postman's wife, *La Berceuse,* now in the Kröller-Müller Museum in Otterlo, Holland. Besides the *Cornfield,* four other Van Goghs, including an *Iris,* are in the Van Gogh Museum in Amsterdam.

Other painters had far fewer canvases, although they were well rep-resented. There were fifty-three drawings, most notably ten Gauguins, ten Matisses, and seven Picassos. There were only two Picasso oils, and not his latest work. There were only three Matisse oils—two landscapes (one lent by Bernard Berenson, who would later present it in 1938 to Prince Paul of Yugoslavia for the Belgrade Museum) and a portrait, *The Woman with Green Eyes*. The portrait received a great deal of attention, was widely reproduced in the press and furiously mocked. Painted in 1908, now known as *The Girl with Green Eyes*, it is in the San Francisco Museum of Modern Art as a bequest of Harriet Lane Levy. It would appear that the picture already belonged to her and was not for sale, listed in the catalogue as belonging to Mme. L., although Clive Bell remembers asking its price.[19] Harriet Levy had shared a flat in Paris with Alice Toklas, who was trying tactfully to leave to join Gertrude Stein in the Rue du Fleurus. When, much to Toklas and Stein's pleas-ure, Harriet decided to return to California in the fall of 1910, she particularly asked that the Matisse be sent to her very carefully.[20]

There were other French painters of interest represented in the exhibition: Maurice Denis with five canvases, one of which, *Ulysses and Calypso*, was bought by the Helsinki museum; André Derain with three—his *Le parc de Carrières, Saint-Denis* was bought by Fry (it is now in the Courtauld); three Odilon Redon, two Albert Marquet; George Rouault with six untitled landscapes; three Paul Signac; Felix Vallotton with four; and Maurice Vlaminck with eight—Clive Bell bought his *Le Pont*. There were also paintings by artists who have achieved lesser levels of recognition: Cross, Friesz, Girieud, Herbin, Laprade, Manguin, Puy, Sérusier, and Valtat. Aristide Maillol was also represented with three sculptures and three drawings. Matisse had more sculptures—seven—than paintings.

Fry's own attitude towards the exhibition can be gathered from the note he wrote in February for the *Burlington* on the acquisition of the Denis and the Cézanne by the Finnish museum. Without being ex-plicit, he makes it clear that, in his opinion, the Finns put the English to shame in terms of taste. He points out that, as Van Gogh was already well represented in the Helsinki gallery, there was no need to acquire a picture by him. He wrote rather defiantly: "The two pictures are admirably chosen as representative of the most striking, and one believes the most promising, of all recent artistic movements." At the same time he compares the Denis, placing it in a "classical" tradition, to the painting of Poussin, Ingres, and Puvis de Chavannes. Of the Cézanne he wrote that it had the "actual material of poetry and [provided] the fullest gratification for the demands of the imagination."[21]

But what did this exhibition mean, other than having acquired fame as a notorious event that moved forward, particularly in the Anglo-American world, the cause of modern art and of modernism? It is always mentioned in that context, and forms one of the chapters in Ian Dunlop's *The Shock of the New* (1972), which discusses seven controversial exhibitions ranging from the Salon des Refusés of 1863 to the International Surrealist Exhibition of 1938.

Desmond MacCarthy wrote the introduction to the simple catalogue (an unillustrated list) based on notes supplied by Fry and on conversations with him. In its modest English way, it was something of a manifesto. In a letter to his mother at the time, MacCarthy asserted somewhat more independence, saying about the preface: "I wrote [it] with technical help from Fry."[22] The brief introduction began with a statement that in a sense was accurate (but contrary to how the exhibition was later seen): "The pictures collected together in the present Exhibition are the work of a group of artists who cannot be defined by any single term." MacCarthy first ventures that they might be called "Synthesists." But quite quickly he reverts to the title of the exhibition as an expansion of that term.

> The Post-Impressionists consider the Impressionists too naturalistic.
>   Yet their own connection with Impressionism is extremely close. . . .
> Nevertheless, the connection of these artists with the Impressionists is accidental rather than intrinsic. . . . Impressionism encouraged an artist to paint a tree as it appeared to him at the moment under particular circumstances. It insisted so much upon the importance of his render-

ing his exact impression that his work often completely failed to express a tree at all; as transferred to canvas it was just so much shimmer and colour. The "treeness" of the tree was not rendered at all; all the emotion and associations such as trees may be made to convey in poetry were omitted.

This is the fundamental cause of quarrel between the Impressionists and the group of painters whose pictures hang on these walls.

Some sentences further on came the most famous remark in the introduction, and one that is, in its slightly ironic English way, quite significant for what was to be the nature of modernism as well as abstraction. MacCarthy wrote that the work of the Post-Impressionists "may even appear ridiculous to those who do not recall the fact that a good rocking-horse often had more of the true horse about it than an instantaneous photograph of a Derby winner." In the rest of the piece, MacCarthy emphasizes the importance of design and "geographical simplicity" in Cézanne, how Van Gogh uses Cézanne's methods to express his intense emotions, and how Gauguin dwells on "the significance of gesture and movement characteristic of primitive art." So too in Matisse, MacCarthy felt that a

search for an abstract harmony of line, for rhythm, has been carried to lengths which often deprive the figure of all appearance of nature. The general effect of his pictures is that of a return to primitive, even perhaps of a return to barbaric, art. . . . [The artist] begins to try to unload, to simplify the drawing and painting, by which natural objects are evoked, in order to recover the lost expressiveness and life. . . . The works of the Post-Impressionists are hardly known in England, although so much discussed upon the Continent. The exhibition organised by Mr. Robert Dell at Brighton last year has been our only chance of seeing them. The promoters of this exhibition have therefore thought it would be interesting to provide an opportunity for a greater number to judge these artists. The ladies and gentlemen on the Honorary Committee, though they are not responsible for the choice of the pictures, by lending their names have been kind enough to give this project their general support.[23]

MacCarthy wrote what might be thought of as a supplement to his preface in a letter to the *Spectator* on November 26 which was based on his experience of those who came in the first few weeks and to answer the charges of "artistic imposture." It was also a reply to the brief hostile review there two weeks earlier. The review began: "In spite of the special pleading of the preface to the catalogue of this strange collection, it seems unjust to make Manet in any way responsible for the excesses of what are now called the Post-Impressionists." The writer did get part of the point, but rejected its virtue. "Post-Impressionism apparently consists in forgetting all past art, and attempting to see the world as it appears to a child when it first begins to draw." The political point was also made, with a smug contrast to the French. "There is really nothing exceptional about these latest examples of French art, granted that a revolution is in progress, for in France a reform movement always has its section who are for barricades, the guillotine, and the Anarchist's bomb." The author did recognize that time might prove him wrong. He concluded: "But while the High Court of time is trying the issue we may refuse to be intimidated into admiration by critics on the look-out for a new sensation."[24]

MacCarthy mentioned that "the epithet 'barbarous' often resounds through the Grafton Galleries," but he chose to see it as a term of praise, particularly of Gauguin, whom the *Spectator* treated rather favorably, not uncommon in reviews that were otherwise hostile. MacCarthy pointed out that these pictures were meant to convey a new message, a sense of the "human burden." Speaking particularly of Van Gogh's *La Berceuse,* he wrote: "it would be a great disaster if artists only painted pictures suitable for the homes of those who can buy their pictures at high prices; not because such pictures cannot be of the finest beauty, but because such a restriction bars out so much beauty of another kind that might find expression in art."[25]

Molly MacCarthy wasn't all that enamored of the exhibition, writing to her mother-in-law about the pictures: "they are thought monstrous by the average public. I belong to that, and they don't give me much pleasure, it must be confessed, but I don't feel I know enough about them yet, but when Roger Fry shows one a statuette like this [squiggle in manuscript] and says it's *wonderful*, I can only see it in the light of the comic spirit."[26]

Looking back at the exhibition in 1945, MacCarthy emphasized the controversial part. "The Press notices were certainly calculated to rouse curiosity. And from the opening day the public flocked, and the big rooms echoed with explosions of laughter and indignation. . . . The people who annoyed me most were, I think, cultivated women who went deliberately into trills of silvery laughter in front of pictures."[27] Occasionally, a viewer would storm into MacCarthy's office and demand that the exhibition be closed. He would reply that he couldn't do that, but he would offer the objector the option of writing down views for posting, an offer that generally calmed down the individual. But, to a degree, the public mood appeared to turn around quite quickly. The controversy brought in lots of viewers, and there were sales.

Fry had not written the introduction of the catalogue, but he did write pieces about the exhibition on November 19, December 3, and December 24 in the *Nation*. On November 19 he began diffidently: "Having been asked to advise on the choice of the pictures and their arrangement in the present exhibition, my remarks on it must be taken as explanatory—in the nature of an apologia—than as the expression of entirely independent criticism." He took the position that the artists were

in reality the most traditional of any recent group of artists. That they are in revolt against the photographic vision of the nineteenth century, and even against the tempered realism of the last four hundred years, I freely admit. . . . These artists have, as it were, stumbled upon the principles of primitive design out of a perception of the sheer necessities of the actual situation. . . . Why should he [the artist] wilfully return to primitive or, as it is derisively called, barbaric art? The answer is that it is neither wilful nor wanton but simply necessary, if art is to be rescued from the hopeless encumbrance of its own accumulations of science; if art is to retain its power to express emotional ideas, and not to become an appeal to curiosity and wonder at the artist's perilous skill. . . . More and more regardlessly they [the artists in the exhibition] are cutting away the merely representative element in art to establish more and more firmly the fundamental laws of expressive form in its barest, most abstract elements. Like the Anarchists, with whom they are compared, they are not destructive and negative, but intensely constructive.

Fry felt that these painters undermined the English belief in work as a creator of value. "If by some miracle beauty could be generated without effort, the whole world would be the richer."

In his second article, Fry went into more detail about Cézanne. "His portrait of his wife has, to my mind, the great monumental quality of early art, of Piero della Francesca or Mantegna. It has that self-contained inner life, that resistance and assurance that belong to a real image, not to a mere reflection of some more insistent reality." About Van Gogh he remarked: "Those who have laughed at this great visionary because he became insane, can know but little of the awful adventures of the imagination. . . . To Van Gogh's tortured and morbid sensibility there came revelations fierce, terrible, and yet at times consoling, of realities behind the veil of things seen."[28]

Fry also gave a lecture about the exhibition, as did others, such as Sickert. Fry was an extremely effective lecturer: at about this time Sickert did a splendid drawing of him posed with a pointer with the rather enigmatic title "Vision, Volumes and Recession." Sickert remained close to Fry, but they were nevertheless aesthetic opponents. Henry Tonks, another painter critic of the exhibition, later did a much more critical drawing of Fry lecturing, exhibited in 1923, which had Clive Bell in an acolyte position incanting the new creed, "Cézannah, Cézannah."[29] As Virginia Woolf mentions in her biography of Fry, Tonks remained obsessed with Fry and what he regarded as his malign power over art criticism, remarking rather excessively, even ludicrously, at the time of Fry's death in 1934 that it was "as if a Mussolini, a Hitler, or a Stalin had passed away."[30]

VISION VOLUMES AND RECESSION

Roger Fry by W. R. Sickert, etching version.

Fry delivered a talk in the last week of the exhibition, on January 9, 1911, that was published in the *Fortnightly Review* in May 1911.[31] In the archives of the Tate there is preserved a hostile account of this lecture, yet in terms of content consistent with the published account. It begins with a description of the lecturer, informing us that the lecture was given at the Dilettante Society, which had space in the rooms above the Gallery.

In a way, Fry was in rebellion against the cultivated amateurism that the Dilettante Society represented. As Woolf mentions in her biography, it was the disdain—indeed more than disdain but rather fury—of the cultivated classes that particularly distressed him. As she points out, it was this very class that had been so fond of Fry when he was giving lectures on the Old Masters. He became aware of the aspects of social veneer of cultivation, the class aspects of taste, and the possibility that this new art might be more "democratic" in its appeal.

She cites the perhaps most notorious example of this, the anger of Wilfred Blunt, the Tory unconventional radical and sexual libertine who one would imagine might be sympathetic to the exhibition. But it was also a matter of generations: Blunt was now seventy, and the exhibition was an affront to his status as an English gentleman, as was particularly evident in his remark about Fry and MacCarthy being, he believed, paid for their work. He was still on the radical side in politics, an anti-imperialist and in favor of Home Rule in Ireland. His diary contains both political commentary and his reaction to visiting the Grafton Galleries on November 15. He considered but rejected the possibility that the exhibition might have been parallel to the *Dreadnought* hoax:

To the Grafton Gallery to look at what are called the "post-impressionist" pictures sent over from Paris. The exhibition is either an extremely bad joke or a swindle. I am inclined to think the latter, for there is no trace of humour in the thing. Still less is there a trace of sense or skill or taste good or bad or art or cleverness—nothing but that sort of gross imbecility which scrawls indecencies on the walls of a privy. The drawing is on the level of that of an untaught child of 7 or 8 years old, the sense of colour that of a tea-board painter, the method that of a schoolboy who wipes his fingers on a slate after spitting on them. . . . In all the 300 to 400 [*sic*] pictures there was not one worthy of attracting the smallest attention even by its singularity or of rousing any feeling but disgust—I am wrong—there was one picture signed "Gauguin" which at a distance had a pleasing effect of colour. . . . Apart from the frames, some of which are good old ones, the whole collection should not be worth £5 and then only for the pleasure it wd. give to make a bonfire of them. Yet two or three of our critics of taste have pronounced in their favour. Roger Fry has written [*sic*] an introduction for the catalogue & Desmond MacCarthy acts as secretary (both doubtless paid). . . . These are not works of art in any sense. They are merely works of impotent stupidity. I met Gay [?] & her daughter Phyllis there, half ashamed to be seen in such a pornographic show.[32]

But Fry's lecture was not trying to cope with this extreme view. The note-taker reported:

Fry is a slim, clean-shaven man, wearing his hair long, a curl at the end and parted in the middle. . . . He is a good lecturer, conversational and easy in style without being impertinent or familiar. Amusing and not aggressive but holding his ground well against an adversary. I thought his lecture one of the most psychologically subtle I had ever listened to, worthy of a Jesuit, but quite sophistical, too clever by half, unconvincing for that reason and, in retrospect, leaving a residuum of complete scepticism as to the validity of his main assumptions.[33]

Fry's lecture was addressed to the doubters, not to those who were enthusiastic about the pictures or those who thought the exhibition was a farce. He had a conspiratorial theory about the opposition to the show which does appear rather exaggerated, that it had been "organised by a few speculative dealers." Presumably they were those who saw that the market for pictures that catered to "sentimental longings" would be undone. Fry was right in that the market for contemporary realist and rather sentimental works, particularly its upper end, was ultimately undermined by the artists whom he exhibited. He stated quite succinctly and powerfully what was the intent of the pictures:

"It is to discover the visual language of the imagination. To discover, that is, what arrangement of form and colour are calculated to stir the imagination most deeply through the stimulus given to the sense of sight."

Fry compares art to music, while recognizing that the relation of art to nature gives its viewers preconceived notions of what a picture should look like. Listeners to music are far less likely to have such expectations. No artist exactly reproduces whatever may have stimulated the work. But how far can the work be from the stimulus for the viewer still to be willing to accept it? In effect, what was coming late to England was an undermining of the popular bourgeois idea of realism. Fry was arguing the modernist dictum:

> Those feelings which belong to the deepest and most universal parts of our nature are likely to be actually disturbed and put off by anything like literal exactitude to actual appearance. . . . These artists, however unconsciously they may work, are gaining for future imaginations, the right to speak directly to the imagination through images created, not because of their likeness to external nature, but because of their fitness to appeal to the imaginative and contemplative life.

In his talk, Fry illustrates his point by claiming greater "reality" for the bowl of fruit in a painting by Cézanne than that on the bar in the Folies Bergère painting by Manet, greater "reality" for Cézanne's portrait of his wife than for the bar girl. "The world of the imagination is essentially more real than the actual world, because it has a coherence and unity which the actual world lacks." In his conclusion, Fry made a sweeping and retrospectively a comparatively just claim for the importance of Cézanne's role: that he

> has recovered for modern art a whole lost language of form and colour. . . . It is one of many expressions of a great change in our attitude to life. We have passed in our generation through what looks like the crest of a long progression in human thought. . . . It seems to me, therefore, impossible to exaggerate the importance of this move-

ment in art, which is destined to make the sculptor's and painter's endeavour once more coterminous with the whole range of human inspiration and desire.

Fry mentioned Sickert, making it clear that he did not rule out debate, as Sickert had given a talk in the gallery just before his. The division between Sickert and Fry emphasizes the "split" quality of the event, as Sickert was one of the most "advanced" painters in England, a disciple of Degas's, and an importer of the influence of French painters. Sickert felt that Fry deliberately wanted to cause a "rumpus" and get attention by including a "nonsense element" in the exhibition. He also felt it was a bit of a ramp by French dealers in order to sell their wares. "Monsieur Matisse obligingly parades before the Grafton Street booth with a string of property sausages trailing from the pocket of his baggy trousers. John Bull and his lady, who love a joke, walk up, and learn a few things, some of which have been known in Europe for a decade, and some for a quarter of a century." Sickert admired Manet, Cézanne (although he believed he was overrated), Van Gogh, and Gauguin, about whom he was particularly enthusiastic, urging that some of his pictures be acquired for the nation. But he attacked in his talk the two who became the giants of French painting in the twentieth century, Matisse and Picasso.[34]

––––––––––

Having ventured into some of the reactions to the exhibition, let us now return to early November and the actual opening. The exhibition, presumably deliberately, had its press view on Guy Fawkes day, Saturday, November 5, 1910, a day traditionally associated with fireworks and explosions. The popular press responded appropriately. Did it help the sense of excitement at the moment that the political crisis was also building up? The suffragettes were turning to more confrontational activities. The very next week, when the exhibition officially opened, Asquith would request a dissolution of Parliament and rather than going forward on the Budget would go to the country on the question of the Lords' veto. The attempt to resolve the situation through the compromise of all party conferences had failed. The system was not working and the Liberal government felt driven to the extreme step of a second election in the same year.

Some of the art critics had a sense of a parallel with the political situation, that the system was being challenged. The anonymous critic in the *Daily Express* wrote on November 9: "There are more shocks to the square yard at the exhibition of the Post-Impressionists of France . . . than at any previous picture show in England. It is paint run mad."[35] Fry wanted to make a mark, at the same time that he continued his ordinary life: the evening of the 5th he went to Haslemere to hear a concert by Aranyi, having heard Casals there two weeks before. The next day, November 6, he went to Cambridge to be with Lady Ottoline on her visit to Goldsworthy Lowes Dickinson. Walter Lamb met her there and commented on the visit in a rather bitchy, complacent, and self-approving way to Clive Bell:

> I heard something of your Parisian speculations from Lady Ottoline and Roger Fry in Dickinson's rooms last Saturday. The lady, whom I met for the first time, impressed me greatly with her architectural grace. . . . Lytton has been staying nearly a week with me: he seemed to be unnaturally healthy, acquiescent, and interested in the young ladies of Newnham. . . . [Grant was] simulating some faint glow of affection for Keynes. . . . Forster, whose new novel everybody thinks so good, and I find myself utterly unable to read, has been whispering impotent nonsense about the flaccidity of civilisation. . . . Bertie [Russell] is very friendly and charming, and I find him not quite such an automobile of intellect as I used to fear.[36]

One phase of Fry's life came to an end on the next day, Monday, November 7, the day of the private view, when he took his wife to York to enter an asylum, the Retreat, where she would spend the rest of her life.[37] He had expressed his intense despair a few weeks before, in a letter to Dickinson on October 15. "I think I could get used to the dullness and greyness of life without love if it weren't for the constant sense of her suffering. This thing seems as diabolically contrived as anything could be. If she could only die—but this is not nothing new—only the trouble has been very acute of late."[38]

There was a counterpoint of public life and personal tragedy. Perhaps his rather frenetic activity was one way of coping with the situation. He wrote to his mother on Christmas day about Helen: "It is wonderful how much goodness & sympathy a tragedy like this brings out though nothing can alter the terrible reality. It hardly bears thinking about. I have to try not to [think] too much or the pain of pity for her constant suffering wld. be too much. . . . I suppose we learn more from suffering than happiness."[39] In 1913 he commented to his mother about his domestic tragedy: "It has made me feel no kind of ambition: any kind of success seems such a tiny thing compared with what I have lost; and with that a kind of recklessness perhaps which has enabled me to say what I really think about art without considering the consequences. All the same, I think if Helen had been well she would have encouraged me to take the line I have and would have faced the risk with me."[40] At the same time as he was coping with his wife, he was deeply involved in the exhibition, giving lectures about it, and defending it in the press. On November 8 "Manet and the Post-Impressionists" officially opened, for a rather long period for a gallery show, until January 15, 1911.

What was Fry like at this time? As we've seen, it was in 1910 that he became closely involved with the Stephen sisters, and the next year he would be Vanessa's lover. With Clive earlier, and Duncan later, Roger was one of the three great loves of her life. Their love started when he went with the Bells to Turkey the following April. Virginia traveled out to help bring Vanessa, who was seriously ill, home, and she too came closer to Roger in their shared concern with a possible repeat of the tragedy of Thoby's death. In her biography, Virginia begins the chapter on the Post-Impressionists with a description: "To a stranger meeting him then for the first time (1910) he looked much older than his age. He was only forty-four, but he gave the impression of a man with a great weight of experience behind him. He looked worn and seasoned, ascetic yet tough."[41] The Post-Impressionist pictures were primarily a platform for a new creation of reality. Looking back in her biography of Fry, she wrote of him at this point: "Under his influence, his pressure, his excitement, pictures, hats, cotton goods, all were connected. Everyone argued. Anyone's sensation—his cook's, his housemaid's—was worth having. Learning did not matter; it was the reality that was all-important."[42]

The exhibition was a great success, or at the very least a *succès de scandale*. There were approximately 25,000 visitors.[43] The *Daily Graphic* reported on the last day of the exhibition that the gallery was thronged with attentive viewers, unlike the first few weeks when individuals would stand in front of the paintings and laugh.[44] In retrospect, the received opinion of the exhibition was that it was hated, and that the gallery-going English public demonstrated itself to be philistine. This was an oversimplification: the reviews were mixed, some were favorable. Indeed, much of informed opinion appeared to change quite rapidly. By the time of the second Post-Impressionist Exhibition of 1912 the tide had turned to a noticeable degree, and the modernism of the paintings was already much more acceptable.

The 1910 exhibition has acquired a legendary reputation of which the alleged distress and contempt it stirred up are part. But the legend is centrally correct that the exhibition was the definitive introduction of modern difficult art into the English-speaking world. It was also an important forerunner for other forms of modernism, particularly by Woolf, Strachey, Keynes, Bell, and Grant. At the end of November Fry commented to his mother about the reaction. "It is odd that people should think that because they don't like a thing it was done specially to insult them but that seems to be the usual reaction on such occasions. There has been nothing like this outbreak of militant Philistinism since Whistler's day. Anyhow it is good for people to have their lives stirred and the show is a huge success never less than 400 a day."[45]

MacCarthy knew the reviews would make the exhibition a great sensation. At the press view, he remembered: "As I walked about among the tittering newspaper critics busily taking notes (they saw at once that the whole thing was splendid copy) I kept overhearing such remarks as

'Pure pornography,' 'Admirably indecent.' Not a word of truth, of course, in this. As M. le Publique I had been careful to exclude too frankly physiological nudes and, indeed at the last moment, instead of hanging two of the pictures, I told Roger they had better be kept, for a time, in my sanctum downstairs."[46]

The exhibition—when it was absorbed, when the exposure to these pictures had been assimilated—was a major reason that Woolf should decide that human character had "changed" and the English would allow themselves to be "modern." The experiences of the members of Bloomsbury were part of the questioning of the certainties of English society that year; they were a challenge to the pieties held by those critics, even the intelligent among them, who were unable to grasp the new.

Though in the first weeks much of the criticism was negative, there was no question that the exhibition was newsworthy from the start. In November there were more than fifty reactions in the press, including not only the reviews but cartoons, and by December the tide had begun to turn and the writings about the paintings were more favorable.

Was it a different world? There was a parody exhibition in December at the Chelsea Arts Club, called "Septule and the Racinistes," that even deceived some critics. Though the paintings were meant to be parodies of Picasso, Cézanne, and Gauguin, apparently they came out more like Tonks and John.[47] But the word *racine* made the modernist point that the aim was to get at the roots of reality rather than the superficial appearance of nature presented in traditional pictures. There was even a costume ball in mid-December given by the Slade students in association with this exhibition, attended by Fry, the Bells, Virginia, and Adrian, as well as James Strachey. They came as native figures from a Gauguin, wearing just a bit of African cloth manufactured in Manchester, and with their bodies painted brown. Once again, as in the *Dreadnought* hoax, they were identifying with those whom the West had dominated. Fry himself attended on Lady Ottoline's urging but without her coming as well. He wrote to her that it was "rather amusing, but I won't tell you about that now." In the same letter he mentioned plans for the next Grafton show. This would be the second Post-Impressionist Exhibition held at the end of 1912 and would include Russian painters as well as French and English. The letter indicates the refusal of the older generation to go along. "I attacked Steer & Tonks about it last night but found them too unsympathetic to make it worth while to try to get them in so it must be only les jeunes—can we manage with them?"[48]

Stella Tillyard, in a reassessment of the exhibition, wishes to lessen Fry's claim to modernism in favor of Ezra Pound, Wyndham Lewis, and the Rebel Art Centre. At the same time she provides a counter-argument for the change of taste of which the introduction of Post-Impressionism in England was a part, the claim that liberals and radicals were looking for a new aesthetic.

> As Arts and Crafts declined, liberals and radicals were left without any suitable visual correlative to their aesthetic. The demand for simplicity and purity cut them off from both idealist and neo-classical academic art, while their dislike of scientific representation cut them off from Impressionist painting which was thought to be almost exclusively a translation of recent optical and colour theory onto canvas. . . . It was the promoters of Post-Impressionism who managed successfully to combine seriousness and largely non-urban subject matter, and to equate both with aesthetic and social radicalism.[49]

Tillyard makes the ingenious but to my mind ultimately unconvincing argument that the reason Fry's assessment was so rapidly accepted was not a sudden change in values. Rather, on or about December 1910, despite his ostensible distancing from the Arts and Crafts movement, Fry was using, according to Tillyard, the language of Arts and Crafts to make modernism acceptable; that the public interested in Arts and Crafts transferred its allegiance to Post-Impressionism, in effect domesticating, as the English so often do, the new and startling. It is true that Fry shared the Arts and Crafts interest in the importance of pattern and design and in the connection between art and life. As Nikolaus Pevsner argued in *Pioneers of Modern Design* (1936, revised 1960), in a view that some find too historically determined, the Arts and Crafts movement was a step on the road to modernism and shares with it a hope to return to essentials, although still expressed through pattern, to get away from the superficial busyness that characterized Victorian design. But all this takes us a long distance from what Fry actually said and wrote about the exhibition. One senses that in part Tillyard's argument derives from the perhaps legitimate irritation that is present at times in studies that touch on members of Bloomsbury—at their claim to primacy as modernists, combined with their style of self-assurance.

Tillyard also gives too much weight to numbers. There was, with the exhibition, a profound sense of break. Those influential, progressive English writers on art, Ross, MacColl, and Ricketts, and those teachers of the advanced young such as William Rothenstein and Henry Tonks at the Slade School, turned on the Post-Impressionists after having in the past championed the new and been, on the whole, very sympathetic to Roger Fry. Tonks even went so far, at the time of the second Post-Impressionist Exhibition two years later, to beg Slade students not to see the pictures, at least according to Paul Nash. "Tonks made one of his speeches and appealed, in so many words, to our sporting instincts. He could not, he pointed out, prevent our visiting the Grafton Galleries; he could only warn us and say how very much better pleased he would be if we did not risk contamination but stayed away."[50] Oliver Brown, the art dealer, remembers that on his way into the first exhibition he met a friend of his father's who said to him, "Don't go in, young man, it will do you harm. The pictures are evil."[51]

Tillyard provides an interesting calculation. Thirteen publications, including five conservative newspapers, came out against the exhibition. Fourteen publications were favorable; of the four newspapers in this group, three supported the Liberal party. Eleven publications were neutral.[52] Tillyard suggests that Virginia Woolf, in her essay and also in her biography of Fry, following his lead, may make the exhibition overly significant. Yet Sickert was also quite right in saying that the exhibition caused a "rumpus." Quite a few of these painters had been exhibited in England before, Cézanne as long ago as 1898 and again in 1906 and

1908. But it is not only hindsight that endows the exhibition with its great impact. The earlier exhibits in England did not have the same influence, and the reaction in 1910 can legitimately be read as conveying an awareness of a significant shift in values and forms of expression.

In looking at the reviewers, it may be best to begin with the voice of the *Times* itself, the paper that was regarded in England as the voice of record, the Thunderer. Although Fry officially kept a low profile, it was certainly known that he was the progenitor of the exhibition; after all, he was quite a recognized figure and up to this point a respectable one. At the same time the anonymous reviewer almost seems to suggest that Fry did not know what he was supporting:

> The catalogue with its cleverly-written Preface, [is] trying to prove that the pictures are not only art, but almost the only logical art, the only possible art, at the present day. Now Mr. Fry is a distinguished scholar and critic, who has made a name by his writing on Bellini and the older art—writing at once sane and learned. It is to be feared that when he lends his authority to an exhibition of this kind, and gives it to be understood that he regards the work of Gauguin and Matisse as the last word in art, the final expression of the genius of to-day, other writers of less sincerity will follow suit and try to persuade people that the Post-Impressionists are fine fellows, and that their art is the thing to be admired. They will even declare all who do not agree with them to be reactionaries of the worst type. . . . [This art] professes to simplify, and to gain simplicity it throws away all that the long-developed skill of past artists had acquired and bequeathed. It begins all over again—and stops where a child would stop. . . . Really primitive art is attractive because it is unconscious; but this [Gauguin] is deliberate—it is an abandonment of what Goethe called the "culture-conquests" of the past. Like anarchism in politics, it is the rejection of all that civilization has done, the good with the bad.

The review was written by C. J. Weld-Blundell, a "Catholic aristocrat and collector."[53] The political analogy to anarchism is specific, as indeed for some time English critics had been making the analogy between French art and anarchism.[54] There was a noticeable increase in the use of political language in the discussion of pictures, and it is hard to believe that this move away from traditional connoisseurship was not connected with the political atmosphere of the day. As political uncertainties were increasingly prevalent in the political sphere, such ideas made themselves felt in the artistic world. The tone of the *Times* review was English superciliousness at its worst, and does support the idea that English taste did need some sort of bomb (an anarchists' bomb?) set under it. The reviewer liked nothing exhibited; even the *Bar au Folies Bergère* he dismissed as an inferior Manet. In his concluding remark—and some of the other reviewers too protected themselves in this way—he made some allowance that he might be wrong: "Whether even so it is in any sense great art is a question that may be left to the decision of Time—*le seul classificateur impeccable.*"[55]

Considering the degree to which the *Times* was read by "everyone" who counted, the review probably had an effect in setting the tone of the reaction. It was perhaps unfortunate that another of the regular reviewers in the newspaper, Arthur Clutton-Brock, had not been assigned the review. In an article in the *Burlington* in January 1911, he was sympathetic to the Post-Impressionists and quite vividly captured the point of the transformation that Fry had in mind. He emphasized the move from representation to expressionism, the search for essence.

> If Cézanne, Gauguin, and Van Gogh were charlatans, they were like no other charlatans that ever lived. If their aim was notoriety, it is strange that they should have spent solitary lives of penury and toil. If they were incompetents, they were curiously intent upon the most difficult problems of their art. The kind of simplification which they attempted is not easy, nor, if accomplished, does it make a picture look better than it is. The better their pictures are, the more they look as if anyone could have painted them who had the luck to conceive them; in fact, they look just as easy as the lyrical poems of Wordsworth or Blake.

About Van Gogh, Clutton-Brock remarked: "He paints the essence and character of rain, as a poet might describe them, with all irrelevant facts eliminated." And of Gauguin: "He does not paint local colour for us, but life itself."[56]

The next major review in the daily press was by Robert Ross, a friend and colleague of Fry's. His negative approach now, however, was no surprise to Fry, for as early as mid-October they discussed the show, and Fry knew that Ross would attack it. At the time he wrote to Lady Ottoline: "I am certain at least that our show will wake people up more than anything that has happened for ages and that at least is something. Ross is already on the war path without any prompting of mine, but I tactfully accused him of purblind prejudice which has stirred him up to greater activity."[57]

The English attitude of ironic disdain was brought out by the situation. The defection of such figures as Ross suggests vividly the sort of seismic break that the exhibition represented. Ross published his review in the *Morning Post* on November 7, with the opening sentence: "A date more favourable than the Fifth of November for revealing the existence of a wide-spread plot to destroy the whole fabric of European painting could hardly have been chosen." Choosing the date of the Gunpowder plot gave an increased emphasis to politics; there was a pervasive tendency to use political language in many of the reviews.

Ross picked out Matisse, Denis, and Vlaminck for particular dislike but remarked about the entire show:

When the first shock of merriment has been experienced there must follow, too, a certain feeling of sadness that distinguished critics whose profound knowledge and connoisseurship are beyond question should be found to welcome pretension and imposture. It is only comparable to the no less deplorable credulity evinced by serious men of science in the chicanery of spiritualism, automatic writing, and the narratives of the neuropath. Public taste has been so often wrong. Its present idols become the paving stones or macadam of the morrow. The pariahs of one generation are prophets for its successor. With these lamentable precedents perhaps it is more regrettable than extraordinary that any charlatanism in art or literature may now enjoy the privilege of examination such as should be only accorded to serious new developments.

And it is an error to suppose that because posterity momentarily reverses a hostile contemporary opinion the original opinion was wrong. . . . The emotions of these painters (one of whom, Van Gogh, was a lunatic) are of no interest except to the student of pathology and the specialist in abnormality. At Broadmoor there are a large number of post-impressionists detained during his Majesty's pleasure. Their works are, however, already the property of the State. The National Art Collections Fund may sleep in peace.

Ross did not like the Cézannes, but he did praise a Maillol figure and Gauguin, "an artist with a fresh idea, a curious technique, and a fantastic visions. He, too, can draw and paint."

Ross reserves his greatest venom for Van Gogh. "Van Gogh is the typical . . . degenerate of the modern sociologists. *Jeune Fille au Bleuet* . . . and *Cornfield with Blackbirds* . . . are the visualised ravings of an adult maniac. If that is art it must be ostracised, as the poets were banished from Plato's republic. [Ross might have thought twice about that comparison.] . . . The only primitives he resembles are the wool-work trophies of our great-grandmothers, though there is less form, less art." He then moves on to attack Matisse:

To the negative silliness of covering canvas with pigment *La Femme aux yeux verts* . . . he has added the primitive and more pristine offence of "modelling." If Van Gogh belongs to the School of Bedlam, M. Matisse follows the Broadmoor tradition in a predilection for mere discords of pigment. . . . To discuss the "pavement art" of MM. Denis, Signac, Henri-Edmond Cross, and Georges Seurat and others would be waste of time, for anyone sufficiently idle and mindless could reproduce them. . . . The relation of M. Henri Matisse and his colleagues to painting is more remote than that of the Parisian Black Mass or the necromantic orgies of the Decadents to the religion of Catholics.

Ross goes so far as to approve the action of the German Emperor in dismissing Hugh von Tschudi from his museum post for buying Post-Impressionists. "I can now understand why the German Emperor dismissed a high official from a Berlin Gallery. And if the movement is spreading (another boast of the catalogue) it should be treated like a rat plague in Suffolk. The source of infection (e.g. the pictures) ought to be destroyed."[58]

Here was one of advanced taste and sympathetic to the new making easy jokes about the pictures. It is almost pathetic to read the defense Ross made of English art in a talk in which, according to his biographer, he denounced the Post-Impressionists, saying "None of them can draw as well as Augustus John, none of them can paint as well as Charles Shannon or Nicholson, none of them could teach as Professor Tonks teaches, because they are not nearly so proficient in the grammar of art."[59]

Laurence Binyon made a similar point in a negative notice in the *Saturday Review*. He felt that much of the exhibition was "childish rubbish." He had some kind words to say about Van Gogh, Gauguin, Denis, Flandrin, and Picasso, but concluded that "none of these paintings could hold a candle to the 'Smiling Woman' of Augustus John which the Contemporary Art Society has, I am delighted to see, acquired for the nation."[60]

Presumably because of Ross's interest, the *Morning Post* devoted a lot of space to letters about the exhibition. These were not from the outraged general public but rather from members of the cultural establishment. As is so frequently the case, those who were in the avantgarde in the previous generation are perhaps even more likely to attack the next wave of the new. Sir Philip Burne-Jones, flying his late father's flag, wrote indignantly to both the *Times* and the *Morning Post*. Many who came to the fore in the 1890s as proponents of more advanced art, and in European terms, as supporters of Impressionism, turned on this newest development.

One of the letter writers, Charles Ricketts, was a prominent figure of the period, a founder of the Vale Press in 1896, active as a designer, particularly for the theater, and eminent as an art critic. Years before, Fry had been a regular visitor to his and Charles Shannon's evenings at their house in London, although it would probably go too far to claim, as William Gaunt does, that Fry had been a disciple of Ricketts.[61] But Ricketts was an ultimate connoisseur, and in its way Post-Impressionism was an assault on tradition, an attempt to "make it new," a change in character. As Fry would later write, when Post-Impressionism became better known in England, it placed the connoisseur on the same level as his servant—not that, presumably, many servants entered the Grafton Gallery.

Ricketts came into the fray with a long letter of November 9 to the *Morning Post*. His position was to regard the Post-Impressionists as a "reactionary movement." The tone taken is a rather grand one of airy dismissal.

> Cézanne was not properly an impressionist, though he borrowed impressionist pictures to copy. He remained for a while only a compromising provincial satellite of the school, till he retired to the country, where he would leave his paintings in the fields, not deeming them worthy to take home, thereby proving that, if a poor painter, he was an astute critic. . . . Mr. Ross is again wrong in suggesting the "Grafton decorations" should be burnt; they might interest the doctors of the body and the students of the sickness of the soul. Let us rather be angry not with the post-impressionist painters—they are doing, perhaps, their best—but with the curious sophistries that preface the catalogue. This, like other wastepaper, might be burnt.[62]

Ricketts later in 1911 expanded his views for an article for the *Nineteenth Century*, but it was not published until 1913. Again, it was the novelty, the lack of tradition which he particularly disliked. "Art is to become young again, but the slate must be cleaned for a new message to appear in the form of a subconscious ecstasy, from which our past and present must be erased, so that we may attain to the synthetic outlook of childhood, in which lies the only possibility of the future. . . . Novelty in itself is valueless. The spirit of beauty and power, of which art is the expression, has centuries behind it; it is as old as thought." (Perhaps it was particularly appropriate that one of Ricketts's most famous works was his illustrations in 1894 for Oscar Wilde's *Sphinx*.) As usual, the political analogy was ready to hand. "To revert in the name of 'novelty' to the aims of the savage and the child—out of lassitude of the present—is to act as the anarchist, who would destroy where he cannot change."[63]

On November 16 Sir William Richmond, a prominent artist and member of the Royal Academy, wrote a letter to the *Morning Post* of total rage, almost a parody of the Colonel Blimp approach, combined with the language of sexual contamination. For instance:

> For a moment there came a fierce feeling of terror that lest the youth of England, young promising fellows, might be contaminated here. On reflection I was reassured that the youth of England, being healthy, mind and body, is far too virile to be moved save in resentment against the providers of this unmanly show. They will not growl at the perpetration of these atrocities, but pity them; but they are, and justly, indignant at the unwisdom of the sorry show. . . . This invasion of depressing rubbish is, thank Heaven, new to our island of sensible and, in their own fashion, poetic people.[64]

Philip Burne-Jones wrote on November 17 about "the cult of ugliness and the anarchy and degradation of art exemplified today by the 'Post-Impressionists.'" He cited the notorious sentence about a rocking-horse, asking, "What has a rocking-horse or an instantaneous photograph got to do with art? . . . One is tempted to suspect that it is a huge practical joke organised in Paris at the expense of our countrymen." In the same issue there was a letter taking issue with Richmond, defending the pictures, by C. Lewis Hind, the art critic who would publish a short book about the Post-Impressionists the following year.[65] The next day Burne-Jones wrote to defend Richmond against Hind. "In the House of Art there are many mansions, in which there is ample room for all, however diverse in aim and achievement, who humbly and faithfully obey her laws. . . . But certain standards must be generally acknowledged—certain rules adhered to if the temple is to be safeguarded from the invasion of the savage and the frankly incompetent."

In the same issue, R. B. Cunninghame Graham, the traveler, socialist, and Scottish nationalist, defended the pictures, comparing the dispute with that between Whistler and Ruskin; Martin Hardie, an artist and official at the Victoria and Albert Museum, denounced the exhibition; and Walter Crane, artist and socialist, wrote a mild letter in which he attempted to take a middle position, seeing the pictures as an unfortunate but perhaps necessary stage. "It may be, indeed, that the Art of portable picture painting has reached its last stage, and must *decompose* before springing into really fresh and healthy life with the growth of new social ideals and a new social order."[66]

Ebenezer Wake Cook, a watercolorist, wrote a letter on November 19 against the exhibition, pointing out that as early as 1904 in his *Anarchism in Art* he had indicated the downhill direction that art was taking, and that this was a culmination of decadence.[67] On November 22 Arthur Severn, Ruskin's friend and disciple, attacked the exhibition; and E. F. Benson, the novelist, wrote a long letter to reprimand Sir William Richmond for his intemperance, and expressed the feeling that it was unwise for artists to criticize other artists, but admitted he had not yet seen the exhibition. On November 26 the art critic Tancred Borenius wrote a strong letter in favor of the exhibition: "It seems to me that the works of the best of them, from Cézanne down to Matisse, evince a most astounding sense of form and power of construction; that they achieve, each in their own way, a pure sensuous beauty of colour, and that their attitude of mind is profoundly poetical."[68]

On November 30, in the *Post,* Jacques-Emile Blanche, with whom Duncan Grant had studied in Paris in 1906, wrote a long but comparatively gentle attack, pointing out that there was no such group as Post-Impressionists in France, that the paintings by Manet (whose biographer he was) were weak examples, and being rather dismissive of the other artists. He does make an interesting comparison between Fry and William Morris, with Fry's emphasis on the importance of pattern: "Pattern, pattern! . . . This word brings us back to the time of William Morris, with associations of wall-papers, artistic materials, chintz."[69] The cumulative impact of Blanche's letter was of a gentle, not notably cogent, denigration.

ATTRACTORS OF ALL SOCIETY: WORKS BY POST-IMPRESSIONISTS.

THE MANET AND THE POST-IMPRESSIONISTS EXHIBITION, AT THE GRAFTON GALLERIES.

Illustrated London News, November 26, 1910.

POST-IMPRESSIONIST EXPRESSIONS—SKETCHES BY FRANK REYNOLDS.

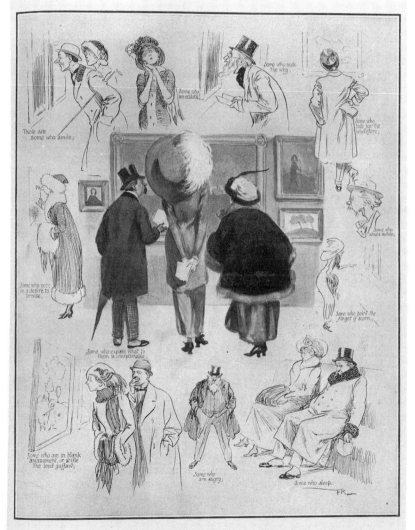

GAZERS AT PAINTINGS FEW APPRECIATE AND FEWER UNDERSTAND: STUDIES AT THE GRAFTON GALLERIES.

The Exhibition of pictures by Manet and the Post-Impressionists, as we noted in our issue of last week under a number of reproductions of examples, is attracting all London to the Grafton Galleries. Without unfairness, it may be said that the success of the show is in large measure a success of curiosity. To the few who appreciate and understand the work there are many who do neither, who go merely to gaze and scoff, and to feel that they have been in the new movement, if not of it.

Illustrated London News, December 3, 1910.

Views were divided in the "quality" Sundays. Frank Rutter wrote a favorable review in the November 13 *Sunday Times;* in the *Observer,* P. G. Konody was negative, asserting that the exhibition "is sending the great majority of London art-lovers into fits of laughter, whilst finding enthusiastic defenders among a small circle of indiscriminating intellectual snobs." Yet he saw distinctive qualities in some of the paintings by Cézanne, Van Gogh, and Gauguin, and in a sense he kept his options open. He did not feel that English collectors would follow the German lead in purchasing French paintings, though "they may even contain a hint of the direction the normal evolution of art may take in the near future. . . . The majority of the pictures at the Grafton Galleries are not things to live with. Germany is welcome to them." He concluded, inaccurately, that "the present exhibition will have to depend more on gate-money than on sales."[70]

The illustrated weeklies also paid attention. In its issue on the press day, November 5, the *Sphere,* under the headline "The Latest Revolt in Art," reproduced three Gauguins, two Van Goghs, and one Cézanne. In the *Illustrated London News* of November 26, there were two pages of illustrations, with neutral comments, of four Van Goghs, two Gauguins, two Manets, two Denises, a Cross, a Vlaminck, and the Matisse of the *Woman with Green Eyes.* The following week, December 3, there was another full page, this time of drawings of viewers by Frank Reynolds, entitled "Post-Impressionist Expressions," giving their varying reactions: "There are some who smile; Some who are ecstatic; Some who see the why, Some who look for the wherefore; Some who peer, in a desire to praise; Some who explain what to them is unexplainable; Some who would imitate; Some who point the finger of scorn; Some who are in blank amazement or stifle the loud guffaw; Some who are angry; Some who sleep."[71] The November 23 issue of the society weekly the *Tatler* devoted two pages to the exhibition, using a philistine and jokey tone, and even devoted one page to a painting by Herbin, printing it twice sideways, and suggesting that it also be turned upside down, making it look like "The 'Daily Mail' Garage at Wormwood Scrubs."[72]

Some of the critics saw the point Fry was making, but rejected it vehemently. In the December issue of the *Connoisseur,* its anonymous critic, although he had some praise, uncharacteristically, for Van Gogh and Picasso, wrote that the paintings were

> work of the extremists . . . [whose] aim [was] . . . not to reproduce the appearance of things, but to express the emotional significance under-lying them. To do this they have discarded the accepted tenets of art as resulting in work too subtle and complicated to arouse the emo-tions, and have gone back to the most simple and primitive forms of expression, those of children and savage races. The result is the nega-tion of art. . . . The exhibition forms a monument of misplaced labour, and fills the spectator with a feeling of regret that men of talent, inspired by high if mistaken ideals, should waste their lives in spoiling acres of good canvas when they would have been better employed even in stone-breaking for the roads.[73]

Fry commented to his father about all the fuss: "I have been the centre of a wild hurricane of newspaper abuse from all quarters over this show of modern French art. I fear you would not like the pictures but I believe them to be serious efforts at a more cohesive art than we have had for several centuries."[74]

In retrospect, it is quite ironic that Arnold Bennett, under the name "Jacob Tonson" in the *New Age,* should have written a very favorable notice. Even earlier, in the December 10 issue of the *Nation,* he had written a letter, appropriately from Paris, in reply to an attack from Robert Morley, in which he came to the defense of Fry. Morley had remarked: "It is impossible to take them seriously. Any child of tender years could spot a canvas over with red, blue, yellow, and black—depict flowers of a shape and hue unknown to Nature, or draw and color figures which one might guess to be intended to represent human beings; but to exhibit such productions seriously! What do these can-vases really show? They reflect the debasement of the lives of the painters living in the Gay City."[75] It is significant, however, that Ben-nett does not support these painters because they are new, or prophets of a new approach, but rather because by not doing so, England is indicating its provinciality, the quality Bennett had come to London (and Paris) to lose. He was in some ways at the forefront of advanced opinion, being one of the first to champion the great Russians such as Dostoevsky and Chekhov. (Tolstoy's reputation was already established, and much attention was paid in England to his death at this very time.)

Morley had said that the paintings could not be taken seriously. Bennett replied:

> Hundreds of the most cultivated minds in Europe take them seriously. Mr. Morley may be referred to your distinguished contributor Mr. Roger Fry. One also thinks at once of Mr. Bernard Berenson. Mr. Berenson has been nourished on the great masters, and his position as the greatest living art-critic is not often seriously challenged. Yet Mr. Berenson takes these pictures seriously. . . . Mr. Morley may argue that all art critics are insane, and that only the plain profane man can be trusted. But numbers of plain profane men take these pictures seriously. I do, for instance.[76]

Bennett was intensely francophile, spent much time in Paris, and was well aware of the paintings of Cézanne and Gauguin. In his more formal review in the *New Age*, he wrote about the reaction to the exhibition:

> The attitude of the culture of London towards it is of course merely humiliating to any Englishman who has made an effort to cure himself of insularity. It is one more proof that the negligent disdain of Continental artists for English artistic opinion is fairly well founded. The mild tragedy of the thing is that London is infinitely too self-complacent even to suspect that it is London and not the exhibition which is making itself ridiculous. . . . In twenty years London will be signing an apology for its guffaw. It will be writing itself down an ass. The writing will consist of large cheques payable for Neo-Impressionist pictures to Messrs. Christie, Manson and Woods.[77]

Bennett went on to recount his own conversion to Cézanne ten years before. Despite his approval of the pictures, his reasons and indeed his very style, that chatty tone, indicate his differences from the Georgians.

Despite his championing of the pictures, he was on the side of realism and entertainment.

Paradoxical, in light of Woolf's essay, as it might be to have Bennett on the side of the Post-Impressionists, it also reinforces the point that the break at the time, though significant, was not necessarily neat. Bennett wrote his piece for the *New Age,* a progressive periodical under the editorship of A. R. Orage, which was quite specific about the idea of a new age dawning in 1910, when "the smug, failed certainties of the bourgeois nineteenth century" were being demolished.[78] The *New Age* saw Post-Impressionism, the funeral of the monarch, Bergson (who lectured in England in 1911), psychoanalysis, and the interest in Russian literature, as all being indications of basic changes in how the world was viewed. In fact, in April one of its critics, Victor Reynolds, had commented on an exhibition of the "Independents" in Paris that future art would "return to primitive sources of inspiration." The regular reviewer, George Calderon, wrote on December 24: "All through the galleries I am pursued by the ceaseless hee-haw of a stage duke in an eye glass." He noted that after seeing the exhibition one noted "how flat, stale and unprofitable have become all those engravings, pictures and statues in the dealers' windows." Katherine Mansfield herself, in the *New Age* circle, felt that she was liberated by seeing two of the Van Gogh paintings.[79]

Even according to the popular press, there was quite a dramatic change in attitude between the opening of the exhibition and its closing. A reporter in the *Daily Graphic* wrote in the issue of January 16, 1911, about the closing:

> The galleries were thronged. Never has there been such a crowd since the Whistler Exhibitions at the New Gallery, and the fact seems to show that public taste in pictures is advancing faster than the critics.... During the first week or two of the exhibition a considerable proportion of the spectators used to shout with laughter in front of Van Gogh's *Girl with the Cornflower,* or Gauguin's *Tahitians....* But on Saturday the general attitude was one of admiration and of regret that an exhibition which has furnished so much food for discussion must close.[80]

It has not been my intention here to explore every comment on the exhibition but primarily just those that, in my opinion, provide interesting evidence of the shift in sensibility that took place that year. The exhibition served as a vehicle, one might almost say a battering ram, for the more advanced European ideas to begin to transform the English scene.

———

Virtually simultaneous with the Post-Impressionists at the Grafton was an exhibition of recent work by Augustus John. Initially the show made a great impression, and for a brief moment it seemed as if he would carry all before him. There was a rather condescending review in the *Times* which nevertheless recognized John's success: "Is there really a widespread demand for these queer, clever, forcible, but ugly and uncanny notes of form and dashes of colour? . . . Chelsea likes it; Chelsea says that 'Mr. John has done what the Post-Impressionists have only been trying in vain to do.'"[81] Until then, John had appeared to be the new progressive force; but the French giants quite rapidly reduced him to a provincial figure, of some interest, but increasingly outside the mainstream. It was as if John, who had been recognized as the "latest word," was suddenly becoming outdated.

Michael Sadler illustrates the point. He would become one of the earliest collectors of modern art in Britain, buying four Gauguins in 1911. But now he was still loyal to John. He wrote in a letter to the *Nation* on December 3, 1910: "The main idea of this new school is to return to the primitive, to get behind the mass of conventional symbol and facile representation that has grown up since the Renaissance . . . [to] express the great truths of art in the simplest and most direct way possible. . . . What they have tried to do is already being done by Augustus John. . . . He is a development, whereas Post-Impressionism is an open breach."[82] Sadler did not mean this as praise of the Post-Impressionists.

Fry in fact liked John's work, although Clive Bell didn't. Fry wrote to Lady Ottoline about John's exhibition: "John's things are extravagantly beautiful & nearly all sold at huge prices." But at the same time, he does not suggest to her that they go to the Chenil Gallery, but rather, "Do tell me when you are coming to town we must go together to the Grafton & really see it."[83] Fry wrote about John in the *Nation* on December 24: "In criticising the very first exhibition which he held in London I said that he had undeniable genius, and I have never wavered in that belief, but I do recognise that Mr. John, working to some extent in isolation, without all the fortunate elements of comradeship and rivalry that exist in Paris, has not as yet pushed his mode of expression to the same logical completeness."[84]

A new force in European art, with Bloomsbury as its dominant English conduit, was coming into view in England: the force of modernism, which would dominate the cultural world until well after the Second World War. Of course there were to be other great avatars of the movement—Yeats, Lawrence, Pound, Joyce, Eliot (who was close to Bloomsbury—the Woolfs' Hogarth Press would publish the first edition of *The Waste Land*). The multiplicity of the Bloomsbury figures—the sense that they had all exits covered—helped them in their ascent. And as John's comparative collapse indicates, their victory was quite rapid; by the time of the second Post-Impressionist Exhibition in 1912 the battle had been practically won, at least among a significant number of the cognoscenti. The short-term derision with which it was greeted seemed much more pro forma.

One of the early indicators of the change can be seen in a correspondence that took place at this time between Eric Gill and William Rothenstein, still in India, who had a sense, I believe, of himself being made somewhat out-of-date. Gill wrote on December 5:

> You are missing an awful excitement just now being provided for us in London: to wit: the exhibition of "post-impressionists" now on at the Grafton Gallery. All the critics are tearing one another's eyes out over it and the sheep and the goats are inextricably mixed up. John says "its a bloody show" & Lady Ottoline says "oh charming," Fry says "what rhythm" & MacColl says "what rot." As a matter of fact those who like it show their pluck, and those who don't, show either great intelligence or else great stupidity.

Gill went on to discuss with Rothenstein the one aspect of his life that he felt was more important, his thoughts that presaged his conversion to Catholicism: "A Religion so splendid & all embracing that the hierarchy to which it will give birth, uniting within itself the artist and the priest, will supplant and utterly destroy our present commercial government and our present commercial age."[85] With the letter Gill enclosed a copy of the engraving he had made for Fry to use as a Christmas card.

Rothenstein wrote to Fry the following March: "There was a shower of cinders one day while I was sitting on the banks of the Ganges & one of the Juggernaut Gods is said to have been found leaning to one side—both facts were accounted for later, I read, by the Post-Impressionist earthquake in London. . . . You will find my work very tame." Rothenstein felt himself increasingly isolated from Fry. The division had been hinted at before, but the exhibition brought about a more definite break, with the New English Art Club, previously a leader of the new wave in English art, now becoming old fashioned. (Fry had resigned from the committee of the NEAC in 1908.)

In the letter Rothenstein tried to minimize the effect of the exhibition. "Art is not an affair of social excitement, no one knows that better than you, & drawing room discussion does nothing any good I think. I fancy it [the exhibition] has been a brilliant & gallant charge of the light brigade—a glorious episode but leaving things very much where they were before."[86] Fry invited Rothenstein to participate in the second show, telling him that Steer and Tonks had already declined, feeling that the NEAC would continue to serve as a venue for the more progressive British artists. Fry had hoped, as he wrote on April 13, that with his commitment from the Grafton to have an annual autumn exhibition there, it "might be used for a general secession exhibition of all non-academy art of any importance."[87] But Fry would not cede control to a committee, as Rothenstein had proposed.

Rothenstein was writing with much more anger a month later in reply to Fry's letter of April 13: "You seem to have been so much offended at my not having found the effect of the Post-Impressionists an unmixed good that you attributed a set desire on my part to oppose your plans for a continuation of Grafton exhibitions." He continued with heavy-handed irony: "As my work is really more academic than revolutionary & my arrogant temper makes me a difficult person to work with, I cannot believe my absence [presumably from the next exhibition] will in any way weaken your position."[88] Writing to Lady Ottoline, Fry characterized this letter as a "declaration of war."[89]

In Rothenstein's view, Fry had abandoned art for theory, a not unfamiliar attack of those holding the older values against those espousing the newer ones (who of course will be attacked in their turn). As Rothenstein wrote in his memoirs, published in 1932: "The minds of [art] experts are more sensitive and better trained than their eyes. Henceforth criticism was to be occupied with a literary or philosophical interpretation of the arts, with elaborate theories about form, which soon became popular among those who wished to be in the fashion. The imaginative side of the painter's nature was now condemned as 'literary.'"[90]

In May 1911 Fry wrote to say how much he liked an exhibition of Rothenstein's work done in India. "I was even tempted to buy one of the drawings"—which does sound a rather bittersweet compliment as presumably it would have been more friendly to buy or not mention the temptation.[91] The misunderstandings continued and the correspondence and friendship tapered off. The Post-Impressionist Exhibition had split the older "advanced" leaders from the newer developments.

Another colleague with whom Fry came to an intellectual parting of the ways was D. S. MacColl, painter and art critic, and at this time keeper at the Tate Gallery, the museum in England that had the greatest commitment to contemporary art. Perhaps appropriately, in 1911 be become keeper of the more traditional Wallace Collection. (These were not complete breaks, and Fry continued to cooperate with MacColl and even Robert Ross in the workings of the Contemporary Art Society. But MacColl would resign from the Society in 1913 over the issue of Post-Impressionism.)

MacColl had led the fight against the Chantry Bequest, which, through the Council of the Royal Academy, bought the most conservative possible pictures for the nation. In his time, he had played a role similar to Fry's on behalf of the younger generation of painters such as Steer and Conder and internationally he had championed Degas, Manet, and Monet. He had now reached his limits. In the preface to a collection of his essays published in 1931 he wrote: "We had to fight, in the earlier period, for seniors and beginners who appeared eccentric against a background of mediocrity. The assumption is now all in favour of eccentricity. . . . The barriers are down, the doors are open, there is a welcome of trumpets and no resistance to what is called 'advanced art.'"[92] He found the Post-Impressionists violated his values, the English tradition that was one of restraint, the classical skills in art, in music, in literature. Wildness and a seeming lack of discipline were not encouraged, but rather individualism within a context of order, self-expression kept under control. It was inevitable that this sense of the weakening of command was made more acute by the political disorder in a society that prided itself on not indulging in the excesses associated with those who were unfortunate enough to live on the Continent.

On the other hand, a critic such as Frank Rutter was explicit, as in the title of his very short book *Revolution in Art*, published by the *Art News*, of which he was the editor. His book was appropriately bound in red. The dedication, underlined and all in capitals, read "TO THE REBELS OF EITHER SEX ALL THE WORLD OVER WHO IN ANY WAY ARE FIGHTING FOR FREEDOM OF ANY KIND, I DEDICATE THIS STUDY OF THEIR PAINTER COMRADES." In the text he was a little less explicit, stating that the connection with the unrest of politics and economics was more likely to be indirect rather than direct. He did comment that "the rebels of art were shot down metaphorically as ruthlessly as the Communists [in the Commune of 1870] were literally. Both had against them not only the organized forces of existing authority but also the general opinion of a majority lazily content with existing conditions." Rutter celebrated imagination rather than the Victorian virtues of work: "The more spontaneous the drawing appears, the more it has the effect of being dashed off in a few joyous moments, the more completely does it express the emotional fulness and technical mastery of its author." He commented of Cézanne and Gauguin that "these two deceased painters are to their younger comrades what Marx and Kropotkin are to the young social reformers of to-day."[93]

That was one side of the divide. On the other were not necessarily philistines but those such as MacColl who had in the past supported the "advanced" side. MacColl's essay on Post-Impressionism did not appear until February 1912 in *Nineteenth Century* because he had been ill, but he had just managed to see the exhibition. He was not happy with the pictures, and he makes the point that:

> You can *think* the concept of a tree, and you can talk about it, since words allude to ideas they do not represent, but you cannot imagine it, and you cannot draw it. . . . [These pictures] were welcomed in the degree in which they renounced with violence the world as it is seen. They were accepted as a promise, queer and doubtful, of a painting that should render the world beneath appearances, the world *unseen*. . . . These distortions of reality were thought, in some unexplained way, to give us "symbols" of a deeper reality than the painter ordinarily represents.[94]

Exactly so.

———

Sir George Savage, the doctor who had treated Virginia Woolf's mental illness in 1910, making the arrangements for her to go to Jean Thomas's rest home, in 1913 organized an exhibition of art by inmates from English asylums. But by that time "no comparison was made between the art of the insane and the modern art of France."[95]

The point was a common one made in 1910 that the Post-Impressionists were mad. Obviously this had some bearing in the case of Van Gogh—although there is now less assurance as to the nature of his illness—but it was carried to the "common sensical" "logical" conclusion that if the artist was mad, the art was bad. T. B. Hyslop, the physician superintendent at the asylums of Bridewell and Bedlam and a painter and a composer himself, made the point forcefully.[96] In 1905 he had written a paper about how degeneration, which was particularly manifested, he believed, in trade unions and feminism, would impede Britain's ability to run the Empire. He gave a talk at the Art Workers' Guild, once a more advanced organization of the Arts and Crafts movement,[97] which was published in the *Nineteenth Century* in February 1911. Roger Fry was in the audience, but there is no record of his making any comment, perhaps because he was no longer a member of the Guild. Significantly, he had resigned in 1910, having been elected in 1900.[98]

Hyslop's lecture in 1911 was a discussion of the art of the insane, but its very title as an article made the parallel explicit: "Post-Illusionism and the Art of the Insane." The lecture on January 13 was listed in the official history of the Guild as "Post-Impressionist Art."[99] He began by retelling the critical comment of a inmate of Bedlam that only half of the pictures shown at the Grafton were "worthy of Bedlam"; that the other half were simply "shamming degeneration or malingering." The rest of the talk, however, made no explicit mention of "Manet and the Post-Impressionists"; Hyslop pointed out that art by the insane is marked by "faulty delineation, erroneous perspective, and perverted colouring, but these form only positive symptoms of decadence, and they do not give us in all cases the measure of the negative lesion which may be due to disease. This holds good not only for the insane artist but also for his critic." For Hyslop, good art was marked by representation and technique, not by the power of vision, the intensity that was the claim of the Post-Impressionists.[100] Madness and degeneracy were common charges. J. Comyns Carr, another figure who had supported the progressive forces in art in the previous generation, remarked that these paintings "seem to me to indicate a wave of disease, even of absolute madness; for the whole product seems to breathe not ineptitude but corruption."[101]

C. J. Holmes in his autobiography reported on the lecture, which, much to his distress, was greeted with great enthusiasm by the audience. He remarked about Hyslop that "his arguments and evidence, however, were based upon such a complete misapprehension of the aims of painting, in all but its most commonplace and trivial aspects, that I was wholly unconvinced." Selwyn Image, who had become Slade Professor at Oxford instead of Fry, spoke in favor of Hyslop's argument (Image, a pioneer himself in the 1880s in his involvement with the Century Guild, was now firmly opposed to the newest developments in art). Fred Brown, a then well-known artist and head of the Slade, spoke against Hyslop. "To my delight he proved to be as little satisfied with the lecturer's evidence as I had been, and said so with his accustomed candour and pluck, His last words, coming as they did with one with his magnificent record, must have made his audience thoughtful: 'All I can say is, that if Van Gogh as an artist was mad, I wish I had a little of his madness.'"[102]

In his own forty-page work on the exhibition Holmes had written: "The insanity of Van Gogh's last years has furnished the enemies of the Post-Impressionists with a cheap cudgel, but taints only a very small proportion of his work. The remainder is of wonderful quality and variety. . . . The haunting power and beauty of his best work is so great as to annihilate all minor objections."[103] But even here he has an instinct for the *mot injuste*, remarking about Van Gogh's painting of an orchard that if he "had consistently maintained the notes he strikes in this exquisite picture he would have been acclaimed, even by the general public, as one of the most delightful of all modern landscape-painters."[104]

Fred Brown had been a founder of the New English Art Club, which welcomed the influence of French art, particularly Impressionism. But the tradition of the Slade was on draftsmanship, on the line, a "real" world, and this art violated such ideas. Brown had initially not liked the exhibition but then changed his mind. As Fry wrote to his father, he was "gratified that Fred Brown, the London Slade Professor who has always been rather antagonistic to my ideas and began by scoffing, wrote me a most generous retraction, saying that he had been completely converted to the ideas embodied by these painters."[105]

But as William Wees has commented in his study of Vorticism, even those of the older generation who were sympathetic were on the other side of the divide. "The 'liberal' position of the Slade became irrelevant in the face of the 'radical' art brought to London by Roger Fry. . . . The Slade's standard could no more accommodate a Gauguin or a Matisse than Asquith's Liberal government could accommodate an Emmeline

Pankhurst or a Sir Edward Carson."[106] The young at the Slade, such as Mark Gertler, were heavily influenced by the new development. Indeed the novel based on Gertler, Gilbert Canaan's *Mendel*, published in 1916, has the exhibition as a central episode. Such artists as the brothers Paul and John Nash, Dorothy Brett, Dora Carrington, Gwen Raverat, C. W. R. Nevinson, William Roberts, and Stanley Spencer were students at the Slade at the time and were unlikely to follow Tonks's directives not to see the new painting.

One should not neglect the class aspect of this controversy. On the Continent, unless it is taking too romantic a view, the artist may well revel in the Bohemian life, in being an outsider, while in England artists generally appear to be much more middle-class figures, much more interested in coming to terms with their society. William Morris had been fully aware of this tendency, and he observed the growing respectability of such organizations at the Art Workers' Guild, which had begun with the idea of fighting established values. This too, according to Fry, had been the course of the New English Art Club.

Such is frequently the fate of avant-garde organizations. But in England the process appears to be accelerated and particularly welcomed. That Bloomsbury was already in the upper middle class may have made it easier for it to be subversive in its values and in its behavior. But for genteel supporters of formerly "advanced" art, Post-Impressionism presented a threat, a potential retrogression into chaos. The point has been made by Julie Codell in an article on the art critic M. H. Spielmann, who regarded both Impressionists and Post-Impressionists as madmen, although he supported some controversial causes; he was, for example, against the removal of Epstein's allegedly obscene sculptures from the Strand in 1908. As Codell writes about Spielmann: "his resistance to modernism was due in part to his desire to salvage artists' reputations from the taint of Bohemianism associated with modernists who were invariably French or French-trained."[107] It was that image that the Post-Impressionist Exhibition, with its emphasis on instinct over cultivation, challenged. It was, inevitably, consciously or not, a commitment to a change in human character.

9

Bloomsbury Emergent

Virginia Woolf's friendship with Roger Fry was just beginning in 1910, and in the division of the arts, made practically in the nursery, between herself and Vanessa, painting was on Vanessa's side. In a letter to Violet Dickinson on November 27 Virginia couldn't resist being a little flippant about the pictures at the exhibition. "Now that Clive is in the van of aesthetic opinion, I hear a great deal about pictures. I dont think them so good as books. But why all the Duchesses are insulted by the post-impressionists, a modest sample set of painters, innocent even of indecency, I cant conceive. However, one mustn't say that they are like other pictures, only better, because that makes everyone angry." It is striking that she went on to mention her own sense of productivity, part of the artistic turmoil of the time and perhaps stimulated by it. "You will be glad to hear that I am seething with fragments of love, morals, ethics, comedy tragedy, and so on; and every morning pour them out into a manuscript book."[1]

The following year there was the scare about Vanessa's health while she and Clive, with Roger and Harry Norton, a close Cambridge friend, were traveling in Turkey. Indeed, the decision to go there and see the Byzantine mosaics had been partially inspired by Fry's point that the

Post-Impressionists were parallel to Byzantine art in succession to Roman naturalism. Virginia went out to help bring Vanessa home, terrified by the similarity of the experience with Thoby, who in 1906 had fallen mortally ill in Greece. Roger nursed Vanessa with great care and they established a close rapport, culminating with his becoming her lover shortly after they returned to England.

This was particularly extraordinary as he had left on the trip with some reluctance under the impression that he was Lady Ottoline's lover; he had asked her to come on the trip as well.[2] The situation seemed characteristically complex. Just before the trip, on April 1, Fry wrote Lady Ottoline a rather breathless and comparatively incoherent love letter which concluded: "I long to be with you to find out together—to understand myself—I feel that I am curiously nothing as though something happened to me when I went through what I did with Helen which has made me a spectator haunting the world a thing of no weight—oh, I can't explain. I don't understand anything to-night only I long to be with you again & help you."[3] But it was probably just shortly before this that Bertrand Russell and Lady Ottoline had launched an affair that was to continue for some years. In November, Fry and Vanessa agonized about whether to tell Virginia about their affair, Vanessa feeling that it would have been easier if Clive were still flirting with Virginia. Although Clive now had other interests, he might well be jealous, and in any case Vanessa did not want to lose him as a friend and father.[4]

Virginia paid homage to Fry in opening a memorial exhibition of his paintings in Bristol in 1935, the year after his death. There she made quite vivid how much he had done in shaping how one thought about the world visually. "The names of Cézanne and Gauguin, of Matisse and Picasso, suddenly became as hotly debated, as violently defended as the names—shall we say?—of Ramsay MacDonald, Hitler, or Lloyd George. . . . Pictures have never gone back to their wall. They are no longer silent, decorous, and dull. They are things we live with, and laugh at, and discuss. And I think I am right in saying that it was Roger Fry more than anybody who brought about this change."[5]

She would write about the exhibition in her biography of Fry, published in 1940, a commission by the family that she had felt unable to refuse and about which she was not totally happy. There she emphasizes that Fry was seen as a vulgarian, violating the received standards of good behavior of the day. "He was amused to find that his own reputation—the dim portrait that the public had drawn of him as a man of taste and learning—was replaced by a crude caricature [literally as well] of a man who, as the critics implied, probably from base motives, either to advertise himself, to make money, or from mere freakishness, had thrown overboard his culture and deserted his standards." As she rightly commented in the biography—reminding us that we mustn't be smug—"It would need to-day as much more courage to denounce Cézanne, Picasso, Seurat, Van Gogh and Gauguin as it needed then to defend them. But such figures and such opinions were not available in 1910, and Roger Fry was left to uphold his own beliefs under a shower of abuse and ridicule."[6]

Fry was full of energy and imagination, and through his lectures, his pen, his gift for friendship, his gift for advocacy, he was able to preach a new doctrine, to become a magnet for younger painters, to bring the interests of the English into the international arena. He was also particularly important not only for making these French painters so much better known in the Anglo-American world but for enunciating ideas about them that made it clearer than had been true before what these pictures meant—at least according to him—that made them more self-consciously part of the movement of modernism. He helped liberate painting from the tyranny of representation and gave it a power that he felt had not been seen in European painting since the Italian primitives.

Another indication of this break, of course, was Virginia Woolf's famous remark. Perhaps this is the point where something more might be said of the creation of that remark, which was, after all, made some fourteen years after the Post-Impressionist Exhibition. It was, as pointed out earlier, a quarrel that Woolf was having with Arnold Bennett, incited by his comment about *Jacob's Room,* her first non-traditional novel, that, whatever its virtues might be, she was incapable of creating character. She herself felt that she was able to do something better, get behind superficial surface description to the essence of character, the message of *Mr Bennett and Mrs Brown.*

Their dispute had begun gently as early as 1917 when Woolf anonymously reviewed in the *Times Literary Supplement* a collection of essays by Bennett, *Books and Persons,* which indeed contained his review of the Post-Impressionists. The collection had the marks of the middlebrow literary establishment she disliked. In his prefatory note, Bennett mentioned that he was dedicating the collection to Hugh Walpole, who had suggested he bring it out, and he also thanked Frank Swinnerton, who would come in on Bennett's side in the dispute, for his help. Her review was favorable, but its praise had a slightly patronizing air about Bennett's professionalism. He was "the father of fifty volumes. The man who speaks knows all that there is to be known about the making of books. He remembers that a tremendous amount of work has gone to the making of them; he is versed in every side of the profession." At the end of the review, she points out the paradox of Bennett's support for the Post-Impressionists.

> These new pictures, he says, have wearied him of other pictures; is it not possible that some writer will come along and do in words what these men have done in paint? And suppose that happens, and Mr Bennett has to admit that he has been concerning himself unduly with inessentials, that he has been worrying himself to achieve infantile realisms? He will admit it, we are sure; and that he can ask himself such a question seems to us certain proof that he is what he claims to be—a "creative artist."[7]

The same month the review was published, July, she and Leonard printed the first publication of the Hogarth Press, *Two Stories,* which contained "Three Jews" by Leonard and her own "The Mark on the Wall," her first writing in a clearly new style, a "modernist" work.

She turned more forthrightly to the attack two years later in her essay "Modern Novels," again in the *Times Literary Supplement,* where she remarked that Wells, Galsworthy, and Bennett, whom she regarded as the most prominent and successful English novelists in the year 1910, were "materialists, and for that reason have disappointed us and left us with the feeling that the sooner English fiction turns its back upon them, as politely as may be, and marches, if only into the desert, the better for its soul. . . . Mr Bennett is perhaps the worst culprit of the three, inasmuch as he is by far the best workman." Woolf put forward a counter-vision, consistent with the experiences of 1910: "The mind, exposed to the ordinary course of life, receives upon its surface a myriad impressions—trivial, fantastic, evanescent, or engraved with the sharpness of steel. From all sides they come, an incessant shower of innumerable atoms, composing in their sum what we might venture to call life itself."[8] That same year she wrote the story "An Unwritten Novel," in which, in my view, the unnamed Mrs Brown is the central figure. Then two years later, in 1921, when the story was published in *Monday or Tuesday,* Vanessa did a woodcut portrait that can be taken as being "Mrs Brown," sitting in the train.

The controversy heated up in 1923 when Bennett made a passing comment on *Jacob's Room* in a piece called "Is the Novel Decaying?" in *Cassell's Weekly,* saying that the characters in it were not alive. Woolf responded in the *New York Evening Post* in November, the first use of the title "Mr Bennett and Mrs Brown." She renewed the attack on Wells, Galsworthy, and Bennett, significantly calling them Edwardian, an era that officially ended with the death of the king in May 1910. "But in lodging such a charge against so formidable a library we must do as painters do when they wish to reduce the innumerable details of a crowded landscape to simplicity." It was not that all previous novelists failed, for she ascribes great vitality to the Victorians for creating memorable characters, unlike, in her view, the Edwardians. But even the Victorians did not achieve the depths in characters that one was taught by the great Russians. The new novelists are in pursuit of the character of Mrs Brown, whom Wells, Galsworthy, and Bennett have completely failed to capture. "The capture of Mrs Brown is the title of the next chapter in the history of literature; and, let us prophesy again, that

Figure by Vanessa Bell.

chapter will be one of the most important, the most illustrious, the most epoch-making of them all."[9]

This essay then provided the impetus for a lecture, "Character in Fiction," for the Cambridge Heretics Society on May 18, 1924, which in its turn was the basis for a longer essay published in T. S. Eliot's *Criterion* in July and then issued as the first in the Hogarth essays series in October, reverting to the first title, *Mr Bennett and Mrs Brown.* As Quentin Bell has said, "it was as near as she came to an aesthetic manifesto."[10]

It was in the lecture and its subsequent versions that the much quoted phrase first appeared: "on or about December 1910 human character changed." (When it is quoted elsewhere, "on" is frequently changed to "in," a comma is frequently inserted after "December" and after "1910," and less frequently "character" is changed to "nature," perhaps excusable as she does refer to Mrs Brown as standing for human nature. It may well have been Woolf herself who inserted the commas; they appeared after her death in *The Captain's Death Bed and Other Essays* in 1950. In his Editorial Note to that volume, Leonard Woolf states that the essays "have, in fact, been revised or rewritten by her" and were likely to have been further changed if she had lived.[11] But I prefer the original punchier version.) The claim she makes is sweeping, that all human relations had shifted, in religion, conduct, politics, and literature. To a degree this is Woolfian hyperbole. Yet in many ways she was right, for the introduction of modernism, for the growing triumph of a new way of looking at the world, for a changed conception of reality. She ended the piece with a similar evocation as in the original brief essay, a characteristic combination of the sweeping and the particular: "We are trembling on the verge of one of the great ages of English literature. But it can only be reached if we are determined never, never to desert Mrs. Brown."[12]

Certainly the members of Bloomsbury were not alone in taking the steps toward modernism. Ezra Pound, who had come from America and was a figure in London at the time, in his "Hugh Selwyn Mauberley" satirized Bennett as "Mr Nixon," on his steam yacht, advising a young poet: "And give up verse, my boy, / There's nothing in it." D. H. Lawrence was becoming increasingly active as a poet and novelist; his first novel, *The White Peacock*, appeared in 1911. Joyce had published his first book, *Chamber Music*, in 1907. Marinetti lectured on Futurism in London in 1910. On the Continent Cubism and the Russian ballet, which would come to London in 1911, had already made their marks. Freud's *Three Essays on the Theory of Sexuality*, the first of his works to be translated into English, was published in the United States in 1910.

In the Bloomsbury circle the most immediate effect of modernism was upon the painters. Fry's painting changed to a degree and he himself became somewhat closer to being a Post-Impressionist. Although his painting was so close to his heart, and perhaps was the activity that was most important to him, the public and indeed the art world itself paid it little mind. But his views of art did receive considerable attention, and he became the most important English art critic of the first half of the century. For him the exhibition was the turning point, as so many of the "cultivated" now regarded him as an anarchist, indeed as an immoralist, and he became the prophet for the young. His critics made the standard remark about the art he championed, to be echoed from then on: that children could have painted as well.

In putting forth his views in "An Essay in Aesthetics" in 1909 Fry anticipated this criticism as an image for what was right about the art he displayed in 1910:

> That the graphic arts are the expression of the imaginative life rather than a copy of actual life might be guessed from observing children. Children, if left to themselves, never, I believe, copy what they see, never, as we say, "draw from nature," but express, with a delightful freedom and sincerity, the mental images which make up their own imaginative lives.
>
> Art, then, is an expression and a stimulus of this imaginative life, which is separated from actual life by the absence of responsive action.

In the course of the essay, he wrote that the way the artist aroused the viewer's emotions was through the rhythm of the line, mass, space, light and shade, and color. He then concluded with a statement about the relation of art to nature.

> The artist's attitude to natural form is, therefore, infinitely various according to the emotions he wishes to arouse. He may require for his purpose the most complete representation of a figure, he may be intensely realistic, provided that his presentment, in spite of its closeness to natural appearance, disengages clearly for us the appropriate emotional elements. Or he may give us the merest suggestion of natural forms, and rely almost entirely upon the force and intensity of the emotional elements involved in his presentment.
>
> We may, then, dispense once for all with the idea of likeness to Nature, of correctness or incorrectness as a test, and consider only whether the emotional elements inherent in natural form are adequately discovered, unless, indeed, the emotional idea depends at any point upon likeness, or completeness of representation.[13]

Yet he would not go as far as Clive Bell, who would enunciate the doctrine of significant form as the key to modern art. Bell had put forth this idea in his first book, *Art,* published in 1914. He thought of that book as part of a larger project he was working on in 1910 which he called the "new Renaissance." In May 1919 in a letter in the *Burlington,* Fry pointed out that "whatever Mr. Clive Bell may have said, I personally have never denied the existence of some amount of representation in all pictorial art. . . . What I have suggested is that the purer the artist the more his representation will be of universals and less of particulars."[14]

Fry certainly felt that the artistic world had improved. In a letter on December 4, 1910, to Eric Gill, he praised his art, but also made a remark that can be taken for what he thought was happening in art in general as represented in Gill's exhibit: "What a queer world it is but you have made it exciting & more full of hope for the future than I had dreamed say ten years go. Then I was mainly interested in myself, a comparatively dull subject & now I suppose it's what you call God."[15]

The Post-Impressionist Exhibition would ultimately have a great effect, and created more of a sense of an international movement than had been true before, no matter how well known the artists were already in France. Ultimately, it broke the "logjam" of taste, so it became easier for many to accept the Fauves and Cubism. It was, in its sense of starting anew, consistent with Bloomsbury's values, which were committed to examining everything afresh, to taking nothing on trust, to questioning received opinions and values. The danger of course was in being engaged too tightly with a new set of values. As Clive Bell wrote, Fry had

> an open-mindedness that made Roger, not only one of the most delightful companions, but one of the most remarkable men of his age. Had a serious student seriously advanced an opinion (say, that Giotto or Cézanne was no good) which called in question his (Roger's) judgment and jeopardized his whole aesthetic, Roger would have listened attentively and sympathetically. And that, not out of urbanity, but because he was genuinely anxious to get at the truth, and always conceived it possible that he might be completely wrong.[16]

More immediately, however, the exhibition had a considerable effect on the painting of Vanessa Bell and Duncan Grant. In the memoir she wrote about Fry in October 1934, Vanessa conveyed a splendid sense of the excitement: "The autumn of 1910 is to me a time when everything seemed springing to new life—a time when all was a sizzle of excitement, new relationships, new ideas, different and intense emotion all seemed crowding into ones life." She did not realize yet how much Roger was at the center of it, but she was seeing much more of him; he would come by Gordon Square and occasionally spend the night in the guest bedroom. She was also extremely worried about the infant Quentin and his inability to gain weight, and it was Roger alone who instinctively understood the situation and gave her support.

But the exhibition was the main event:

> The world of painting—how can one possibly describe the effect of that first Post Impressionist exhibition on English painters at the time? . . . It is impossible I think that any other single exhibition can

ever have had so much effect as did that on the rising generation. The fuming and storming of the elders added to the fun of course. . . . Here was a sudden pointing to a possible path, a sudden liberation & encouragement to feel for oneself which were absolutely overwhelming. . . . It was as if at last one might say things one had always felt instead of trying to say things that other people told one to feel. Freedom was given one to be oneself & that to the young is the most exciting thing that can happen.[17]

Despite the power of the experience, Vanessa's illness, caused by a miscarriage the following year in Turkey, lasted in its full effects for two years or more and meant that she painted far less. It was partially psychological and was not dissimilar to the depressions experienced by her father and sister. But the illness in its way served to emphasize the time as one of recovery and of starting in a new direction. She and Roger came closer and closer, culminating in their becoming lovers, until her affections were engaged, in 1913, by Duncan Grant. But Roger would remain, with Clive and Duncan and her sons, one of the most important men in her life.

Even her illness served as a mark for the transformation, a reversal, of the story her sister was writing in *The Voyage Out*. There Vanessa provided a model for Helen Ambrose, the strong aunt. But in terms of her health she had some resemblance to Rachel, but with a happier outcome. She may have painted less, but what she did was of great power and was a new departure, heavily influenced by the exhibition: most strikingly the magnificent *Studland Beach* of 1911, perhaps done before the trip to Turkey; paintings of 1912 such as *Frederick and Jessie Etchells in the Studio* and a portrait of Virginia Woolf; and a portrait of Lytton Strachey of 1913. (Fry too did a *Studland Bay* in 1911 that is striking in its freedom.) The exhibition had liberated the painter in Vanessa. It was if one had discovered a new land, and indeed Clive Bell referred to Cézanne in his *Art*, published in 1914, as "the Christopher Columbus of a new continent of form."[18]

With Duncan Grant, the effect can be seen in his extraordinary *The Tub* of 1912, which in terms of color and composition is a very modern picture. Also striking is his painting of three male nudes, perhaps of 1911, probably unfinished, and rarely seen as it is on the reverse side of Bell's *Studland Beach*. The effect may not have continued so strongly with Bell and Grant, but they were painting on the other side of a divide from where they had been before the exhibition. It might be said that Grant became a modern painter with the exhibition. One can look at his *The Lemon Gatherers* of 1910 that Vanessa Bell had liked so much; it is a strong, interesting painting. But he did another version of it in 1912, simplified in terms of color and form, also reworked in 1919, and one can see there the influence of the exhibition.[19] So too the exhibition had a considerable influence upon design in Britain, introducing there the bolder and more abstract conceptions that we associate with the modern vision.

Grant too at this time became much closer to Roger Fry. The writers in the group appeared to be slower in their appreciation than the artists. Keynes wrote to Grant on November 15: "What is your final view about the Frenchmen?—they don't find much favour here—even Dickinson was rather outraged."[20] Yet Keynes recognized that there needed to be a secession from the New English Art Club, that it was no longer serving its purpose in representing the more advanced English art, particularly as it had rejected the painting Grant had been working on.[21] At the end of November Grant had gone down to Guildford to paint alongside Fry, whom he hadn't known particularly well before. "I thought Roger Fry extremely nice but rather exhausting—he makes up his mind so extraordinarily quickly." Fry and Grant became collaborators on the Borough Polytechnic murals in the summer of 1911 which also included other artists, Frederick Etchells, Bernard Adeney, and Albert Rutherston (Rothenstein's brother). Fry was the director of the project, and his mural depicted elephants, in the part that has survived, in the London Zoo. As Frances Spalding points out,[22] Grant was heavily influenced in his work by what Bell and Fry must have told and shown him about the Byzantine art they had seen on their trip, which Fry thought had so much similarity to Post-Impressionist art. Grant's mural *Bathers*, of stylized naked male figures leaping into the sea, now in the Tate, is an exciting and new sort of work. Richard Shone has called it "the most radical painting produced in that year in England."[23]

As we have seen, Forster in 1911 felt that Fry had painted a Post-Impressionist portrait. Forster's relationship to Bloomsbury always had its rather tangential aspect, so too his enthusiasm for the pictures was muted. Edward Marsh, that man about the arts, took his friend Forster to the private view, and Forster wrote to him rather diffidently afterward that "Gauguin and Van Gogh are too much for me."[24] As for Fry, he thought that Forster was quite hopeless in his approach to art.

In a sense, the pictures may have suggested qualities more basic than Forster wished to cope with. He had reached a plateau of fame with *Howards End* and a plateau of love with Masood. Neither situation gave him total satisfaction. But the resolution of his feelings about Masood, even though it was unsatisfactory, made him realize how important his homosexuality was to him. At the same time that he was working on his talk on the feminine note in literature, he was thinking of writing an essay on pornography and sentimentality, and commented in his diary on October 25: "To work out:—The sexual bias in literary criticism, & perhaps literature." As early as December 19 he was moving toward a different sort of novel. "Desire for a book. To deal with country life & possibly Paris. Plenty of young men & children in it, & adventure. If possible pity & thought. But no love making—at least of the orthodox kind, & perhaps not even of the unorthodox. It would be tempting to make an intelligent man feel towards an intelligent man of lower class what I feel, but I see the situation too clearly to use it."[25]

He was writing erotic stories which he knew could not be published, he was working on the manuscript of "Arctic Summer" which wouldn't work out, and in 1913 he began *Maurice* which he knew couldn't be published. "Arctic Summer" was, in some senses, an attempt to come to terms with Fry, or rather to disagree with him, as the central character, Martin Whitly, needs to liberate himself from Fry's belief in form. One critic believes Forster was inspired by the debate in the *Nation* in the autumn over the exhibition, the issue of form versus content, as well as the articles about militarism, stimulated by the publication of Norman

Angell's *The Great Illusion,* reflected in the other central character in the story, Clesant March, an army officer. Indeed Forster was working on the manuscript of *Arctic Summer* while Fry was painting him.[26] In my view, he was not able to come to terms with these problems involving sexuality and politics, and the significance of his relationship with Masood, until *A Passage to India* in 1924. Nineteen-ten had marked a triumph with *Howards End,* but also the beginning of a long wait until his next major publication, and his last novel.

For the story of the Bloomsbury group, and the history of modernism, 1910 had been a year of considerable importance. Virginia Woolf had meant her aphorism half seriously. Through the exhibition, England came closer to continental culture than had been true for a hundred years or more. Long before the Chunnell, the country became somewhat less insular. Before there had been an awareness of European culture, but now England was to a greater degree part of that culture. Bloomsbury was certainly an elite group, yet its ideas emphasized, at least in theory, the "democracy" of art, of sensibility, the equality of the aesthetic reaction.

In many ways, Edwardian England, in its materialism and indeed vulgarity, was the apotheosis of the bourgeois world. Although perfectly aware that they were part of that world and that the income it bestowed allowed them to lead the artistic life, the members of Bloomsbury were nevertheless dedicated to challenging that world's unexamined assumptions. Cézanne represented a blow for personal freedom—an escape from the tyranny of the line, of draftsmanship, as expressed by Tonks at the Slade—a commitment to personal values that was the heart of Bloomsbury's beliefs. Truth and expressiveness were more important than comfort or beauty, beauty that was associated with the representation of the natural world. Bloomsbury, in its rather decorous English way, was challenging, in its search for the reality under appearance, the basic assumptions of its society. Although there are comparatively few specific references in their writings and correspondence of the time to the violent events of the year—in the world of labor, the fight for the suffrage, the class antagonism over the issue of the House of Lords and the Budget, the unresolved problem of Ireland—all contributed to a sense of unrest that perhaps at the time, and certainly in retrospect, made Virginia Woolf feel that the world was dramatically changing.

One could also argue that Bloomsbury's own experiences during the year, and particularly the exhibition itself, had a profound effect upon its members and on the course of modernism, certainly in the English-speaking world. Virginia Woolf in her writing more and more approached the condition of painting, particularly Post-Impressionist art. In varying degrees, the members of Bloomsbury already shared an aesthetic philosophy in G. E. Moore's *Principia Ethica* of 1903 which Virginia had carefully read in 1908. It emphasized the importance of art and personal relationships, of states of mind, and the discovery of a true reality, as in Bishop Butler's aphorism opposite its title page: "Everything is what it is, and not another thing." The Bloomsbury world was in many ways a private one, even though its younger members were actively pursuing their careers in the world of serious journalism and beginning to write the books for which they would be remembered. But they were not yet modernists. The furor over the exhibition, but more significantly the impact of Cézanne, helped propel these writers and artists into a new, fresh, different, indeed a changed world of human character.

I have chosen to concentrate on activities in which Bloomsbury was involved in 1910. Certainly on the public stage the exhibition received a great deal of attention and, over the years, so has *Howards End*. Fry and Forster, peripheral figures in Bloomsbury's world at the beginning of the year, were much more part of it at the end. One could exhaustively investigate the entire culture for signs of the change Woolf indicated. But such a pursuit, even if possible, would probably be inconclusive. Other than Fry and Forster, members of Bloomsbury were still in an emergent state from which their accomplishments and influences rippled out over the years to come. But their experiences in 1910 were critical. They had participated in essential shaping events, significant in themselves and for their world, both in personal ways but also for the history of the modern movement in the twentieth century.

NOTES

INTRODUCTION

1. Virginia Woolf, *Mr Bennett and Mrs Brown* (London, 1924), pp. 4–5.
2. Roger Fry, *Vision and Design* (London, 1920), pp. 192–193.

1. VIRGINIA WOOLF I

1. For this and other useful biographical information see Alan and Veronica Palmer, *Who's Who in Bloomsbury* (Brighton, 1987).
2. Virginia Woolf, "Old Bloomsbury," in Jeanne Schulkind, ed., *Virginia Woolf: Moments of Being* (Sussex, 1976), pp. 173–174.
3. Clive Bell papers, Trinity College, Cambridge, 3 10 (14).
4. Leonard Woolf to Lytton Strachey, Feb. 1, 1909, in Leonard Spotts, ed., *Letters of Leonard Woolf* (San Diego, 1989), pp. 145–146.
5. Strachey to Woolf, Aug. 21, 1909, ibid., pp. 148–149.
6. Leonard Woolf, *Beginning Again* (London, 1964), p. 35.
7. Strachey papers, British Library Add. Mss. 60659, Vanessa to James Strachey, July 2 [1909].
8. Clive Bell papers, Trinity College, Cambridge 3 10 (2).
9. Clive Bell, *Old Friends* (London, 1956), p. 31.
10. Virginia Woolf to Janet Case, Jan. 1, 1910, in Nigel Nicolson and Joanne Trautmann, eds., *The Letters of Virginia Woolf* (New York, 1975) I, 421. Although Virginia had not yet married, in references, and in the text, I will call her by the name by which she became best known.
11. Strachey Papers, British Library, Add. Mss. 60659, Vanessa to Lytton, Oct. 27 [1909].

2. THE DREADNOUGHT HOAX

1. I use Abyssinia and Ethiopia interchangeably; although the former was probably more common then and the latter now. By a nice coincidence Leonard Woolf wrote

extensively about the area in his *Empire and Commerce in Africa: A Study of Economic Imperialism* (London, n.d. [1920]). It was quite an influential book in its time. There (p. 139), Woolf remarks: "In the following pages I propose to call the whole block of territory which includes Abyssinia, Eritrea, and the the three Somalilands, Ethiopian Africa."

2. Virginia Woolf, *The Voyage Out* (first published 1915), end of chapter 4. The possible connection between the passage and the *Dreadnought* incident I owe to Jane Wheare, *Virginia Woolf: Dramatic Novelist* (London, 1989), p. 48.

3. Quoted in David Dilks, *Neville Chamberlain* (Cambridge, 1984), I, 116.

4. Quentin Bell, *Virginia Woolf* (New York, 1972), I, 146.

5. Adrian Stephen, *The "Dreadnought" Hoax* (London, 1936), pp. 7–8, 16.

6. See Michael Holroyd, *Lytton Strachey* (New York, 1968), I, 406.

7. See Michael Holroyd, *Augustus John* (New York, 1975), pp. 536–537.

8. See Joseph Hone, "Horace Cole: King of Jokers," *Listener,* April 4, 1940, pp. 674–675, for this and other details. Adrian stated that they knew all along that Fisher was on the ship. Hone was an Anglo-Irish man of letters and an early biographer of Yeats. Presumably he knew Cole through the Anglo-Irish connection.

9. Bell, *Virginia Woolf,* I, 157.

10. I am grateful to my colleague Susan Treggari for discussing this point with me. James Michie translated the stanza thus: "One bride alone, among the many, honoured / The torch of marriage, proved a shining liar / To her oath-breaking father and for all time / Stands as a paragon." *The Odes of Horace* (London, 1987), Book 3, Ode XI, lines 33–36.

11. Strachey Papers, British Library, Add. Mss. 60659, Vanessa to Lytton, Jan. 12 [1910].

12. Charleston papers, King's College, Cambridge, copy, Vanessa Bell to Marjorie Snowden, Feb. 13, 1910, 31 Box D.

13. Hone, "Horace Cole," p. 674.

14. Admiralty Papers, Public Record Office, Kew Gardens, London ADM 1/8792. All the documents and newspaper stories quoted are from this file, unless otherwise indicated.

15. Stephen, *"Dreadnought" Hoax,* p. 27.

16. Bell, *Virginia Woolf,* I, 159.

17. Berg Collection, New York Public Library, Dorothea Jane Stephen to Virginia Woolf, March 3, 1910.

18. I owe this point to S. P. Rosenbaum.

19. *Letters of Virginia Woolf,* Woolf to Dickinson [Feb. 14, 1910], I, 422.

20. See Norman Sherry, *The Life of Graham Greene: 1904–1939* (New York, 1989), I, 4. The novelist's first name was actually Henry, but apparently he never used it; the civil servant's first name was William. The novelist thought his uncle would have

secretly relished the hoax, according to Christopher Hawtree, letter to author, June 24, 1994. See Christopher Hawtree, "The Battleship that Was Taken for a Ride," *Daily Telegraph*, Feb. 24, 1990. Also see Virginia Nicholson, "The Dreadnought Hoax," script of performance at Charleston, May 29, 1994 (script courtesy of Quentin Bell).

21. This term presumably inspired Lytton Strachey for a piece he wrote in January 1914 in the *New Statesman* in which an African chief, "Bonga-Bonga," has an interview with a Cabinet member, speaking parody English, with the point that the British government is no more liberal and civilized, perhaps less, than the African state. "Bonga-Bonga in Whitehall," Jan. 17, 1914, rpt. in Lytton Strachey, *Characters and Commentaries* (London, 1933), pp. 175–180.

22. British Library, Add. Mss. 58120A, Grant to Keynes, Feb. 9, 1910; Add. Mss. 57930, Keynes to Grant, Feb. 12, 1910.

23. *Daily Mirror*, Feb. 15, 1910.

24. *Western Daily Mercury*, Feb. 15, 1910.

25. *Dorchester Mail*, Feb. 18, 1910.

26. For a full record of questions in Parliament see *Hansard*, Feb. 24, 1910, col. 339–340; March 2, 1910, col. 832. The surviving pages of Woolf's account are in Bell, *Virginia Woolf*, I, 213–216.

27. *Letters*, I, 423 [?8 March 1910].

28. Bell, *Virginia Woolf*, I, 214–215.

29. Ibid., p. 215.

30. Virginia Woolf wrote: "Willy Fisher explained that since my brother's mother was his own Aunt, the rules of the Navy forbade any actual physical punishment." I, 215.

31. *Times* (London), Aug. 10, 1970.

32. This is Virginia Woolf's version; Adrian has the episode taking place near Hendon, an outskirt of London (p. 41).

33. The episode was far more directly evoked in Woolf's short story of 1920, "A Society." See Susan Dick, *The Complete Shorter Fiction of Virginia Woolf* (San Diego, 1985), pp. 118–130.

3. VIRGINIA WOOLF II

1. Nigel Nicolson and Joanne Trautmann, eds., *The Letters of Virginia Woolf* (New York, 1975), Woolf to Violet Dickinson, Feb. 27, 1910, I, 422.

2. See Louise A. DeSalvo, *Virginia Woolf's First Voyage* (Totowa, N.J., 1980), p. x.

3. *Letters* I, 449. The "terrible ructions" were not further specified. A draft exists of an extraordinary letter from Clive to Lytton marking their disagreements, but it was probably written some time later. Olivier Bell, who was kind enough to show me a copy, believes that Virginia may have typed the letter and Leonard may have edited it; he did

not return to England until June 1911. In any case, it may never have been sent. But it is well worth giving here in part as it demonstrates how rocky the course of Bloomsbury friendship might be. "Dear Lytton . . . I should be even more obtuse than you suppose had I not perceived long ago that you despised me. Your arrogant manners, your condescending attitude, the things that you are in the habit of saying to our common acquaintances, leave no doubt as to your feelings. . . . My manners you find florid and vulgar, over emphatic and underbred, when you infer—wrongly as I think—that my appreciations are more or less blunt and that I am deficient in sensitiveness to the finer shades of thought and feeling. . . . Your intellect is not powerful but well trained. . . . You see part of life clearly but it is a very small part. . . . You are so selfish that you have lost the power of seeing what people feel. . . . You are clever, brilliant even, charming but you are very far from being that genius to whom one could pardon anything. . . . Do you suppose that Thoby was or Vanessa is blind to my florid ways? When one cares, such superficial things become a joke, an attraction almost, not a source of constant irritation and excuse for studied contempt. Intimacy, you know, and have known for some time, is impossible between us. Is it not then a little indecent, incongruous a little with that refinement and sensibility of yours that you should continue to use my house as a hotel? . . . At Gordon Square the coin in which you pay is no longer current, and I fear you have no other."

4. Virginia Woolf Papers, University of Sussex Library, Clive Bell to Virginia Stephen [May 7, 1908].

5. See Jane Dunn, *A Very Close Conspiracy: Vanessa Bell and Virginia Woolf* (London, 1990), p. 142, and Quentin Bell, *Virginia Woolf* (New York, 1972), I, 212.

6. Virginia Woolf Papers, University of Sussex Library, Clive Bell to Virginia Stephen [?Sept. 6, 1910]

7. See Stephen Trombley, "The Morality of Madness: Sir George Henry Savage," in *All That Summer She Was Mad: Virginia Woolf: Female Victim of Male Medicine* (New York, 1982), pp. 107–158.

8. See Vanessa Bell to Virginia Woolf, Oct. 25, 1904, in Regina Marler, ed., *Selected Letters of Vanessa Bell* (New York, 1993), p. 20. At the time of Virginia's earlier problems Vanessa wrote to her about Savage: he said "'There is one thing I want to tell you most seriously—I will have no fees.' I said he must let us pay him, as we had taken up so much of his time and could do nothing in return, but he then pointed to the photograph he has of Father, and said that he was proud to do anything for his children, and that the only thing he cared about was that you should get well. It was quite extraordinarily nice of him, when one thinks of his being the greatest man on his subject in England and what his time is worth."

9. See Janet Oppenheim, *Shattered Nerves* (New York, 1990), pp. 107–108.

10. British Library, Add. Mss. 60659, Vanessa to Lytton Aug. 26 [1909]. In Marler, *Letters of Vanessa Bell,* p. 86.

11. Virginia Woolf Papers, Adrian Stephen to Saxon Sydney-Turner April 6, 1910.

12. British Library, Add. Mss. 57932, Strachey to Grant, April 4, 1910.

13. Saxon Sydney-Turner papers, Huntington Library, San Marino, California, Clive Bell to Sydney-Turner, n.d. In the same letter Bell recommends the poems of Frances Cornford, a close friend of Brooke's. "Read them. They are not unmusical, and they strike me as expressing a very interesting mind and character." Bloomsbury at this point was developing a rather affectionate if slightly patronizing relationship with the group Woolf would christen the "neo-pagans." Younger, they were somewhat the reverse of the Bloomsbury figures—they tended to be more conventional in fact, while seemingly more free and easy in their living style.

14. Morrell papers, Harry Ransom Humanities Research Center, University of Texas at Austin (hereinafter HRC), Clive Bell to Ottoline Morrell, April 5, 1910.

15. Alan and Veronica Palmer, *Who's Who in Bloomsbury* (Brighton, 1987), p. 192.

16. Andrew McNeillie, ed., *The Essays of Virginia Woolf* (New York, 1986), I, 338.

17. Virginia Woolf Papers, Clive Bell to Virginia Woolf, ?Spring, 1910.

18. Berg Collection, New York Public Library, Vanessa to Virginia, June 24 [1910].

19. Tate Archives, London, Vanessa Bell to Clive Bell, June 22 [1910] 8010.2.29.

20. Ibid., June 24 [1910] 8010.2.30.

21. Ibid., n.d. [?June, 1910] 8010.2.33.

22. Ibid., n.d. [?June 10, 1910] 8010.2.35.

23. Virginia Woolf Papers, Clive Bell to Virginia Stephen [June 6, 1910].

24. *Letters*, I, 425 [June 6, 1910].

25. For details see Donald A. Laing, *Clive Bell: An Annotated Bibliography of the Published Writings* (New York, 1983), pp. 50–56.

26. Berg Collection, Vanessa to Virginia, June 25 [1910].

27. *Letters*, I, 428–429 [June 24, 1910].

28. Tate Archives, Vanessa Bell to Clive Bell, n.d. [June 1910] 8010.2.32.

29. Marler, *Letters of Vanessa Bell*, Vanessa to Clive [June 23, 1910], p. 92.

30. *Letters*, I, 431, July 28, 1910.

31. Berg Collection, Vanessa to Virginia [?July 5, 1910].

32. Ibid., July 17, 1910.

33. Ibid., July 20, 1910.

34. Ibid.

35. Ibid., Clive to Virginia [?Jan 25, 1911].

36. Ibid., Vanessa to Virginia, July 27, 1910.

37. Ibid., Aug. 5 [1910].

38. As Quentin Bell has remarked: "I was born in August 1910 and am therefore coeval with the First Post-Impressionist exhibition. In fact, I might almost claim that we were twins, conceived about the same time and in much the same part of Bloomsbury. While the British public was howling with rage at Van Gogh's sunflowers

and Cézanne's bathers I too was howling, but in a much more rational way." Quentin Bell, "Retrospect: Autobiographical Essay," in *Bad Art* (Chicago, 1989), p. 216.

39. Berg Collection, Vanessa to Virginia, Aug. 1 [1910].

40. Tate Archives, Vanessa to Clive, Aug. 26 [1910], 8010.2.40.

41. Ibid., Aug. 27 [1910], 8010.2.41.

42. Ibid., Aug. 29 [1910], 8010.2.42.

43. British Library, Add. Mss. 59730B, Keynes to Grant, Aug. 29, 1910.

44. Tate Archives, Vanessa to Clive, [n.d.], 8010.2.46.

45. Berg Collection, Clive to Virginia, Dec. 30, 1910.

46. Ibid.

47. *Letters*, I, 432 [August 1910].

48. Ibid., I, 442, to Vanessa, Dec. 25 [1910].

49. Virginia Woolf Papers, [?Aug. 21, 1910].

50. *Letters*, I, 434.

51. Ibid., I, 434–435.

52. Tate Archives, Sept. 7 [1910], 8010.2.50.

53. Ibid., Oct. 7 [1910], 8010.2.57.

54. British Library, Add. Mss. 58120A, Grant to Keynes, Oct. 13, 1910.

55. Tate Archives, Oct. 10 [1910], 8010.2.59.

56. McNeillie, *Essays*, I, 340–344.

57. For dates see Edward Bishop, *A Virginia Woolf Chronology* (London, 1989).

58. *Letters* [?14 Nov. 1910], I, 439.

59. Berg Collection, Dec. 25, 1910.

60. DeSalvo, *First Voyage*, p. 64. See Louise A. DeSalvo, ed., *Melymbrosia by Virginia Woolf* (New York, 1982), pp. xix–xxii. DeSalvo exaggerates, I believe, but it is of interest, and does fit with her argument that the earlier version was more political, that she makes the following statement, in the latter book, about the novel "*Melymbrosia* bristles with social commentary and impresses one with Woolf's engagement with the most significant problems of Edwardian and Georgian England. In its pages the following contemporary issues are examined: the trade union movement and labor unrest; the suffrage movement and increasing militancy; the parliamentary debates, which threatened to alter the very structure of British government; the issues of whether artists, writers, and musicians or politicians did more good for society; the effect of political leaders like Balfour and Lloyd George; the Lords' rejection of the budget; the problem of reconciling humanism with empire building; the effect of the declining birthrate upon the empire; whether women owed it to their country to produce many children; the changes occurring in religion; the effect of new developments in psychology; the contradictions within liberalism; the Irish nationalist movement; the protectionist movement; legislation affecting the welfare of the poor, the aged, and women; the limited means society provided women who needed to earn their living; the impos-

sibility of crossing class lines to marry; the effect of illegitimacy upon personality; legislation affecting the education of women; the need to secure foodstuffs to feed a population whose agricultural productivity had declined; the allure of less circumscribed ways of social and sexual behaviour; the excitement of airplanes; the problem of road repair; the impending spectre of war with Germany; the Moroccan crisis; the effect of the revolution in Portugal; the problems of developing naval power; the issue of the Dreadnoughts; colonialism and its origins" (pp. xxxvi–xxxvii). The mind reels. See also Elizabeth Heine, "Virginia Woolf's Revisions of *The Voyage Out*," in Virginia Woolf, *The Voyage Out* (London, 1990), pp. 399–452.

61. *Letters*, Feb. 28, 1916, II, 82. Comment pointed out by Heine in "Revisions," p. 409.

62. *Essays*, I, 348.

63. *Letters*, I, 438 [Nov. 24, 1910].

64. Ibid., I, 440 [Nov. 27, 1910].

65. Berg Collection, Clive to Virginia, n.d

66. *Letters*, I, 442.

67. Ibid., I, 445–446.

4. Artists and Others

1. Point made by Judith Collins in a panel discussion, "Post-Impressionism: Pure and Applied," *Charleston Newsletter* 23, June 1989, p. 12.

2. See Frances Spalding, *Roger Fry* (Berkeley, 1980), p. 58.

3. See John Pope-Hennessy's remark: "Within its limits, Fry's *Bellini* is an absolutely first-rate book. I said this one day to Berenson; he replied, 'Of course, my dear, I wrote it', and it is strongly Berensonian." John Pope-Hennessy, "Roger Fry and the Metropolitan Museum of Art," in Edward Chaney and Neil Ritchie, eds., *Oxford, China and Italy: Writing in Honor of Sir Harold Acton and his 80th Birthday* (London, 1984), p. 233.

4. Walter Sickert in the *New Age*, May 2, 1910, quoted by Anna Robins, "Feuds and Factions at the New English Art Club," in *The New English Art Club Centenary Exhibition* (London, 1986), p. 13.

5. HRC, Fry to Lady Ottoline Morrell, n.d.

6. HRC, Fry to Morrell, Oct. 14, Nov. 23, 1910.

7. Pope-Hennessy, "Fry and the Metropolitan," pp. 229–235.

8. Denys Sutton, ed., *Letters of Roger Fry* (New York, 1972), I, 32.

9. Pope-Hennessy, "Fry and the Metropolitan," p. 239.

10. Fry Papers, King's College, Cambridge, Fry to Sir Edward Fry, Feb. 14, 1910; in Sutton, *Letters*, I, 327.

11. Belle da Costa Greene Archives, Morgan Library, F. Misc. II: Fry to J. P. Morgan, Dec. 27, 1909; to Morgan, July 12, 1910 (in Sutton, *Letters*, I, 335); Roger

Fry to Belle da Costa Greene, Oct. 15, 1910; Fry to Greene, Dec. 28, 1910 (in Sutton, *Letters*, I, 338); Greene to Fry, Jan. 19, 1911.

12. Fry Papers, Fry to Lady Fry, July 7, 1910.

13. Sutton, *Letters*, I, 328.

14. Fry Papers, Fry to Sir Edward Fry, Feb. 19, 1910.

15. Fry to Trevelyan, June 27, 1910; to Clive Bell, June 28, 1910, Sutton, *Letters*, I, 334–335.

16. R. C. Trevelyan Papers, Trinity College, Cambridge, Forster to Trevelyan, Feb. 26, 1910, RCT3 19.

17. Ibid., 22, August 18, 1910.

18. For details about the picture and its acquisition see Anthony Bailey, *Responses to Rembrandt* (New York, 1994). As Bailey points out (p. 118), Dzików, where Fry went, though Polish speaking, was then within the Austro-Hungarian Empire..

19. Fry Papers, Fry to Lady Fry, April 24, 1910. Mostly published in Sutton, *Letters*, I, 330. Frick sent "a draft on the Morgan bank . . . for $293,162.50 which may have included a commission for Fry on top of the £60,000 for Count Tarnowski." Bailey, *Responses to Rembrandt*, p. 5.

20. Osbert Sitwell, ed., W. R. Sickert, *A Free House!* (London, 1947), p. 350.

21. *The Annual Register: A Review of Public Events at Home and Abroad for the Year 1910* (London, 1911), p. 101.

22. Fry to Helen Fry [May 1910], in Sutton, *Letters*, I, 331.

23. Fry Papers, Fry to Lady Fry, July 7, 1910.

24. HRC, Fry to Morrell, Dec. 28, 1910.

25. See for the history of the Contemporary Arts Society, *British Contemporary Art 1910–1990* (London, 1991), with chapters on the early years by Judith Collins and Richard Cork and on the present by Marina Vaizey.

26. Fry to MacColl, March 16, 1909, in Sutton, *Letters*, I, 317.

27. Robert Gathorne-Hardy, ed., *Ottoline: The Early Memoirs of Lady Ottoline Morrell* (London, 1963), p. 167.

28. Contemporary Art Society Archives, London, Minute Book.

29. *Annual Report*, Contemporary Art Society, December 1911.

30. CAS Archives, Dec. 5, 1912, Minute Book.

31. Judith Bumpus, "The Contemporary Art Society," *Art and Artists*, 193 (1982), pp. 5–6.

32. See Eric Gill, *The Engravings* (London, 1990), #10.

33. Gill Papers, William Andrews Clark Library, Los Angeles, Fry to Gill, Dec. 4, 1910.

34. HRC, Fry to Morrell, Nov. 30, 1910.

35. See Miranda Seymour, *Ottoline Morrell: Life on the Grand Scale* (London, 1992), p. 107.

36. Collins, "The Origins and Aims of the Contemporary Art Society," *British Contemporary Art,* p. 22.

37. Gill Papers, Fry to Gill, Feb. 18, 1911.

38. Ibid.

39. For these details see Judith Collins, *Eric Gill: Sculpture* (London, 1992), pp. 72–73.

40. Fiona MacCarthy, *Eric Gill* (New York, 1989), p. 104.

41. Fiona MacCarthy, "The Word Became Flesh," review of a Gill sculpture exhibition, *Times Literary Supplement,* Dec. 25, 1992, p. 14.

42. Keynes Papers, King's College, Cambridge, J. Knewstub to Keynes, Feb. 6, 1911, PP 69/11.

43. Ibid., Knewstub to Keynes, Aug. 3, 1912.

44. MacCarthy, *Gill,* p. 104.

45. *Annual Register,* p. 100.

46. Courtesy Quentin Bell, Vanessa Bell, "Memories of Roger Fry," October 1934, p. 2.

47. *Times,* Nov. 26, 1910, p. 6.

48. Frank Rutter, *Art in My Time* (London, 1933), p. 125.

49. Joseph Hone, *The Life of Henry Tonks* (London, 1939), pp. 99–100, quoting Rutter, *Art in My Time.*

50. *Times,* Nov. 1, 1910, p. 11.

51. Points made in Eric Hobsbawm, *The Age of Empire: 1875–1914* (New York, 1987), p. 221.

52. See J. B. Bullen, ed., *Post-Impressionists in England* (London, 1988), p. 3.

53. See Benedict Nicolson, "Post-Impressionism and Roger Fry," *Burlington,* Jan. 1951, 93, p. 11.

54. Quoted in Virginia Woolf, *Roger Fry* (London, 1940), p. 112.

55. Anon., *Burlington,* Feb. 1908, 12, pp. 272–273; in Bullen, *Post-Impressionists in England,* pp. 42–43.

56. Roger Fry, "Letter," *Burlington,* March 1908, 12, pp. 374–376; in Bullen, *Post-Impressionists in England,* pp. 44–48.

57. Rutter, *Art in My Time,* pp. 114–115.

58. Osbert Sitwell, ed., *A Free House or the Artist as Craftsman: Being the Writings of Walter Richard Sickert* (London, 1947), p. 208.

59. First published in 1936 as *Pioneers of the Modern Movement,* then in subsequent revised editions with the revealing subtitle *From William Morris to Walter Gropius.*

60. Included in Roger Fry, *Vision and Design* (London, 1920).

61. Ian Dunlop, *The Shock of the New* (New York, 1972), pp. 124–125.

62. Richard Shone, *Bloomsbury Portraits,* 2nd ed. (London, 1993), p. 36. The painting is dated ?1902 but Shone suspects it is 1906–07.

63. Christopher Reed, "Apples: 46 Gordon Square," *Charleston Newsletter*, June 1989, 23, p. 22.

64. I am indebted to Stella Tillyard for the opportunity to read her paper "'Illustration, Illustration All the Time': W. R. Sickert, Virginia Woolf and Early Modernism" (March 1989).

65. *Times*, July 11, 1910, in Bullen, *Post-Impressionists in England*, pp. 89, 91.

66. Fry Papers, Fry to Grant, Nov. 9, 1910.

67. Vanessa Bell, "Memories," p. 3.

68. Clive Bell, *Old Friends* (London, 1956), p. 80.

69. I owe these points to letter, Diane Gillespie to author, Nov. 15, 1992.

70. Jeanne Schulkind, ed., *Virginia Woolf: Moments of Being* (Sussex, 1976), p. 175.

71. Woolf, *Roger Fry*, pp. 149–150.

72. *Times*, April 28, 1938, quoted in Anne Olivier Bell, ed., *The Diary of Virginia Woolf* (London, 1984), V, 365.

73. Sandra Jobson Darroch, *Ottoline* (New York, 1975), p. 83.

74. Berg Collection, Vanessa to Virginia [?July 10, 1910].

75. By one of those splendid coincidences, Peppard Cottage played Howards End in the movie, as James Ivory was not satisfied with using the actual house, Rooks Nest, in Hertfordshire where Forster had lived, and which was the model for the fictional Howards End.

76. See Seymour, *Ottoline Morrell*, p. 72.

77. Michael Holroyd ed., *Lytton Strachey by Himself* (London, 1971), pp. 122–123.

78. British Library, Add. Mss. 57932, Lytton Strachey to Duncan Grant, April 4, 1910.

79. HRC, Lamb to Morrell, ?June, 1910.

80. Keynes Papers, King's College, Cambridge, Keynes to Strachey, July 10, 1910, PP 45/316/4/166.

81. Ibid., Strachey to Keynes, PP 45/316/4/167–168.

82. HRC, Lamb to Morrell, Nov. 20, 1910.

83. HRC, Strachey to Lady Strachey, Nov. 30, 1910.

84. HRC, Lamb to Morrell n.d., [?Dec. 1910].

85. HRC, Strachey to Morrell, Dec. 8, 1910.

86. HRC, Fry to Morrell, Nov. 23, 1910.

87. Ibid., Nov. 30, 1910.

88. Ibid., Dec. 7, 1910.

89. *Letters*, Jan. 1, 1911, I, 448–449.

90. HRC, Lamb to Morrell, Dec. ?, 1910.

91. HRC, Helen Maitland to Ottoline Morrell, Dec. 28, 1910.

92. Keith Clements, *Henry Lamb: The Artist and His Friends* (Bristol, 1985), p. 178. This biography is very useful for details of Lamb's life.

93. HRC, Strachey Papers, Strachey to Lady Strachey, May 22, 1910.

94. Desmond MacCarthy Papers, Lilly Library, Indiana University, Bloomington, Strachey to MacCarthy, June 7, 1910.

95. James Strachey, Preface, to Lytton Strachey, *Spectatorial Essays* (London, 1964), p. 7.

96. Holroyd, *Lytton Strachey*, I, 456.

97. *Spectatorial Essays*, p. 44, reprinting *Spectator* review of March 12, 1910.

98. HRC, Strachey to Lady Strachey, Sept. 27, 1910.

99. Holroyd, *Lytton Strachey*, I, 459.

100. Ibid., p. 460.

101. Point made by John Beer, "The 'Civilisation' of Bloomsbury," in Richard Cork and Boris Ford, eds., *The Edwardian Age and the Inter-War Years* (Cambridge, 1989), p. 198.

102. Duncan Grant in Joan Russell Noble, ed., *Recollections of Virginia Woolf* (London, 1972), pp. 19–20.

103. British Library, Add. Mss. 57930B, Keynes to Grant, July 10, 1910.

104. Keynes papers, King's College, Cambridge, Keynes to father, Jan. 27. 1910, PP 45/168/7/15.

105. Keynes to Grant, Oct. 15, Oct. 20, 1909, quoted in R. F. Harrod, *The Life of John Maynard Keynes* (London, 1952), p. 149.

106. See Elizabeth Johnson, ed., *The Collected Writings of John Maynard Keynes: Activities 1906–1914, India and Cambridge* (London, 1971), XV, 44–59.

107. Keynes papers, King's College, Keynes to father, Oct. 1. 1910, PP 45/7/93.

108. British Library, Add. Mss. 57930, Keynes to Grant, March 3, 1910.

109. British Library, Add. Mss 57993 Grant to Strachey, April 15, 1910.

110. British Library, Add. Mss. 59730B, Keynes to Grant, Oct. 11, 1910.

111. Quotations from Charles H. Hession, *John Maynard Keynes* (New York, 1984), pp. 79–80.

112. British Library, Add. Mss. 58120A, Grant to Keynes, Dec. 18, 1910.

113. British Library, Add. Mss. 57930B, Keynes to Grant, Feb. 4, Feb. 6, 1910.

114. British Library, Add. Mss. 58120A, Grant to Keynes, May 19, 1910.

115. Keynes Papers, Keynes to his parents, June 26, 1910, PP 45/16/87/39.

116. Robert Skidelsky, *John Maynard Keynes* (New York, 1983), I, 257–258.

117. D. E. Moggridge, *Maynard Keynes: An Economist's Biography* (London, 1992), plates 9 and 10, and pp. 838–839.

118. British Library, Add. Mss. 60672, Keynes to James Strachey, Sept. 17, 1910.

119. Keynes Papers, Keynes to Strachey, Sept. 24, 1909, PP 45/316/4/152.

120. Ibid., Keynes to Strachey, Oct. 3, 1910, PP 45/316/4/169.

121. Much of this information from Skidelsky, *Keynes*, pp. 252–257.

122. British Library, Add. Mss. 57930B, Keynes to Grant, June 6, 1910.

123. British Library, Add. Mss. 58120A, Grant to Keynes, June 10, 1910.

124. Skidelsky, *Keynes*, p. 256.

125. Regina Marler, ed., *Selected Letters of Vanessa Bell* (New York, 1993), Vanessa Bell to Clive Bell [June 23, 1910], p. 93.

5. E. M. FORSTER

1. Forster to Florence Barger, Dec. 24, 1911, quoted in P. N. Furbank, *E. M. Forster: A Life* (New York, 1977), I, 206.

2. Ibid., p. 208. See Evert Barger, "Memories of Morgan," *New York Times Book Review*, Aug. 16, 1970, pp. 2, 32–35. It should be noted that at this point "queer" simply meant peculiar. According to the *OED*, it did not come to mean homosexual until the 1920s in the United States and the 1930s in Britain.

3. For details about the college see David Lelyveld, *Aligarh's First Generation* (Princeton, 1978). For the Stracheys and India see Charles Richard Sanders, *The Strachey Family, 1588–1932* (Durham, N.C., 1953). John Strachey had written a defense of Warren Hastings, *Hastings and the Rohilla War,* in 1892. Leslie Stephen's brother, the eminent jurist Sir James Fitzjames Stephen, had written an earlier defense of Hastings, *The Story of Nuncomar and the Impeachment of Sir Elijah Impey,* in 1885.

4. Keynes Papers, King's College, Cambridge, Morison to Keynes, Dec. 31, 1911, A/11/B.

5. Jalil Ahmad Kidwai, ed., *Forster-Masood Letters* (Karachi, 1984), p. 56.

6. Quoted in R. W. Noble, "Dearest Forster"—"Dearest Masood," *Encounter,* June 1981, 56, p. 62.

7. Forster Papers, King's College, Cambridge, Locked Diary, March 19, 1910.

8. Many of Forster's letters to Masood have been published in Jalil Ahmad Kidwai, ed., *Forster-Masood Letters*. Some are to be found in Mary Lago and P. N. Furbank, eds., *Selected Letters of E. M. Forster,* vol. I: 1879–1920 (Cambridge, Mass., 1983).

9. King's College, May 9, 1910.

10. King's College; Furbank, pp. 193–194; Kidwai, pp. 101–102.

11. King's College, Locked Diary, Nov. 13, 1910.

12. King's College; Kidwai, pp. 61–62.

13. King's College, Locked Diary.

14. Kidwai, p. 103; Furbank, p. 194.

15. *Times* (London), Nov. 20, Dec. 8, 12, 1910.

16. Tate Gallery Archives, Vanessa to Clive, n.d., 8010.2.62.

17. *Times* (London), Dec. 17, 1910.

18. *Annual Register* (London, 1911), p. 106.

19. Ibid., p. 104.

20. Ibid., p. 102.

21. King's College, Locked Diary, July 21, Dec. 29, 1910. Forster did make another declaration the following August when Masood and he were vacationing together in Tesserete in Switzerland. He commented on the trip in his diary on December 31, in the last entry for 1911. "The first week was incoherent joy, though the detail escapes me. Towards the end Masood grew tired of the place and of me and it was less pleasant, but it was clear he liked me better than any man in the world, so I did not mind. Near the beginning, I spoke, seeing that after all he did not realise. He was surprised and sorry and put it away at once. It has made either no difference, or a good difference. I have seen the worst of him, but all is well. I bear his going better now, for we shall never be nearer, & do seem firm at last.—A happy but uncreative holiday."

22. King's College, Forster to Masood, Jan 1, 1911.

23. King's College, Forster to Masood, ?January, 1911.

24. Diary Jan. 25, 1911.

25. May 23, 1923, Kidwai p. 81.

26. King's College, Feb. 13, 1924.

27. E. M. Forster, "Seyd Ross Masood," in *Two Cheers for Democracy* (London, 1951), p. 292.

28. King's College, Aug. 18, 1910.

29. *Selected Letters,* Aug. 22. 1910, p. 114.

30. King's College, Locked Diary.

31. Ibid., Sept. 19, Sept. 29, 1910.

32. Ibid., Feb. 19, 1910.

33. Morrell Papers, Harry Ransom Humanities Research Center, University of Texas at Austin, Jan. 16, 1911.

34. Clive Bell Papers, Trinity College, Cambridge, "Lytton Strachey," 3 10 (4).

35. Arnold Bennett, *Books and Persons: Being Comments on a Past Epoch* (London, 1920 [first pub. 1917]), pp. 208–209.

36. James Hepburn, ed., *The Letters of Arnold Bennett* (London, 1966), Feb. 6, Feb. 9, 1910, I, 132–133.

37. Arnold Bennett, *The Journal of Arnold Bennett* (New York, 1933), pp. 359, 402.

38. Christopher Hassall, *A Biography of Edward Marsh* (New York, 1959), p. 169. Three figures of a somewhat older generation, Marsh, A. C. Benson, and Edmund Gosse, were interested in the younger writers and artists of the time. Marsh sent Gosse *Howards End* which he, rather interestingly, vehemently hated. He felt that the end of the book was full of "lurid sentimentality, preposterous morals." A. C. Benson recorded in his diary that Gosse felt *Howards End* "was a vile, obscene, decadent book. . . . that Forster had prostituted charming gifts to a sickening lust for popularity, and so on." Ann Thwaite, *Edmund Gosse* (Chicago, 1984), p. 441. Gosse at this time was deeply involved in establishing an Academy of Letters that

in its sense of the official stood for much that Bloomsbury despised. See David Newsome, *On the Edge of Paradise: A. C. Benson The Diarist* (Chicago, 1980), p. 276. Ironically, *Howards End* received some sort of award from the Academy the following June. Forster wrote to Malcolm Darling: "All the jests that I have been cracking at the Academy's expense must be hastily forgotten. Will they order me a laurel wreath from the florists, or will it be placed on my brows by Mr Edmund Gosse in person? Shall I have a medal for Misconduct too?" Forster Papers, HRC, Forster to Darling, June 5, 1911.

These men both were titillated by and officially disapproved of the apparent homosexual behavior of the younger generation, as Benson observed at King's after the Founder's Feast of 1909: "The public fondling and caressing of each other, friends and lovers sitting with arms enlaced, cheeks even touching, struck me as curious, beautiful in a way, but rather dangerous." Newsome, p. 246. Gerald Shove wrote a little more brutally about what he imagined were the events after the same Feast the following year: "I suppose there were no rapes; just blithering sottish drunkenness, a little groping and a cock-stand or two." Keynes Papers, Shove to Keynes, Dec. 29, 1910, PP 45/296. Keynes himself could be a little disapproving of the excesses of such occasions, writing to Duncan Grant about a feast the previous June. "On Monday we had one of our terminal debauches and everybody became very tipsy. Private lusts are now pressed, in my opinion, or are beginning to be to a point where they interfere with good fellowship. If one hasn't the spirit to carry off an adventure when sober, it's better, I think, not to try when drunk." British Library, Add. Mss. 57930B, Keynes to Grant June 16, 1910. The sexual differences between the generations become clear in Benson's reaction, in 1924, to his beloved George Rylands' account of life while he was working for the Hogarth Press: "They seem to live with each other rather promiscuously, expected to have love-affairs and yet not to be sentimental." Newsome, p. 365.

39. *Times Literary Supplement*, No. 453, Sept. 15, 1910, p. 328.

40. James Hepburn ed., *Arnold Bennett: The Critical Heritage* (London, 1981), p. 248.

41. Ibid., p. 256.

42. Philip Gardner, ed., *E. M. Forster: The Critical Heritage* (London, 1973), pp. 130–160.

43. HRC, Nov. 12, 1910; *Selected Letters*, I, 117.

44. Marsh Papers, Berg Collection, New York Public Library, Nov. 6, 1910.

45. Locked Diary, Dec. 8, 1910.

46. Forster Papers, Nov. 21, 1910.

47. HRC, Sept. 22, 1910.

48. Marsh Papers, Aug. 22, 1910.

49. Locked Diary, Sept. 5, 1910.

50. Malcolm Darling Papers, Box 51, Centre of South Asian Studies, Cambridge University, May 11, 1907.

51. Feb. 10, 1910, *Selected Letters*, p. 104.

52. Darling Papers, Box 51, May 3, 1910. As Darling wrote to his mother on February 15: "India is hard enough on married couples, but it is downright cruel to the children. This is in fact no country for them." *Selected Letters*, p. 109.

53. June 29, 1910, *Selected Letters*, p. 108.

54. Aug. 12, 1910, ibid., p. 110.

55. Aug. 22, 1910, ibid., p. 114.

56. HRC, Sept. 4, 1910.

57. HRC, Sept. 22, 1910, part quoted in *Selected Letters*, p. 111.

58. Nov. 21, 1910, *Selected Letters,*, p. 111.

59. HRC, Forster to Josie Darling, Feb. 17, 20, 1911; to Malcolm Darling, Feb. 22, 1911.

60. E. M. Forster, "Liking Being Alive," *Library Chronicle of the University of Texas at Austin,* new series, no. 23, 1983, pp. 75–79. The words indicated as crossed out in the text are not given here. See also Anne-Marie Roman, "'Liking Being Alive' and E. M. Forster's Aestheticism," ibid., pp. 63–73. Contrary to Lago and Furbank, Roman assumes that Forster did finally consent to be a godfather. I have not found an explicit statement in which he finally declines, but I would hesitate to disagree with Forster's biographer.

61. Roman, ibid., p. 68.

62. Ibid., p. 73.

63. Locked Diary, Dec. 8, 1910.

64. Material from Furbank, pp. 192–193. The paper appears to be a revision of a talk he had given to the Apostles in October. See Elizabeth Heine, Introduction to E. M. Forster, *Arctic Summer and Other Fiction* (London, 1980), pp. xii–xiii.

65. Forster Papers, Notes for paper "Feminine Note in Literature," ff. 90–106.

6. QUAKES IN BRITISH SOCIETY

1. Neal Blewett, *The Peers, the Parties and the People* (Toronto, 1972), p. ix.

2. Figures from Hugh W. Stephens, "Party Realignment in Britain, 1900–1925," *Social Science History*, 6:1 (1982), pp. 35–66.

3. British Library, Add. Mss. 57930A, Keynes to Grant, May 22, 1910.

4. British Library, Add. Mss. 58120A, Grant to Keynes, May 19, 1910.

5. *Times,* Review of the Year, Dec. 31, 1910, p. 9.

6. Keynes Papers, King's College, Cambridge, n.d., PP 45/316/4/158–159.

7. Ibid., Jan. 8, Jan. 12, 1910, PP 45/168/7/10, 7/13.

8. Forster Papers, Harry Ransom Humanities Research Center, University of Texas at Austin, Oct. 14, 1910.

9. Mary Lago and P. N. Furbank, eds., *Selected Letters of E. M. Forster*, vol. I: 1879–1920 (Cambridge, Mass., 1983), Jan. 20, Feb. 10, 1910, pp. 103–105.

10. Keynes Papers, Strachey to Keynes, Jan. 17, 1910 PP 45/316/4/160–161.

11. Berg Collection, New York Public Library, Sydney Waterlow Diary, 1910, Nov. 28, 1910.

12. R. F. Harrod, *The Life of John Maynard Keynes* (London, 1952), Dec. 6, 1910, p. 155.

13. *Hansard*, 5th series, vol. 7, Nov. 15, 1910, col. 87.

14. *Times*, Nov. 19, 1910, p. 13.

15. Virginia Woolf, *The Voyage Out* (London, 1915), p. 109.

16. Ibid., pp. 38, 73, 43–44, 72, 84–85.

17. See Lisa Tickner, *The Spectacle of Women* (Chicago, 1988), pp. 16–18.

18. British Library, Add. Mss. 58120A, Grant to Keynes, n.d. [Jan. 1910].

19. Barbara Strachey, *Remarkable Relations* (New York, 1982), pp. 247–248.

20. For the role of the NUWSS at this time see Leslie Parker Hume, *The National Union of Women's Suffrage Societies, 1897–1914* (New York, 1982), pp. 81–91.

21. *Hansard*, 5th series, Nov. 18, 1910, cols. 106–107.

22. Ibid., col. 137.

23. *Times*, Dec. 6, 1910, p. 3.

24. Ibid., Dec. 1, 1910.

25. Ibid., Dec. 31, 1901 p. 11.

26. Virginia Woolf, *Mr Bennett and Mrs Brown* (London, 1924), pp. 4–5.

27. David Smith, "Tonypandy 1910: Definitions of Community," *Past and Present* (May 1980), p. 170.

28. *Times*, Dec. 31, 1910, p. 10.

29. See Charles Townshend, "One Man Whom You Can Hang If Necessary': The Discreet Charm of Nevil Macready," in John B. Hattendorf and Malcolm H. Murfett, eds., *The Limitations of Military Power* (London, 1990), pp. 146–148.

30. Hans Koning, "The Eleventh Edition," *New Yorker*, March 2, 1981, p. 67.

31. Ibid., p. 83.

32. See James Bryce, Prefatory Note to "Handy Volume" edition of *Encyclopedia Britannica* (London, ?1915), pp. vii–viii.

33. For much of the information in these paragraphs see Herman Kogan, *The Great EB* (Chicago, 1958), and, to an extent, Gillian Thomas, *A Position to Command Respect: Women and the Eleventh Britannica* (London, 1992).

34. Stella Benson Collection, Cambridge University Library, Diary, Dec. 13, 1910, Mss. 6769.

35. *Hansard*, Nov. 18, 1910, cols. 85, 135.

36. *Times,* Dec. 3, 1910, p. 14.

37. Ibid., Dec. 8, Dec. 9, 1910, p. 7.

38. Ibid., Dec. 21, 1910, p. 11.

7. ON THE WAY TO POST-IMPRESSIONISM

1. Desmond MacCarthy, "Bloomsbury," in *Memories* (London, 1953), p. 175. There is a longer manuscript version in the Desmond MacCarthy Papers, Lilly Library, Indiana University, Bloomington.

2. MacCarthy, *Memories,* pp. 180–183.

3. Fry Papers, King's College, Cambridge, Fry to Lady Fry, May 30, 1910.

4. MacCarthy Papers, MacCarthy to Molly MacCarthy, Sept. 8, 1910. Also see Hugh and Mirabel Cecil, *Clever Hearts: Desmond and Molly MacCarthy* (London, 1990), p. 107.

5. Fry Papers, Diary, 1910.

6. Frances Spalding, *Roger Fry* (Berkeley, 1980), p. 131.

7. Cecil and Cecil, *Clever Hearts,* pp. 107–108.

8. Roger Fry, *Vision and Design* (London, 1920), p. 191.

9. Desmond MacCarthy, "Roger Fry and the Post-Impressionist Exhibition of 1910" (1945), in *Memories* (London, 1953), p. 179. There are two versions of this piece. "The Art-Quake of 1910," in the *Listener,* February 1, 1945, pp. 123–124, 129, is marginally different.

10. Fry Papers.

11. MacCarthy Papers, part quoted in *Clever Hearts,* p. 109.

12. Private Collection, MacCarthy to Moore, Sept. 14, 1910.

13. MacCarthy Papers, Desmond MacCarthy to Molly MacCarthy, Sept. 15, 1910.

14. According to Clive Bell, "How England Met Modern Art," *Art News,* Oct. 1950, p. 24.

15. *Memories,* p. 180.

16. Ian Dunlop, "The Post-Impressionists" in *The Shock of the New* (New York, 1972), p. 135.

17. *Memories,* pp. 180–181.

18. Fry Papers.

19. For her time in France see Robert Gathorne-Hardy, ed., *Ottoline: The Early Memoirs of Lady Ottoline Morrell* (London, 1963), pp. 186–200.

20. Ottoline Morrell Papers, Harry Ransom Humanities Research Center, University of Texas at Austin, Sept. 22, 1910.

21. Denys Sutton, *Letters of Roger Fry* (London, 1972), I, 337.

22. Tate Gallery Archives, Oct. 9, 10, 1910, 8010.2.58, 59.

23. Dunlop, "The Post-Impressionists," p. 125.

24. Rothenstein Papers, Houghton Library, Harvard University, Fry to Rothenstein, n.d, postmark June 3, 1910; in Sutton, *Letters of Roger Fry*, I, 332–333.

25. See Donald A. Laing, *Roger Fry: An Annotated Bibliography of the Published Writings* (New York, 1979).

26. Rothenstein Papers, Fry to Mrs Rothenstein, Aug. 22, 1910.

27. Ibid., Fry to Rothenstein, n.d.

28. *Vision and Design,* pp. 190–191.

29. William Rothenstein, *Men and Memories* (New York, 1932), p. 212.

30. Fry Papers, Rothenstein to Fry, n.d.

31. Robert Speaight, *William Rothenstein* (London, 1962), p. 245.

32. *Letters,* Jan. 2, 1910, I, 327.

33. Rothenstein Papers, Fry to Mrs Rothenstein, Aug. 22, 1910.

8. The Exhibition

1. Fry had never liked Sargent's work, but he did cite him at the end of December as a supporter of at least Cézanne, although the statement was grammatically ambiguous. Sargent was moved to remonstrate: "The fact is that I am absolutely sceptical as to to their [the Post-Impressionists] having any claim whatever to being works of art, with the exception of some of the pictures by Gauguin that strike me as admirable in color, and in color only." *Nation,* Dec. 24, 1910, Jan. 7, 1911; J. B. Bullen, *Post-Impressionists in England: The Critical Reception* (London, 1988), pp. 148, 153. See Quentin Bell, "John Sargent and Roger Fry," *Burlington,* Nov. 1957, 99, 380–382. Fry replied on January 14 that he had had a private letter from Sargent earlier in which he had expressed admiration for Cézanne and that was the only painter he had meant. "I learn, for the first time, from his letter to the *Nation* what his opinion of the other artists shown at the Grafton Gallery is." *Nation,* Jan. 14, 1911, 8, 646.

2. Ian Dunlop, *The Shock of the New* (New York, 1972), p. 141.

3. Hugh and Mirabel Cecil, *Clever Hearts: Desmond and Molly MacCarthy* (London, 1990), Nov. 17, 1910, p. 112. Part in MacCarthy Papers, Lilly Library, Indiana University, Bloomington.

4. C. J. Holmes, *Notes on the Post-Impressionist Painters: Grafton Gallery, 1910–11* (London, 1910), p. 7.

5. C. J. Holmes, *Self and Partners (Mostly Self): Being the Reminiscences of C. J. Holmes* (London, 1936), p. 280.

6. Clive Bell, "Review," *Athenaeum,* Jan. 7, 1911, p. 19.

7. Holmes, *Notes,* pp. 39–40.

8. *Nation,* Dec. 24, 1910; Bullen, *Post-Impressionists in England*, pp. 150–151.

9. Holmes, *Self,* p. 282.

10. *Times Literary Supplement*, Dec. 22, 1910, p. 517.

11. *Manet and the Post-Impressionists* (London, 1910), n.p.

12. Fry Papers, Copy Fry to Holmes, n.d.

13. Private Collection, copy MacCarthy to Edward Marsh, Sept. 26, 1910.

14. Virginia Woolf, *Roger Fry* (London, 1940), p. 152.

15. Desmond MacCarthy, "The Art-Quake of 1910," *Listener*, Feb. 1, 1943, p. 124.

16. Ibid.

17. See *Impressionist and Post-Impressionist Masterpieces: The Courtauld Collection* (New Haven, 1987), no. 3, n.p. Some details of the pictures in the exhibition are from Benedict Nicolson, "Post-Impressionism and Roger Fry," *Burlington*, Jan. 1951, 93, 11–15.

18. Bell, "Review," p. 24.

19. Ibid., p. 26.

20. See James R. Mellow, *Charmed Circle: Gertrude Stein and Company* (New York, 1974), p. 151.

21. Roger Fry, "Acquisitions by the National Gallery at Helsingfors," *Burlington*, Feb. 1911, 18, 293.

22. MacCarthy Papers, Nov. 8, 1910.

23. Bullen, *Post-Impressionists in England*, pp. 94–99.

24. *Spectator*, Nov. 12, 1910, pp. 797–798.

25. Bullen, *Post-Impressionists in England*, pp. 127–128.

26. MacCarthy Papers, Molly MacCarthy to Louise MacCarthy, Nov. 8, 1910.

27. Desmond MacCarthy, *Memories* (London, 1953), pp. 182–183.

28. Bullen, *Post-Impressionists in England*, pp. 120–124, 129–134.

29. Reproduced in Dunlop, *Shock of the New*, pp. 156–157.

30. Quoted in Woolf, *Fry*, p. 158.

31. Bullen, *Post-Impressionists in England*, pp. 166–179.

32. Blunt Diaries, Fitzwilliam Museum, Cambridge MS 406–1975, pp. 51–53; part published in Woolf, *Fry*, pp. 156–157, and Wilfred Blunt, *Diaries* (New York, 1922), II, 329–330.

33. Tate Archives, Anon., "The Post-Impressionists."

34. *Fortnightly Review*, Jan. 1911; in Bullen, *Post-Impressionists in England*, pp. 154–166.

35. Published Nov. 9, 1910; in Bullen, *Post-Impressionists in England*, pp. 105–106.

36. Charleston papers, King's College Cambridge, copy Lamb to Clive Bell, Nov. 8, 1910, XII, 64.

37. Fry Papers, Diary.

38. Virginia Woolf Papers, University of Sussex, copied out by Virginia Woolf; letter printed in Sutton, *Letters of Roger Fry*, I, 337, with these sentences omitted.

39. Fry Papers, Fry to Lady Fry, Dec. 25, 1910.

40. Sutton, *Letters of Roger Fry*, March 28, 1913, I, 366. It is significant, I think, that Sutton chooses to end the first volume of the letters, in the middle of the year, with this letter.

41. Woolf, *Fry*, p. 149.

42. Ibid., pp. 152–153.

43. Figure given by S. K. Tillyard, *The Impact of Modernism* (London, 1988), p. 81.

44. Published January 16, 1911; in Bullen, *Post-Impressionists in England*, p. 183–184.

45. Fry Papers, Nov. 24, 1910.

46. *Listener*, p. 124.

47. Nicolson, "Post-Impressionism and Roger Fry," p. 13.

48. HRC, Dec. 17, 1910.

49. Tillyard, *Impact of Modernism*, pp. 39–40.

50. Paul Nash, *Outline* (London, 1949), p. 93.

51. Oliver Brown, *Exhibition* (London, 1968), p. 39.

52. Tillyard, *Impact of Modernism*, pp. 92–95.

53. Ibid., p. 93. See also p. 105 for Weld-Blundell's belief in "a social reform programme which fused temperance and religious revivalism with rural resettlement, rearmament, and the demise of party politics."

54. See Bullen, *Post-Impressionists in England*, p. 15.

55. *Times*, Nov. 7, 1910, p. 11.

56. Bullen, *Post-Impressionists in England*, pp. 193–201.

57. HRC, Oct. 14, 1910.

58. Bullen, *Post-Impressionists in England*, pp. 100–104.

59. Robert Ross, "Present and Future Prospects of English Art," (?October 10, 1910 lecture at Liverpool, no source given), p. 21; cited in Maureen Borland, *Wilde's Devoted Friend: A Life of Robert Ross* (Oxford, 1990), p. 152.

60. Laurence Binyon, "The Post-Impressionists," *Saturday Review*, Nov. 12, 1910, 110, 609–610.

61. William Gaunt, *Aesthetic Adventure* (London, 1945), p. 197.

62. Bullen, *Post-Impressionists in England*, pp. 106–108.

63. Rpt. in Charles Ricketts, *Pages on Art* (London, 1913), pp. 149–164. See also J. G. P. Delaney, *Charles Ricketts* (Oxford, 1990), pp. 246–249.

64. Bullen, *Post-Impressionists in England*, pp. 114–117.

65. *Morning Post*, Nov. 17, 1910, p. 3.

66. Ibid., Nov. 18, 1910, p. 10.

67. Bullen, *Post-Impressionists in England*, pp. 117–120.

68. *Morning Post*, Nov. 26, 1910, p. 4.

69. Ibid., Nov. 30, 1910, p. 5.

70. *Observer,* Nov. 13, 1910, p. 9.

71. *Illustrated London News,* Nov. 25, 1910, pp. 824–825.

72. *Tatler,* Nov. 23, 1910, pp. 228–229.

73. *Connoisseur,* Dec. 1910, 28, 315–316.

74. Fry Papers, Nov. 24, 1910.

75. *Nation* Dec. 3, 1910, 8, 406.

76. Ibid., Dec. 10, 1910, 8, 443.

77. *New Age,* Dec. 1910, Bullen, *Post-Impressionists in England,* pp. 134–136.

78. The phrase is Charles Muscatine's in "The Public Humanities and the Academic," in *Federation of State Humanities Councils Annual Report 1993,* p. 3.

79. For material on the *New Age* and quotations see Wallace Martin, *The New Age under Orage* (New York, 1967), pp. 131–135.

80. Bullen, *Post-Impressionists in England,* pp. 183–184.

81. *Times,* Dec. 5, 1910, p. 14.

82. *Nation,* Dec. 3, 1910, 8, 405–406. Sadler's and Bennett's letters were part of an extensive correspondence in the *Nation* about the exhibition, including two letters attacking the show from Henry Holiday, a stained-glass maker who was a prominent member of the Arts and Crafts world, who called it "an impudent sham." Dec. 24, 1910, 8, 539.

83. HRC, Dec. 7, 1910.

84. Bullen, *Post-Impressionists in England,* p. 149.

85. Walter Shewring, *Letters of Eric Gill* (London, 1947), pp. 34–36, corrected on the basis of original in Rothenstein Papers, Houghton Library, Harvard, MS Eng 1148 (569).

86. Fry Papers, March 19, 1911.

87. Rothenstein Papers, Fry to Rothenstein, April 13, 1911; in Sutton, *Letters of Roger Fry,* I, 345.

88. Fry Papers, April 17, 1911.

89. HRC, April 22, 1911.

90. Rothenstein, *Men and Memories,* p. 216.

91. Rothenstein Papers, May 31, 1911.

92. D. S. MacColl, *Confessions of a Keeper and Other Papers* (New York, 1931), p. vi.

93. Frank Rutter, *Revolution in Art* (London, 1910), pp. 15, 12, 18.

94. MacColl, "A Year of Post-Impressionism," in *Confessions,* pp. 218–224.

95. Bullen, *Post-Impressionists in England,* pp. 31–32.

96. Both Savage and Hyslop are discussed at some length in Stephen Trombley, *All That Summer She Was Mad: Virginia Woolf: Female Victim of Male Medicine* (New York, 1982); see p. 216. See also Anne Olivier Bell, "Letter," *Virginia Woolf Miscellany,* Spring 1980, 14. 7. Hyslop was one of the doctors (the other was Savage) consulted in 1912 by

Leonard Woolf when he was considering the question of whether or not they should have children in the light of Virginia's mental state. Savage was much more cheerfully positive, feeling that children might do Virginia a world of good, although he had written about the inadvisability of the mad having children. Hyslop suggested that they wait for a year and a half before deciding.

97. See Peter Stansky, *Redesigning the World* (Princeton, 1985).

98. Woolf, *Fry*, p. 156.

99. H. J. L. J. Massé, *The Art Workers' Guild, 1884–1934* (Oxford, 1935), p. 116.

100. Bullen, *Post-Impressionists in England*, pp. 209–210.

101. Quoted in Ulysses L. D'Acquila, *Bloomsbury and Modernism* (New York, 1989), p. 10.

102. Holmes, *Self and Partners,* pp. 280–281.

103. Holmes, *Notes,* p. 14.

104. Ibid., pp. 25–26.

105. Fry to Sir Edward Fry, Nov. 24,1910, Sutton I, 338.

106. William C. Wees, *Vorticism and the English Avant-Garde* (Toronto, 1972), p. 31.

107. Julie F. Codell, "Marion Henry Spielmann and the Role of the Press in the Professionalization of Artists," *Victorian Periodicals Review* (Spring 1989), 22, 1, p. 10.

9. Bloomsbury Emergent

1. Nigel Nicolson and Joanne Trautmann, eds., *The Letters of Virginia Woolf* (New York, 1975), I, 440.

2. Morrell Papers, Harry Ransom Humanities Research Center, University of Texas at Austin, Feb. 12, 1911.

3. Ibid., April 1, 1911.

4. Tate Gallery Archives, London, see Vanessa Bell to Fry, Nov. 15, 1911, 8010.8.40.

5. Virginia Woolf, "Roger Fry," in *The Moment and Other Essays* (London, 1947), pp. 83–84.

6. Virginia Woolf, *Roger Fry* (London, 1940), pp. 157–159. It is not clear that opinion among the "cultivated" classes had turned around completely by 1940. In 1953 a member of the National Art Collections Fund wrote about a grant to help purchase the *Portrait of André Derain* by Matisse for the nation: "I do not wish in any way to subscribe to the freak compositions turned out by the so-called modern school." Another wrote "I cannot believe it was the intention of the Founders [one of whom was Fry] that members subscriptions should be used for buying modern daubs which are bound to lose their present value when this age of ugliness has passed." Nicholas Goodison, "Taste

and Patronage: Ninety Years of the National Art Collections Fund," *Art Quarterly,* Spring 1994, 17, p. 30.

7. *Times Literary Supplement,* July 5, 1917, rpt. in Andrew McNeillie, ed., *The Essays of Virginia Woolf,* II (San Diego, 1987), 128–132.

8. *Times Literary Supplement,* April 10, 1919, rpt. in McNeillie, *Essays of Virginia Woolf,* III (San Diego, 1988), 30–37. A revised version was published in her *The Common Reader* in 1925.

9. *New York Evening Post,* Nov. 17, 1923, rpt. in *Nation and Athenaeum,* McNeillie, *Essays,* III, 384–389.

10. Quentin Bell, *Virginia Woolf* (New York, 1972), II, 104. Quite a few subsequent commentators, admirers of Bennett, have maintained that it was an unfair attack and that he was a much better writer than Woolf gave him credit for being. She was deeply hurt by his attack on her alleged inability to depict character and she did not necessarily claim to be fair in controversy. As James Hepburn has remarked: "It was not an original attack, and discussions of it in recent years have agreed that it was ill-considered [that is, that Bennett had been praised for his psychological subtlety] and that it attacked Bennett on Woolf's own weakest point. But in its time it was a signpost for the young, and since then it has been commonly been offered as a key document of the revolution in life and literature in the twentieth century. It was doubtless the most influential and damaging piece of criticism of Bennett that ever appeared." James Hepburn, ed., *Arnold Bennett: The Critical Heritage* (London, 1981), p. 442.

11. Virginia Woolf, *The Captain's Death Bed and Other Essays* (London, 1950), p. 7. In Leonard Woolf's four-volume edition of *Collected Essays* (London, 1966), "in" makes its appearance (I, 320).

12. The manuscript of the lecture is published in McNeillie, III, 501–517, and the *Criterion* version in III, 420–438. The pamphlet version was only minimally revised. See for discussion of the dispute between Bennett and Woolf, Samuel Hynes, "The Whole Contention between Mr Bennett and Mrs Woolf," *Edwardian Occasions* (New York, 1972), pp. 24–38, and Irving Kreutz, "Mr Bennett and Mrs Woolf," *modern fiction studies* (Summer 1962), 8, 103–115. See also Margaret Drabble, who in *Arnold Bennett* (New York, 1974) claims that that their works in fact were similar and that it was class that really divided them. For commentary at the time, see Robin Majumdar and Allen McLaurin, *Virginia Woolf: The Critical Heritage* (London, 1975), pp. 112–147.

13. Roger Fry, *Vision and Design* (London, 1920), pp. 14, 25.

14. Roger Fry, "Mr MacColl and Drawing," *Burlington,* Aug. 1919, 35, 84–85.

15. William Andrews Clark Library, Los Angeles, Fry to Gill, Dec. 5, 1910.

16. Clive Bell Papers, Trinity College, Cambridge, "Anecdotes, for the use of a future Biographer, illustrating certain peculiarities of the late Roger Fry" (May 1937), Box 32, p. 9. See also Clive Bell, "Roger Fry," in *Old Friends* (London, 1956), pp. 62–91.

17. Courtesy Quentin Bell, Vanessa Bell, "Memories of Roger Fry," Oct. 1934, pp. 7–9.

18. Clive Bell, *Art* (London, 1914), p. 207.

19. Figures 4 and 5 in Simon Watney, *The Art of Duncan Grant* (London, 1990).

20. British Library, Add. Mss. 57930B, Keynes to Grant, Nov. 15, 1910.

21. Ibid., Dec. 6, 1910.

22. Frances Spalding, *Roger Fry* (Berkeley, 1980), p. 149.

23. Richard Shone, "Charleston Painters at the R.A.," *Charleston Newsletter,* April 1987, p. 14.

24. Christopher Hassall, *A Biography of Edward Marsh* (New York, 1959), p. 168.

25. Forster Papers, King's College, Cambridge, Locked Diary, Dec. 19, 1910.

26. See Elizabeth Heine, ed., Introduction, to E. M. Forster, *Arctic Summer and Other Fiction* (London, 1980). Quotation from diary, p. xvi. See also P. N. Furbank, *E. M. Forster: A Life* (New York, 1977), I, 207–210.

ACKNOWLEDGMENTS

As readers of the manuscript I am deeply indebted to Quentin and Olivier Bell, S. P. Rosenbaum, the anonymous readers of Harvard University Press (and at the Press Aida Donald, Camille Smith, and Elizabeth Suttell), Marina Vaizey, as well as Regina Maler and Susan Bell. My greatest debt, as before, is for the numerous readings by William Abrahams, who rigorously tested my style and my ideas, whose extremely helpful criticisms sometimes made me despair, but whose ultimate approval was the greatest of pleasures.

Many others assisted in the making of this book. I am grateful for time at the Center for the Advanced Study of the Behavioral Sciences, where in that Shangri-la I started to work on this book. The staff of the Stanford University Libraries and the Stanford History Department rendered assistance in innumerable ways. I am also grateful to Patricia Barnes, Tony Bradshaw and Polly Vaizey of the splendid Bloomsbury Workshop, Helmiriitta Sariola and Leena Ahtola-Moorhouse of the Museum of Finnish Art, Helsinki, Cassian de Vere Cole, Andrew McNeillie, Frances Spalding, Reid J. Schar, Kristin Zimmerman, and Alex Scott.

Librarians were of great help, most notably Jacqueline Cox at the Modern Fiction Archives at King's College, Cambridge, and Cathy Henderson at the Harry Ransom Humanities Research Center at the University of Texas at Austin. I am grateful for the assistance they rendered me and for help from the staff of other libraries—Trinity College, Cambridge; the British Library; the Centre of South Asian Studies, Cambridge University; the Public Record Office; Magadalene College Library, Cambridge; Houghton Library, Harvard University;

Tate Gallery Archives; Archives of the Contemporary Art Society, London; Sussex University Library; Lilly Library, Indiana University; Berg Collection, New York Public Library; J. P. Morgan Library, New York—where I was so kindly allowed to consult manuscript holdings.

For permission to quote and reproduce I am grateful to the Society of Authors as the literary representative of Quentin Bell for the words of his parents, Clive and Vanessa Bell; Angelica Bell for the images by Vanessa Bell; for the words and images of Duncan Grant, Estate of Duncan Grant © 1978 courtesy Henrietta Garnett; King's College, Cambridge, and the Society of Authors as the literary representatives of the E. M. Forster Estate; the Society of Authors as the literary representative of the Estate of Virginia Woolf; the Society of Authors as agents for The Strachey Trust; Annabel Cole for the words and images of Roger Fry; the Provost and Scholars of King's College, Cambridge, for unpublished writings of J. M. Keynes, copyright © 1996; and Hugh Cecil for words of Desmond MacCarthy. Acknowledgment for illustrations appears in the list of illustrations.

Chapter 5 was published in an earlier version in Susan Pedersen and Peter Mandler, eds., *After the Victorians: Private Conscience and Public Duty in Modern Britain; Essays in Memory of John Clive* (London, 1994), and is used with permission.

INDEX